DISCARD

The Fight for the Soul
of the Democratic Party

The Fight for the Soul of the Democratic Party

The Enduring Legacy of Henry Wallace's Antifascist, Antiracist Politics

John Nichols

VERSO

London • New York

First published by Verso 2020
© John Nichols 2020

All rights reserved

The moral rights of the author have been asserted

1 3 5 7 9 10 8 6 4 2

Verso
UK: 6 Meard Street, London W1F 0EG
US: 20 Jay Street, Suite 1010, Brooklyn, NY 11201
versobooks.com

Verso is the imprint of New Left Books

ISBN-13: 978-1-78873-740-1
ISBN-13: 978-1-78873-741-8 (UK EBK)
ISBN-13: 978-1-78873-742-5 (US EBK)

British Library Cataloguing in Publication Data
A catalogue record for this book is available from the British Library

Library of Congress Cataloging-in-Publication Data
A catalog record for this book is available from the Library of Congress
Library of Congress Control Number: 2019957421

Typeset in Sabon by MJ & N Gavan, Truro, Cornwall
Printed and bound by CPI Group (UK) Ltd, Croydon CR0 4YY

For my mother, Mary K. Nichols, the truest progressive I know, and for David Panofsky, who told me about his uncle Erwin

Contents

Preface

Why We Concern Ourselves with the History of Political Parties

America's future is linked to how we understand our past. For this reason, writing about history, for me, is never a neutral act.
—Howard Zinn

Political parties have histories. In many countries, these histories are told with reverence and respect for their roles in breaking the bonds of colonialism or battling fascism, in defining the character of a country or in opposing malignant tendencies. Not so in the United States. The histories of our major political parties are rarely told. Rather, parties are understood as mere shells into which great men and women climb when they need a place on the ballot or a separate fund-raising apparatus. Dixiecrat segregationists decamp from the Democratic ballot line to the Republican line, transforming both parties. The youngest of Franklin Roosevelt's New Deal Democrats lived long enough to watch in horror as the rules they had established to protect Americans from Wall Street speculation were undone by Bill Clinton and his "New Democrats."

The path I took in writing this book began with a consideration of how the Republican Party of Abraham Lincoln and the Radical Reconstructionists of the 1860s became the party of Donald Trump and the xenophobic white nationalists of the 2010s. I wondered how it had changed so drastically that it made a lie of Dwight Eisenhower's 1954 observation that "should any political party attempt to abolish social security, unemployment insurance, and eliminate labor laws and farm programs, you would not hear of that party again in our political history."

There are no more Eisenhowers in the Republican Party, and that explains a lot. The supposed "adults in the room," the Paul Ryans and the Mitch McConnells, undoubtedly recognized the absurdity and awfulness of the Tea Party agenda of 2011, yet they adopted it largely without question. They thought they could control the right-wing base of their party. Instead, they forged a party that was ripe for takeover by Trump, a charlatan who wore his bigotry on his sleeve. If the Republican Party bartered off most of what was noble in its history long before Trump began to seriously consider a presidential bid, the hustler who wrote *The Art of the Deal* merely closed the deal.

But what of the Democratic Party? In the 2010s, the Democrats were as inept and visionless as the Republicans were calculating and cruel. When Trump assumed the presidency after a 2016 election that the Democrats should have won by a landslide, bolstered by a Republican Congress that was ready to follow the lead of a desperate and damaged narcissist, the crisis came into focus. It was not the Republican Party that was ruining our politics. Rather, the lack of a coherent and appealing opposition to the Republicans was the problem.

So what were the roots of that crisis? It is too shallow to blame Hillary Clinton or the bumbling strategists that mounted her 2016 campaign. It is too easy to point an accusatory finger at the consultants and candidates who kept losing to the empty suits that Mitch McConnell was running for the Senate. Something much deeper was amiss. The Democratic Party had abandoned what was visionary in its past to become the managerial party of Bill Clinton and the surrender caucus that showed up whenever the party was in a position to prevail. For some, it was sufficient to see President Clinton and the New Democrats as the source of the disease. But that was also shallow. The Democratic Party began pulling its punches long before both Clintons arrived on the scene.

The more I traced the roots of the decay of a party that could not beat Nixon or Reagan or George H.W. Bush or George W. Bush or Donald Trump, the closer I got to the last days of Franklin Roosevelt's presidency—and to the great unraveling that began when Harry Truman was maneuvered onto the 1944 Democratic ticket by the party bosses and Southern segregationists who knew FDR was dying and wanted to bury the New Deal with him. Truman, who was willing to compromise with the bosses, established a pattern of ideological and strategic concession by the party that extends to this day. But Truman did not just grab the nomination, the vice presidency and the promise of the presidency in a vacuum. He came to power after a struggle. The more I focused on that definitional fight, the clearer it became that the lost soul of the Democratic Party was a man. And his name was Henry Wallace.

Wallace has been so thoroughly written out of our popular history that he is often confused with a politician who was his polar opposite, Alabama segregationist George Wallace. Even those who know bits and pieces of the good Wallace's story imagine him as a tragic figure who, after a brief moment of New Deal glory, was ruined by the excesses of his idealism. Wallace was an idealist; arguably, with Eleanor Roosevelt, Wendell Willkie and A. Philip Randolph, one of the greatest idealists among the cadre of dreamers who remade America in the late 1930s and early 1940s. Indeed, the bare-bones biography of Henry Wallace is sufficient to identify him as one of the most striking political figures in U.S. history.

A progressive Republican editor and farmer from Iowa who supported Roosevelt in the 1932 campaign that realigned American politics, Wallace became an original member of FDR's cabinet and turned the Department of Agriculture into the roaring engine of the New Deal. He so impressed the president that, in 1940, Roosevelt forced the Democratic Party to accept Wallace as his running mate in an audacious bid for a third term. After an overwhelming election victory on the eve of

World War II, Wallace emerged as the liberal conscience of the administration, championing the fight against fascism abroad and racism at home. He was controversial and so uncompromising that the bosses took advantage of an ailing and distracted Franklin Roosevelt to force him off the ticket in 1944, making way for the more malleable Truman. Yet FDR kept him close, making Wallace his secretary of commerce for a fourth term in which the original New Dealers dreamed of advancing the radical vision of Four Freedoms abroad and an Economic Bill of Rights at home.

When Roosevelt died in 1945, the dream began to fade. Yet Wallace refused to give it up. He fought for a time within the Democratic Party, objecting to Truman's compromises at home and abroad. He warned of the dawning of a Cold War— and of the domestic Red Scare that would extend from it. He attempted to maintain the popular-front coalition that had elected and re-elected Roosevelt, welcoming farm-state populists and urban intellectuals, civil rights campaigners and the defenders of immigrants, feminists and militant trade unionists, socialists and communists.

Wallace was no communist; he was a progressive capitalist who preached the anti-monopoly gospel of the upper Midwest, and who believed that honest competition and diplomacy as opposed to militarism and hubris could keep the postwar peace. As FDR and Willkie had before their deaths, Wallace refused to be drawn into the anti-Communist fervor that the monopolists and the segregationists had ginned up in hopes of undoing the unity of antifascist purpose that had moved America well to the left during World War II. He was skeptical of the Soviet Union. He recognized it as a rival, and a threat. Yet Wallace refused to accept that the threat would be well or wisely answered with a "cold war." Even as his reservations regarding the Soviets grew, Wallace held out for diplomacy, and for peace.

At home, Wallace recognized the dark machinations of the economic royalists who sought to renew the supremacy they had enjoyed in the pre–New Deal moment. He warned, even before the war was finished, that wealthy and powerful men would seek to divide the nation in order to further enrich and empower themselves. Wallace dared to identify the threat posed by these men as that of an "American Fascism," just as he dared to compare homegrown racists with the Nazis of Germany. He spoke these dangerous truths before it was fashionable, and for this he was labeled a communist dupe, a mystic, a zealot.

The Democrats who feared a new New Deal, and who were not prepared to fight as hard to "win the peace" as they had to win World War II, determined to erase the memory of the man who fought the hardest to maintain FDR's legacy. They largely succeeded, but in so doing they undid the visionary ambition that had characterized their party in the period of its greatest strength. This is a tragic story of abandoned values and missed opportunities.

Wallace made the work of his rivals easier. He gave up on the Democratic Party and in 1948 mounted a poorly thought-out and ill-timed independent Progressive presidential bid. While the threat that Wallace's candidacy posed would briefly pull Truman to the left, it failed to pull many votes. And it gave Wallace's detractors an opening to unleash a furious assault on the man they portrayed as clueless and calculating, marginal and dangerous. Wallace made plenty of political missteps, and this book does not imagine that they should be ignored. In fact, it focuses on a number of them. But the antiracist, antisexist champion of peace and progress ended up on the right side of history far more frequently than his critics.

After the collapse of his desperate 1948 bid to forge a "Gideon's Army," Wallace was consigned to the political wilderness. He retreated to a farm in upstate New York, where the man whose proposals to reform capitalism were ridiculed as naïve engaged in pioneering agricultural research. His work would eventually revolutionize farming and form the basis for multibillion-dollar endeavors. He built a fortune so great that, to this day, it helps to sustain the Wallace Global Fund's support for struggles against racism and violence, poverty and disease, climate change and the rise of the corporate state.

The fund maintains the memory of its namesake, recalling that "Henry A. Wallace was deeply concerned by what he saw as the rise of a corporatist state that concentrates power in the hands of the few and wields unchecked authority at the expense of the common good." It takes as its mission the work of promoting "an informed and engaged citizenry, to fight injustice and to protect the diversity of nature and the natural systems upon which all life depends."

That is a fair assessment of what Henry Wallace was all about, a subject that this book will examine in significantly more detail in Chapter 1. The ensuing chapters set the scene for and explore the fights that he waged not only against segregationists and party bosses but also, more importantly, against the surrender of the New Deal ethic of going big and going bold. These chapters rely heavily on Wallace's own words, quoting at length from the speeches and articles the man produced during those few years when everything was up for grabs. They draw also from the champions and the critics of Wallace in his time, from the inheritors of his legacy and from the historians who have wrestled with it. They conclude with an extended examination of the ongoing struggle for the soul of the Democratic Party that began in July 1944 and remains unresolved. The final interviews were done on the 2020 campaign trail.

The story of the party's rejection of Wallace, and of the bolder, more visionary politics that he proposed, tells us much that we need to know—not just about the decline of Democrats from the New Deal era to now, but about the decay of our politics in general. And, more hopefully, about the prospects for reversing that decline and decay.

For 75 years, the Democratic Party has refused to unify around the principles that Wallace outlined in his address to the

1944 Democratic National Convention. "The future," Wallace proposed, "belongs to those who go down the line unswervingly for the liberal principles of both political democracy and economic democracy regardless of race, color or religion." In 1944, the party bosses and the segregationist senators who aligned with them thought Wallace's calculus was wrong. The partisan descendants of those who constrained the Democratic Party's vision then have never stopped trying to constrain it.

The Democrats have had their outstanding leaders and their outstanding moments over the past three quarters of a century. But there has been no consistency of purpose; no steadiness of vision. The party has been whipsawed by campaign donors and consultants, by of-the-moment strategists and "Third Way" think tanks that, invariably, counsel against going down the line unswervingly for progressive principles. Even now, Democrats wrestle with the question of whether to be so bold, so visionary, so truthful and so willing to take risks on behalf of economic and social and racial justice as was Henry Wallace.

As the Republican Party has moved toward the extremism that Eisenhower feared and that Wallace suggested might take the form of an American fascism, the Democratic Party has tried to occupy the middle ground. Whenever it has moved tentatively to the left, the advocates for this progression—the George McGoverns, the Shirley Chisholms, the Jesse Jacksons, the Tom Haydens—have been quickly sidelined by the insiders. The approach might be defensible, politically if not morally, were there a record of steady success. But that record does not exist. America is not a right-wing country, yet through most of the postwar era it has been governed by steadily more right-wing Republican presidents.

Even when Democrats have prevailed, they have struggled to advance the progressive agenda that polls show most Americans desire. The last two Democratic presidents lost their governing majorities in the Congress midway through their first terms, and the two Democratic presidents before them were so badly derailed by domestic and foreign policy missteps that they could not secure re-election.

If we step back and observe with an honest eye the history of our political parties, we see a story of stark and unsettling contrasts. Republicans do not win every election. Yet their party has pulled the country steadily to the right, controlling and corrupting the federal courts, initiating and maintaining endless wars and extending the reach (and the budgets) of the Pentagon, imposing austerity in order to fund tax cuts for the rich. The planet has burned. Nationalism, xenophobia and racism have been mainstreamed. No survey suggests that this is what America wants. Yet this is what we have. Why? Because we lack an adequate opposition. The Democrats have bent, again and again and again, to the demands of investment-bank campaign donors, apologists for the military-industrial complex, and Third Way hucksters.

Democrats have been able to renew their electoral fortunes when they unite with independents to upend the worst excesses of the Republicans. Yet Democrats have not been capable of maintaining the energy and enthusiasm necessary to keep power and to advance an agenda that is both truly progressive and truly necessary. In recent years, they have expended most of their energy fighting to preserve gains made decades ago. So the balance keeps tipping to the right. This pattern has held since the 1940s, the decade in which the critical fight for the soul of the Democratic Party was lost. It will continue until a new fight for the soul of the Democratic Party is waged, and won.

This book encourages the fight in the form of a series of historical essays that come to a point. This is not a whole history of the Democratic Party. Rather, it is an examination of a moment in the party's history, of a brief period when a definitional choice was made. The Democrats opted for compromise in the mid-1940s. It was the wrong choice. And it has haunted the party, and the nation, since that time.

Historical knowledge is always necessary. But it is most necessary when everything is again up for grabs, as is now the case. A new generation of reformers and radicals, of grassroots activists and visionary idealists, has stepped up. They are on the move. They seek to remake the Democratic Party as a fighting force that might win the future. Their successes in reframing and renewing the party in which they have chosen to make their stand invite us to consider the prospect that was outlined by the anthropologist Claude Lévi-Strauss in *Tristes Tropiques*: "If men have always been concerned with only one task— how to create a society fit to live in—the forces which inspired our distant ancestors are also present in us. Nothing is settled; everything can still be altered. What was done but turned out wrong, can be done again. The Golden Age, which blind superstition had placed behind (or ahead of) us, is in us."

Henry Wallace is not a distant ancestor. There are still a few old radicals who remember marching at his side. What he did turned out wrong, not because his values were wrong but because they were ahead of the time. Now, perhaps, what turned out wrong can be done again. Perhaps, the lost soul of the Democratic Party can be found.

1

The Prophetic Politics of Henry Wallace

How FDR's Vice President Anticipated the Dangerous Times That Have Engulfed America

Watchman, what of the night?
—Isaiah 21:11–12, King James Version

A modern Isaiah, seeing the possibilities of modern transporta-
tion and communication, and observing the national barriers
imposed by the nations of the world against each other since the
war, would cry out against international injustices. He would go
to the people of the different nations with his message and call
for a New Deal among nations. He would do this with vigor and
immense earnestness even though, from the immediate practical
point of view, his message might be premature.
—Henry Agard Wallace, *Statesmanship and Religion*, 1934

In the summer of 1948, when his own fight against American
fascism had been lost but he still refused to surrender the radical
hope of a future framed by justice and peace, Henry Wallace
would ask Pete Seeger to sing a favorite song. The words and
music had been submitted by a young college instructor named
Dick Blakeslee to the "People's Songs" project that Seeger, Alan
Lomax, Lee Hays and a handful of others launched after World
War II to champion a revival of old folk music and new songs
of work, struggle and idealism. Blakeslee's lyrics sampled from

Bible verses and ranged across American history. Yet his song closed in the moment, or, rather, in the moment that Wallace had hoped to create:

> I was with Franklin Roosevelt's side on the night before he died.
> He said, "One world must come out of World War Two,
> Yankee, Russian, white or tan," he said, "a man is still a man.
> We're all on one road, and we're only passing through."

As they traveled the backroads of North Carolina and the other segregated states where Wallace challenged racial hatred, Seeger would sing the words "a man is still a man." A thousand miles to the north, a Jewish teenager from Montreal learned those words from a socialist summer-camp counselor. They inspired an interest in folk music that proved to be transformative for Leonard Cohen. Years later, Cohen would add a slight variation to "Passing Through" as he sang the song from the concert stages of Europe and the Americas. After the line "One world must come out of World War Two" he would whisper "... ah, the fool." Those who know something of Cohen's wry romanticism, and the political penchants of the man who challenged his adopted United States ("the cradle of the best and of the worst") with the slyest protest song of his time ("Democracy Is Coming to the USA"), will recognize that this was no insult. Rather, it was an invitation to reconsider casual notions of wisdom and folly.

Wallace and Seeger barnstormed across the segregated South for a doomed third-party campaign for the presidency, that of a New Party, which came to be known as Progressive. They were demanding that the United States make real the promise of World War II as a liberation struggle meant to defeat fascism abroad and at home. They knew they were being portrayed as nostalgic New Dealers who refused to give up on the hope that died with Franklin Roosevelt; as dupes of the Soviet Union in a nascent Cold War; as naïve idealists. Yet they persevered, in the face of the physical violence of the Jim Crow South and the ideological violence of a dawning Red Scare. This was not just their own political project; it was the mission that FDR had outlined in the last months of his life.

"We cannot be content," explained Roosevelt in the waning days of World War II, "no matter how high [the] general standard of living may be, if some fraction of our people—whether it be one-third or one-fifth or one-tenth—is ill-fed, ill-clothed, ill-housed, and insecure." Recognizing that "true individual freedom cannot exist without economic security and independence," the president warned, "necessitous men are not free men. People who are hungry and out of a job are the stuff of which dictatorships are made." And he proposed to address the threat of future fascisms with "a second Bill of Rights under which a new basis of security and prosperity can be established for all—regardless of station, race, or creed."

The Democratic Party that in 1940 nominated Roosevelt and Wallace would, as the decade wore on, abandon FDR's certainty that "an economic declaration of rights, an economic constitutional order" was "the minimum requirement of a more permanently safe order of things." But despite that surrender, Wallace refused to abandon the New Deal and the promise of Wendell Willkie's manifesto *One World* and FDR's Four Freedoms and Second Bill of Rights. He could not accept that an unjust order built upon the crumbling foundations of racism, monopoly and militarism would need to be maintained for decades, and then generations, because his own Democratic Party had lost its nerve—and its faith.

Wallace, a brilliant writer and thinker and an accomplished editor, cabinet member, vice president, presidential candidate and businessman, never suggested it would be easy to end segregation and sexism, address poverty and inequality, upend the military-industrial complex and avert nuclear war. Rather, with the support of Albert Einstein, W.E.B. Du Bois, a young Betty Friedan and a younger Noam Chomsky, he argued that this program was an urgent necessity that could not be cashiered as political concession or electoral compromise. His supporters circulated posters with the picture of an African-American youth and the message: "A black child born on the same day in the same city as a white child is destined to die 10 years earlier. ... We are fighting for those 10 extra years."

Wallace embraced a "new liberalism," asserting: "A liberal is a person who in all his actions is continuously asking, 'What is best for all the people—not merely what is best for me personally?' Abraham Lincoln was a liberal when he said he was both for the man and the dollar, but in case of conflict he was for the man before the dollar. Christ was the greatest liberal of all when he put life before things." He identified as a patriotic American who believed "in using in a nonviolent, tolerant and democratic way the forces of education, publicity, politics, economics, business, law and religion to direct the ever-changing and increasing power of science into channels which will bring peace and the maximum of well-being both spiritual and economic to the greatest number of human beings."

These were not uncommon notions at a time when political leaders, having survived the Great Depression and thwarted Adolf Hitler, imagined a new world order of peace and prosperity, freedom and equality. Clement Attlee, Aneurin Bevan, Jennie Lee, a young Michael Foot, a younger Tony Benn and the British Labour Party preached another version of this social gospel as they set out to win the peace in 1945 with a "Let Us Face the Future!" campaign on behalf of a national health-care system, the nationalization of basic industries and a redistribution of wealth from *Downton Abbey* elites to the toiling masses. Tage Fritjof Erlander, Einar Henry Gerhardsen and the Scandinavian social democrats echoed that message as they forged the model of the modern social welfare state. Jawaharlal Nehru, Bhimrao Ramji Ambedkar and Rajkumari Amrit Kaur joined their voices to the chorus as they saw off British colonialism and announced that "at the stroke of the midnight hour, when the world sleeps, India will awake to life and freedom."

In America, however, Wallace was deemed dangerous by the Southern power brokers, the patronage bosses, the corporatists and the monopolists who were quite happy to bury the New Deal with FDR. The men who schemed to divert the postwar march of democracy disdained Henry Wallace. And he disdained them. Their corruptions, their calculations, he warned, were the stuff of "American Fascism."

From the mid-1940s onward, Wallace was prepared to name the enemies of human progress. He shared Paul Robeson's view that the danger for the United States in the postwar era lay "in the resurgent imperialist and profascist forces in our own country." As the second highest-ranking official in the country, he did not hesitate to make the appropriate, yet too rarely spoken, connection between Hitler's preachments about racial "purity" and the language of Southern segregationists who also spoke of a "master race."

For Wallace, a breaking point came in the summer of 1943, after racial violence flared in Detroit, leaving thirty-four dead (including seventeen African Americans at the hands of the police). Wallace traveled to the city and addressed a mass meeting of labor and civic organizations. "We cannot fight to crush Nazi brutality abroad and condone race riots at home," he told the crowd. "Those who fan the fires of racial clashes for the purpose of making political capital here at home are taking the first step toward Nazism." Wallace warned: "There are powerful groups who hope to take advantage of the President's concentration on the war effort to destroy everything he has accomplished on the domestic front over the last 10 years. Some people call these powerful groups 'isolationists,' others call them 'reactionaries' and still others, seeing them following in European footsteps, call them 'American Fascists.' "

Those were jarring words from the vice president of the United States, but Henry Wallace chose them carefully. Starting when he was Roosevelt's secretary of agriculture, Wallace studied foreign languages so that he could speak directly with the leaders and planners of the fight against Hitler and his Axis. He traveled widely and consulted often with those who had resisted the rise of fascism in Europe and who were resisting its pull in Latin America and Asia. He made a study of the threat, and he intended to speak about it in an American context. He proposed a broad definition of this charged term that could apply to the racists, warmongers and monopolists who manipulated media and politics to maintain their grip on America.

Speaking to that 1943 mass meeting in one of the nation's great industrial centers, Wallace warned that "the people of America know that the second step toward fascism is the destruction of labor unions. There are midget Hitlers here who continually attack labor. There are other demagogues blind to the errors of every other group who shout, 'We love labor, but ...' Both the midget Hitlers and the demagogues are enemies of America. Both would destroy labor unions if they could. Labor should be fully aware of its friends and of its enemies."

Wallace ripped into industrialists. "We know that imperialistic freebooters using the United States as a base can make another war inevitable," he warned. "Too many corporations have made money by holding inventions out of use, by holding up prices and by cutting down production."

Could the schemes of the midget Hitlers, the imperialist freebooters, the American fascists be stopped? "Shouldering our responsibilities for enlightenment, abundant production and world cooperation, we can begin now our apprenticeship to world peace," Wallace said. "There will be heart-breaking delays—there will be prejudices creeping in and the faint-hearted will spread their whispers of doubt. But ... nothing will prevail against the common man's peace in a common man's world as he fights both for free enterprise and full employment.

"The world," pledged Henry Wallace, "is one family with one future—a future which will bind our brotherhood with heart and mind and not with chains!"

Segregationists, the captains of industry and the big-city bosses of the Democratic Party were determined to destroy Wallace, and for the most part they succeeded. They denied him the vice-presidential nomination at the 1944 Democratic National Convention and, by extension, the prospect of the presidency, for it was well understood that, were a Roosevelt-Wallace ticket to be re-elected in 1944, an ailing Roosevelt would in all likelihood be replaced by his vice president. They drove Wallace from the powerful cabinet position that FDR had chosen for him, secretary of commerce, in the Truman administration. In the late 1940s, they elbowed the former vice president to the margins of American politics and then shoved him into the shadows. Eventually, they reimagined our history and our politics so aggressively, and so completely, that Wallace's warnings were laughed off as a sort of political madness while generation after generation of centrist Democrats neglected fundamental economic and social challenges. Ultimately, FDR's New Deal coalition collapsed and a yawning space was opened for the sort of "American fascist ... who in case of conflict puts money and power ahead of human beings." Only with the arrival of Donald Trump on the political scene—to the accompaniment of headlines like the CBC's that asked: "Flirting with Fascism: America's New Path?"—did the full consequence of that failure reveal itself.

Wallace was prophetic. He raised the prospect of a totalitarianism, of a soft fascism, lurking beneath the facade of democracy in the United States. What he suggested was unimaginable for many in his time, as it is for many in this time. Yet as the U.S. slides further down democracy indexes, even those compiled by corporate-friendly groups like the Economist Intelligence Unit, there must be a recognition that established norms are being diminished, that standards are being disregarded. Wallace urged us to be on the alert for moments such as this. More importantly, he outlined ideals and agendas for avoiding them.

There were those in his time who worshiped Wallace as a hero, and those today who do the same. But Wallace would have been the first to tell you about his flaws. He was constantly reassessing his stances, based on new information, and he was quite capable of acknowledging when he had been wrong. His mistakes are a part of his story. Indeed, they help us to make sense of why an exceptionally popular and extraordinarily talented American leader came so close to the presidency, only to be quickly and thoroughly marginalized.

Any political assessment of Wallace must look at the whole man. Even his sharpest critics acknowledged that Wallace was known for "modesty, human decency, competence, energy, and receptivity to new ideas," as essayist Dwight Macdonald said. Wallace was confident that it was possible to reason to a better world. FDR described his vice president as "Old Man Common Sense," but James Farley, the Democratic National Committee chairman, saw Wallace as "a wild-eyed fellow" who might scare away party backers in the South with his talk of eliminating the poll taxes and "white primaries" that locked in segregationist power. Certainly there was nothing of the traditional back-slapping campaigner in Wallace. He arrived on the national scene with few political skills, and turned too frequently for counsel to others who lacked those skills. "I love him as much as you do," novelist Dashiell Hammett confided to playwright Lillian Hellman, "but you simply cannot make a politician out of him."

Yet Franklin Roosevelt did make a politician out of Henry Wallace, at a moment in 1940 when the 32nd president of the United States was under assault by conservatives in both parties. By choosing Wallace as his running mate, historian Doris Kearns Goodwin suggests, FDR elevated a leader who was "as strong or stronger than he was on those liberal issues" that mattered most then. Goodwin has argued that FDR promoted Wallace from his cabinet to the vice presidency not to be a party man but to be "a weapon against the conservatives."

Wallace was against the conservatives, wherever he found them, and at every stage of his life. A born-and-bred "Party of Lincoln" Republican who became a Teddy Roosevelt Bull Moose Progressive in 1912, he then returned to the Republican fold and remained there until he embraced Wisconsin Senator Robert M. La Follette's independent Progressive campaign of 1924. Wallace rejoined the Republicans and worked to steer the party to the left, in tandem with his influential father, who served as secretary of agriculture in the Harding and Coolidge administrations. As Herbert Hoover's Republican presidency imploded in 1932, Wallace signed on with FDR and became the most ardent New Deal Democrat. After Roosevelt's death and his expulsion from the inner circles of power and the Democratic Party, Wallace launched his New Party project, which became the Progressive Party, to mobilize the left for the 1948 election. Eight years later, Wallace voted for Dwight Eisenhower because of the Republican president's recognition that domestic programs would be cheated to feed the Pentagon, and because the old soldier saw the threat posed by the military-industrial complex. Toward the end of his life, Wallace displayed considerable enthusiasm for Lyndon Johnson's Great Society programs. Yet, before he died in 1965, Wallace was expressing dread over LBJ's lurch toward war in Southeast Asia.

There were plenty of liberal Democrats who loved Wallace's passions and policies but distanced themselves from his campaigning because they feared it was simply too bold for the times. Wallace brought some failures upon himself. He could be strategically inept. He erred in his assessments of particular people and particular policies, at home and abroad. He was a deeply religious man who explored the spiritual traditions of his own Christian faith and other traditions with an enthusiasm that sparked ridicule and concern. He was, as wise historians always say with a poignant pause, a complex man. With the exceptions of Thomas Jefferson, Abraham Lincoln, William Jennings Bryan and a handful of others, he was as fascinating a figure as the ferment surrounding the American presidency has yet produced. The story of how the editor of an Iowa agricultural journal, *Wallace's Farmer*, became the most controversial vice president in the twentieth century has inspired fine biographies. In 2000's *American Dreamer*, former Iowa senator John Culver and journalist John Hyde renewed interest in Wallace by ably explaining how the son of Calvin Coolidge's secretary of agriculture came to define New Deal liberalism and mounted a doomed 1948 challenge to Truman as the nominee of a party that welcomed radicals, socialists and communists. Filmmaker Oliver Stone and historian Peter Kuznick collaborated on *The Untold History of the United States*, a 2012 book and television series; in it, they advanced the argument that, had Wallace remained on Roosevelt's ticket and succeeded FDR in 1945, "there would not have been this Cold War. There would have been the continuation of the Roosevelt-Stalin working out of things. Vietnam wouldn't have happened." The Stone-Kuznick project was hailed by former Soviet president Mikhail Gorbachev and journalist Glenn Greenwald, savaged by neo-conservatives and dismissed by Princeton history professor Sean Wilentz as "a skewed political document." In truth, Wallace remains so controversial that every examination of the man inspires excitement and enthusiasm, objection and acrimony.

The debate about Wallace and a presidency that might have been has often distracted us from an understanding of what Wallace's fights in the mid-1940s were about, and how they defined the Democratic Party. It is the purpose of this book to renew that understanding. The abandonment of progressive populism by the Democrats, along with the redistributionist policies that FDR developed and popularized, did much to destroy the New Deal coalition. Ronald Reagan would exploit that in the 1980s, winning landslide victories by drawing so-called "Reagan Democrats" to the extreme right. This opened a void in American politics that would be filled first by the self-serving politics of corporate "centrists" in both parties and then, as neoliberalism failed to answer the needs of the great mass of people, by the right-wing populism of Donald Trump. There are many wise observers who believe that the Democratic Party cannot be reformed. But a reflection on Wallace raises a question in this moment of political, economic and social ferment, of Bernie Sanders and Alexandria Ocasio-Cortez and resurgent democratic socialism and Elizabeth Warren's promise of "big, bold structural change": Might today's Democratic Party take up where FDR and his vice president left off, and become an alternative to the overt and covert American fascism Wallace warned us about?

Answering this in the affirmative is the mission of an insurgency within the Democratic Party that has grown from Sanders's 2016 presidential bid and the efforts of a new generation of activists who have often operated outside the political arena but now seek to transform electoral debates about domestic and foreign policy. This makes Wallace's struggle more than an isolated story from an all-but-forgotten past.

Trump's election created a sense of urgency. But Democrats must know something about how it all fell apart in order to see how it all might be put together again. In the search for answers, it is easy to be drawn to the 1948 campaign, as it provided a rare glimpse of what multiparty competition might look like in a country dominated by the two "old parties" that so frustrated Wallace and his contemporaries, and that still frustrate the majority of Americans who tell pollsters they long for different and better political options. The 1948 race offered more plot twists than all but a handful of campaigns in American history, along with a dramatic conclusion that produced the greatest wrong headline of all time: "Dewey Defeats Truman." Truman was, of course, not defeated, and his victory defined the Democratic Party going forward.

There have been significant examinations of the 1948 campaign in general and of Wallace's crusade in particular. Curtis D. MacDougall's deeply reported 1965 text, *Gideon's Army*, tells an essential story, as does Thomas Devine's thoughtful 2013 book,

Henry Wallace's 1948 Presidential Campaign and the Future of Postwar Liberalism. For those on the old left who remember it, and for a rising generation of young leftists, the 1948 campaign has become the electoral equivalent of the Spanish Civil War, where a Gideon's Army of campaigners armed with leaflets and placards takes the place of the Abraham Lincoln Brigade. For guardians of the status quo, the 1948 campaign is something else altogether: a blunt instrument to pull out whenever they feel it necessary to warn against what Wallace described as a "keep the door open" popular-front politics that makes common cause with socialists, communists, social justice crusaders and radical reformers. The contention is less intense now than it was in the days when Democrats shuddered at the mention of the term "Wallace-ite" and its successor: "McGovernism." History will circle back to the 1948 campaign and it will continue to evoke radically different interpretations of what was, and what might have been. More books will be written on Wallace's presidential bid in general, and its courageous challenge to racism in particular.

But this book begins with a recognition that, by 1948, the guardians of the New Deal ethic had already lost. The Democratic Party had already compromised the ideals of the Four Freedoms and the Economic Bill of Rights. Despite the best efforts of Wallace and his most prominent allies, FDR's Democratic Party died when it rejected the man whom Eleanor Roosevelt described as "peculiarly fitted to carry on the ideals which were close to my husband's heart." The power within the party passed to the men who expelled Wallace from the vice presidency and who were more than ready to join in a two-party dance, where the tune would eventually be called by the neoliberal theorists favored by Wall Street, and the neoconservatives who did the bidding of a military-industrial complex always seeking a new war to fight.

The deck was then—as it is now—so effectively stacked against those seeking to break the grip of the two major parties

that the rebels were thwarted long before Election Day. That was what happened to Wallace in 1948. When his New Party project was initially imagined in 1947, the former vice president was addressing crowds that packed some of the nation's largest stadiums and arenas, his speeches were reproduced in their entirety in daily newspapers and regularly broadcast nationwide by radio networks, he had a following in every state and polls suggested that at the very least he could expect to secure the strongest third-party vote since Robert M. La Follette took 16 percent of the total in 1924. Yet as Election Day 1948 approached, the fear that Wallace's vote might tip the contest to Republican Thomas Dewey convinced even true believers to cast their ballots for a candidate they frankly despised: Harry Truman.

Wallace finished fourth, behind Truman, Dewey and South Carolina governor Strom Thurmond of the segregationist States' Rights Party, better known as the Dixiecrats. While Thurmond carried four Southern states, Wallace carried none, and the number crunchers noted that the substantial vote totals he attained in the labor and left-wing strongholds of Detroit and Brooklyn probably tipped Michigan and New York to Dewey. Even Wallace would eventually admit that the 1948 campaign was something of a fiasco. As radical journalist and Wallace backer I.F. Stone mused, "In thirty minutes, cross-legged, saying 'Oom' with alternative exhalations, I can conjure up a better third-party movement than Wallace's."

It had not been so four years earlier, however, and that is why this book places its primary focus on the nomination fight of 1944. Then, Henry Wallace came agonizingly close to turning the Democratic Party into something strikingly distinct from what it has become. Had he prevailed, a radically different party might have emerged from the war. We would have gotten to the future sooner.

The battle for the soul of the Democratic Party has been waged, with varying degrees of intensity, since the Democratic National Convention of 1944 that rejected Wallace. In 2017, when members of Congress made themselves "the legislative arm of the resistance" to Donald Trump, in the words of Congressional Progressive Caucus co-chair Mark Pocan, they did not do so as mere foes of his presidency. They spoke as advocates for a bolder agenda than Democrats had embraced for a very long time. Pocan and CPC co-chair Pramila Jayapal proposed a "21st-century economic policy" to restore the power of workers and their unions, a power denied them since conservative Republicans and segregationist Democrats overturned the essential infrastructure of the New Deal by enacting the Taft-Hartley Act of 1947.

When Representative Alexandria Ocasio-Cortez demanded a "Green New Deal" agenda, she and her allies borrowed not just a name but the thrilling ambition of the partisans who cheered when Roosevelt said of his presidency, "We had to struggle with the old enemies of peace—business and financial monopoly, speculation, reckless banking, class antagonism, sectionalism, war profiteering. ... Never before in all our history have these forces been so united against one candidate as they stand today. They are unanimous in their hate for me—and I welcome their hatred."

Today's progressives speak of a next politics that refuses, in the words of Representative Ro Khanna, "to be limited by the compromises and the mistakes of the past." To be so unlimited, the advocates of this next politics of the Democratic Party must recognize what they are up against. They are not just fighting the Third Way compromises of contemporary centrists. They are fighting Democrats who claim the mantle of FDR but battle as vigorously as the economic royalists of old to avert a new New Deal.

Henry Wallace was attacked and then dismissed because he proposed "a century of the common man and woman." Almost eighty years of that century have passed since his dismissal, and his fight for the future is largely forgotten. This is what must change. Just as young radicals with groups like the Democratic

Socialists of America are freeing the political discourse from the Red-Scared caution of their elders by embracing the word "socialist," Democrats must free their party from the mental shackles of Wall Street and the generous campaign donations proffered by the "bundlers" for fossil-fuel combines and the military-industrial complex. Progressives, no matter what their partisanship or independence, must free their minds and dream again of the peace and prosperity Henry Wallace championed.

2

Hope in a Time of War

*Four Freedoms, One
World and the Dream of
Overcoming Our Imperialisms*

> *Men need more than arms with which to fight and win this kind
> of war. They need enthusiasm for the future and a conviction
> that the flags they fight under are in clean, bright colors.*
> —Wendell Willkie, *One World*, 1943

> *Ours must be a generation that will distill the stamina and
> provide the skills to create a war-proof world. We must not
> bequeath a third bloodbath to our children.*
> —Henry Wallace, *America Tomorrow*, 1943

America has always had a radical streak, going back to the days
when Thomas Paine began his call for the revolution of 1776
with the words: "Perhaps the sentiments contained in the following pages, are not YET sufficiently fashionable to procure them
general favour; a long habit of not thinking a thing WRONG,
gives it a superficial appearance of being RIGHT, and raises at
first a formidable outcry in defense of custom."

Paine proposed a radical response. "O! ye that love mankind!
Ye that dare oppose not only tyranny but the tyrant, stand
forth! Every spot of the Old World is overrun with oppression,"
he wrote in *Common Sense*, which would inspire not just the
American Revolution but revolutions in France, Haiti and

beyond. "Freedom hath been hunted round the globe. Asia and Africa have long expelled her. Europe regards her like a stranger and England hath given her warning to depart. O! receive the fugitive and prepare in time an asylum for mankind."

General George Washington ordered that another of Paine's pamphlets, *The American Crisis*, be read aloud to the soldiers huddled in the cold at Valley Forge. What distinguished Paine's writings from the traditional call to arms, however, was a vision of what might come after victory. This is not merely the fight for survival. This is what writer Rebecca Solnit meant when she described "hope" to me as "a seizing of possibilities and an embrace of uncertainty, a sense that the future is yet to be determined, and our interventions may help determine it." It is the "why" in "Why We Fight"—the promise that the struggle is not to renew an old order but to initiate a new one.

Perhaps this is why, after many years of neglect in which he was virtually written out of American history, Paine was brought back into the picture by FDR. In the early days of World War II, historian and Paine biographer Harvey Kaye recalls: "Americans faced their gravest crisis since the Civil War. The Japanese assault on Pearl Harbor had propelled the United States into the Second World War, a global conflict in which the very survival of freedom, equality and democracy were at stake. And things did not look good at all. Germany had conquered most of Europe, Japan had overrun East Asia, and on every front from the Atlantic to the Pacific the Axis powers were advancing. At home, the reports of military disasters and setbacks triggered criticism of the government's handling of the war, rumors of invasion and a sense of despair, if not defeat."

Kaye explains: "Roosevelt understood that he needed to firmly engage American collective memory and imagination. Rallying support for the New Deal, he had regularly evoked historical images and personages such as Jefferson and Lincoln. But on this occasion, the nation's 32nd president would reach even more deeply into America's Revolutionary heritage, to the very crucible of war out of which the United States had emerged."

Just ten weeks after America's entry into World War II, on February 23, 1942, with a bow to the 210th anniversary of George Washington's birth, FDR gave one of his "fireside chats" on national radio and identified "a most appropriate occasion for us to talk with each other about things as they are today and things as we know they shall be in the future." Speaking on a day when a Japanese submarine shelled coastal targets near Santa Barbara, California, the president was remarkably frank in spelling out the details of the new crisis. "We have most certainly suffered losses—from Hitler's U-boats in the Atlantic as well as from the Japanese in the Pacific—and we shall suffer more of them before the turn of the tide," he conceded. "But, speaking for the United States of America, let me say once and for all to the people of the world: We Americans have been compelled to yield ground, but we will regain it. We and the other United Nations are committed to the destruction of the militarism of Japan and Germany. We are daily increasing our strength. Soon, we and not our enemies, will have the offensive; we, not they, will win the final battles; and we, not they, will make the final peace."

This was an example of the lofty rhetoric that the president who popularized the phrase "we have nothing to fear but fear itself" in the midst of the Great Depression was capable of employing in dire circumstances. But for the conclusion of one of the most important addresses of his presidency, FDR turned to the words of another wordsmith in another time of war.

"The task that we Americans now face will test us to the uttermost," he said, acknowledging the challenge that lay ahead. "Never before have we been called upon for such a prodigious effort. Never before have we had so little time in which to do so much. 'These are the times that try men's souls.'"

Roosevelt noted, with only slight embellishment, that:

Tom Paine wrote those words on a drumhead, by the light of a campfire. That was when Washington's little army of ragged, rugged men was retreating across New Jersey, having tasted naught but defeat. And General Washington ordered that these great words written by Tom Paine be read to the men of every regiment in the Continental Army, and this was the assurance given to the first American armed forces.

The United States was not just waging a necessary fight against fascism, Roosevelt made clear; it was fighting to begin the world anew. "We of the United Nations are agreed on certain broad principles in the kind of peace we seek," he told tens of millions of listeners. "The Atlantic Charter applies not only to the parts of the world that border the Atlantic but to the whole world; disarmament of aggressors, self-determination of nations and peoples, and the four freedoms—freedom of speech, freedom of religion, freedom from want, and freedom from fear."

Even before the United States had entered into the war, FDR devoted time and energy to crafting a vision of what would come after. This was vital work, as his was a war-weary and war-wary land. The experience of World War I, a fight of kings and kaisers into which the U.S. had been drawn at immense human and material cost, had soured Americans on seemingly distant conflicts. The "war to end all wars" had enriched munitions merchants but it had left a generation of young men shell-shocked and receptive to the isolationist appeals of Charles Lindbergh and his America First Committee.

Freda Kirchwey, editor of the *Nation* magazine, recognized the challenge. "Before its total, uncompromising demands are laid upon them," she explained as the daunting prospect of American involvement in a second world war emerged, "the people of America must learn that this war is their war." Labor unions and civil rights groups, leaders like A. Philip Randolph of the Brotherhood of Sleeping Car Porters and H.L. Mitchell of the

Southern Tenant Farmers Union, First Lady Eleanor Roosevelt and dramatist Lillian Hellman, all championed the view that America must fight not merely to defeat fascism but to win a new world in which the root causes of bigotry, demagoguery, inequality and injustice would be addressed.

The poet Langston Hughes put it more bluntly, writing in a 1943 reflection on the racial violence that had flared in cities such as Beaumont, Texas, and Detroit, Michigan: "You jim crowed me/ Before hitler rose to power/ And you're STILL jim crowing me/ Right now, this very hour.../ Yet you say we're fighting/ For democracy/ Then why don't democracy/ Include me?" The *Pittsburgh Courier*, a widely circulated African-American newspaper during the war years, launched what it referred to as the "Double V" campaign, which demanded victory over fascism abroad and racism at home.

Woody Guthrie, whose guitar featured the slogan "This Machine Kills Fascists," joined the Merchant Marine and the National Maritime Union, a militant CIO union with multi-racial leadership from its founding in the 1930s, and became a member of the unionized fighting force that braved U-boats to deliver supplies and save soldiers and sailors. In "Talking Merchant Marine," he sang of preparing to drop a depth charge on the Nazis:

> Walked to the tail, stood on the stern,
> Lookin' at the big brass screw blade turn;
> Listened to the sound of the engine pound,
> Gained sixteen feet every time it went around.
> Gettin' closer and closer, look out, you fascists.
>
> I'm just one of the merchant crew,
> I belong to the union called the N.M.U.
> I'm a union man from head to toe,
> I'm U.S.A. and C.I.O.
> Fightin' out here on the waters to win some
>   freedom on the land.

Roosevelt saw this bigger picture. He knew that the politics of the moment demanded a bold assertion not merely of military necessity but of postwar possibility—a vision rooted in the premise that the fascist threat had to be met with weapons and with ideas. It was a call to arms as urgent and meaningful as that of the battlefield trumpet.

FDR was not alone in this understanding. Indeed, it was the essential premise of liberal and progressive thinking in the early 1940s, and the basis for the essential divide in debates about the contribution that the Democratic Party would make to postwar politics. Americans, Henry Wallace counseled in 1943, expected a serious response to the question "What will we will get out of the war?" The answer could not be a transitory period of "peace" characterized by the recessions, depression, authoritarian power grabs and simmering conflict that marked the interlude between World War I and World War II. "We shall decide sometime in 1943 or 1944 whether to plant the seeds for World War No. 3," Wallace contended. To avert that prospect, FDR's vice president argued his party and his country must champion "the new democracy, the democracy of the common man," embracing "not just the Bill of Rights but also economic democracy, ethnic democracy, educational democracy and democracy in the treatment of the sexes." Author Max Lerner wanted a crusade on behalf of "militant democracy" as an antidote to authoritarianism, while Kirchwey proposed "A New Deal for the World." Historian Norman Markowitz argues that "social liberals came to enthusiastically define the war as a revolutionary struggle and to look to America to redeem her own revolutionary heritage by uniting with the forces that sought the destruction of colonialism and by working to construct international organizations to eliminate the social and economic inequalities that produce war."

These arguments extended from the vision that Roosevelt outlined in the "Four Freedoms" speech, his epic 1941 State of the Union address to Congress and the American people in which he outlined his own radical hope. Recently re-elected to an unprecedented third term as president, FDR recognized lingering economic challenges at home, but he was increasingly focused on global threats. The United States was not at war, but the president knew that the conflicts raging across Europe and Asia would soon go global.

To a greater extent than any president since Lincoln, FDR was an obsessive speedwriter. He was capable of delivering off-the-cuff comments that charmed the reporters who covered him and the politicians who debated with him. But when he delivered speeches to conventions or the Congress, he devoted hours of his precious time to identifying each epic turn of phrase. According to the Franklin D. Roosevelt Presidential Library and Museum account of the drafting of the "Four Freedoms" address, "as with all his speeches, FDR edited, rearranged and added extensively until the speech was his creation. In the end, the speech went through seven drafts before final delivery."

Roosevelt worked late into the night in the White House study with aides Harry Hopkins, Robert Sherwood and Samuel Rosenman. According to the FDR Library, the president said he had an idea for how to close the speech. "As recounted by Rosenman: 'We waited as he leaned far back in his swivel chair with his gaze on the ceiling. It was a long pause—so long that it began to become uncomfortable. Then he leaned forward again in his chair. ... He dictated the words so slowly that on the yellow pad I had in my lap I was able to take them down myself in longhand as he spoke.'"

These were the words that Roosevelt dictated:

In the future days, which we seek to make secure, we look forward to a world founded upon four essential human freedoms.

- The first is freedom of speech and expression—everywhere in the world.
- The second is freedom of every person to worship God in his own way—everywhere in the world.

- The third is freedom from want—which, translated into world terms, means economic understandings which will secure to every nation a healthy peacetime life for its inhabitants everywhere in the world.
- The fourth is freedom from fear—which, translated into world terms, means a worldwide reduction of armaments to such a point and in such a thorough fashion that no nation will be in a position to commit an act of physical aggression against any neighbor—anywhere in the world.

Roosevelt saw the Four Freedoms as program, not preachment. "That is no vision of a distant millennium," he told Congress. "It is a definite basis for a kind of world attainable in our own time and generation. That kind of world is the very antithesis of the so-called new order of tyranny which the dictators seek to create with the crash of a bomb. To that new order we oppose the greater conception—the moral order. A good society is able to face schemes of world domination and foreign revolutions alike without fear."

The president framed this as an innately American project. "Since the beginning of our American history, we have been engaged in change—in a perpetual peaceful revolution—a revolution which goes on steadily, quietly adjusting itself to changing conditions—without the concentration camp or the quick-lime in the ditch," he said. "The world order which we seek is the cooperation of free countries, working together in a friendly, civilized society."

Before the year was finished, FDR would lead the United States into the war with his post–Pearl Harbor designation of December 7, 1941, as "a date which will live in infamy." It would be a fight for the future. America would make itself "the arsenal of democracy," but the emphasis would be on achieving sufficient democracy so that the arsenal—all arsenals—would become less necessary. FDR understood the American disinclination toward war; if it was necessary to fight against the aggression of Hitler and Mussolini, then the fight needed to have as its end "a worldwide reduction of armaments to such a point and in such a thorough fashion that no nation will be in a position to commit an act of physical aggression against any neighbor—anywhere in the world." This was a contemporary restatement of the Paine-ite impulse: "If there must be trouble, let it be in my day, that my child may have peace."

The "Four Freedoms" were not Roosevelt's final word on what the United States would fight for in World War II. In 1944, in the midst of the war, he would use another State of the Union address to outline a "Second Bill of Rights," which would come to be referred to as an "Economic Bill of Rights."

But the Four Freedoms speech set the stage for FDR's win-the-war, win-the-peace message, by providing what the president believed to be "a definite basis for a kind of world attainable in our own time and generation." His vice president, Henry Wallace, would crystalize the message in July 1943, as the war raged in Europe and the Pacific. "Along with Britain, Russia and China," he said, "our nation will exert a tremendous economic and moral persuasion in the peace."

But, added Wallace, who was speaking that day to a multiracial audience in Detroit, "many of our most patriotic and forward-looking citizens are asking: 'Why not start now practicing these Four Freedoms in our own back yard?' Yes, they are right! A fuller democracy for all is the lasting preventive of war. A lesser or part-time democracy breeds the dissension and class conflicts that seek their solution in guns and slaughter."

That debate about how to prevail in the conflict at hand and prevent the next engaged the United States in the early 1940s. The war had to be won. But, so, too, did the peace. To achieve both ends, FDR believed it was necessary to secure the high ground in American politics going forward. In 1944 he sought re-election as an ailing man, aged beyond his years, so that he might shape the future as the leader of a new Democratic Party. That new kind of party, he hoped, would link liberal

Democrats, liberal Republicans and progressive independents in a movement that might finally overwhelm the Southern segregationists and the conservatives of both the old parties. Roosevelt, Wallace and many others believed that the end of World War II could be a pivot point in American history, where the greatest generation, having beaten fascism overseas, would return with a determination to beat reaction at home.

The great political debate of the war years gave rise to two clear camps, which formed in and around the two major parties. One side sought a postwar regression toward the America that existed before the war and before the New Deal, as was the fervent hope of right-wing fabulists such as *Chicago Tribune* publisher Robert McCormick. Even then, the country had its "Make America Great Again" contingent.

The other side saw the New Deal and the united front against fascism as a blueprint for postwar progress. They might quibble about approaches and agendas, but these liberal internationalists seemed to have the upper hand. For a brief moment during World War II, the isolationists were isolated, as prominent Republicans such as Wendell Willkie and New York mayor Fiorello La Guardia aligned with Roosevelt. The best of the liberal internationalists knew that greatness could be achieved only when segregation, sexism and poverty were addressed. America was "the hope of the world" and had to continue to acquit itself as such, announced La Guardia, who was elected to his position as the nominee of the party of Lincoln but identified as a New Dealer. An ardent advocate for social-welfare programs at home and abroad, La Guardia served after World War II as the director general for the United Nations Relief and Rehabilitation Administration, putting into practice a view he had expressed from his days as a young congressman serving after World War I: "You cannot preach self-government and liberty to people in a starving land." La Guardia was a frequent ally and sometime candidate of the Socialist Party, like a number of progressive Republicans in that time, and he preached that economic security was necessary for the full enjoyment of freedom. "Only a well-fed, well-schooled and well-housed people can enjoy the blessings of liberty," he argued.

The son of an Italian Catholic immigrant father and a Jewish immigrant mother from Trieste whose own sister was interned in a Nazi concentration camp, La Guardia was a predictable Republican ally of FDR and the visionary politics of the World War II era. Wendell Willkie was not. As president of the Commonwealth & Southern Corporation, the nation's largest utility holding company, during the 1930s Willkie emerged as an outspoken critic of the Roosevelt administration's ambitious Tennessee Valley Authority, which supplied electrical power to Southern and border states in competition with Commonwealth & Southern. Willkie, himself a former Democrat, became such a prominent and effective critic of Roosevelt's policies that *Time* magazine identified him as "the only businessman in the U.S. who is ever mentioned as a presidential possibility in 1940." A grassroots mobilization by Willkie for President clubs across the country captured the imagination of Republican leaders and secured him the nomination in one of the great political upsets of the 20th century. In the words of biographer Bill Severn, Willkie "openly admitted that the New Deal had accomplished many needed reforms ... and approved most of the goals if not the methods of the Roosevelt foreign policy."

As a challenger to FDR, Willkie's appeal was his freshness. Roosevelt, a man aged beyond his years by struggles with polio and other physical maladies, faced enormous demands as he wrestled with an unstable economy and global threats. The president remained personally popular, yet there were doubts about his policies—especially when it came to preparation for a war that a great many Americans hoped to avoid. FDR's decision to seek an unprecedented third term brought an outcry from critics inside his own Democratic Party and inspired hope among Republicans. The GOP had suffered the worst defeat in the party's history in 1936, but there was a sense that Roosevelt might be vulnerable to the right challenger in 1940. Ten years younger than the incumbent and possessed of a boyish charm that softened his image as a titan of industry, Willkie projected a combination of youth and competence.

Roosevelt countered the Willkie challenge with a political masterstroke. He replaced the uninspiring vice president of his first two terms, John Nance Garner, and made the Democratic ticket fresh, and young, by insisting that the party nominate as his running mate a candidate who projected just as much energy and idealism as Willkie—and who, like the Republican nominee, had never before sought elected office. The man FDR chose as his new running mate was Secretary of Agriculture Henry Wallace.

While Wallace's addition to the 1940 Democratic ticket frustrated the big-city bosses and segregationists, it electrified the CIO union activists, rural populists, African Americans and young people who had come to see Roosevelt's secretary of agriculture as the keeper of the New Deal flame. The first of FDR's close associates to publicly champion a third-term candidacy, Wallace had framed the 1940 election campaign even before it began as a struggle for political and economic democracy. And against fascism.

Roosevelt "wanted a leading outspoken, anti-fascist on the ticket given what he knew we were up against in the 1940s," explains historian Peter Kuznick. Wallace saw the rise of Hitler and Mussolini as an existential threat, and he warned about it in passionate terms at a time when groups like Friends of New Germany and the German American Bund openly celebrated Hitler and prominent figures like Charles Lindbergh were peddling crude nativism and anti-Semitic tropes at huge "America First" rallies. The Iowan shared the concerns expressed by popular authors like Sinclair Lewis, whose 1935 novel *It Can't Happen Here* imagined the election of a demagogue to the presidency and an American turn toward fascism.

Wallace openly scorned the America First rhetoric that was mouthed not just by Republicans but by prominent Democrats. "We must remember that down through the ages one of the most popular political devices has been to blame economic and other troubles on some minority group," Wallace warned in a 1939 speech in New York. The text of that speech, according to biographer Russell Lord, "aroused fervent interest among important leaders, intellectual and political, of racial minority groups," and was circulated in the White House by a key adviser to the president, Samuel Rosenman, a New York Supreme Court justice who was a prominent member of the American Jewish Committee.

"The survival and strength of American democracy are proof that it has succeeded by its deeds thus far," Wallace continued. "But we all know that it contains the seeds of failure. I for one will not be confident of the continued survival of American democracy if millions of unskilled workers and their families are condemned to be reliefers all their lives, with no place in our industrial system. I will not be confident of the survival of democracy if half our people must be below the line of a decent nutrition, while only one tenth succeed in reaching good nutritional standards. I will not be confident of the survival of democracy if most of our children continue to be reared in surroundings where poverty is highest and education is lowest."

After FDR made Wallace his running mate, he focused on the work of the presidency, while Wallace hit the campaign trail with a vigor that led *New York Times* columnist Arthur Krock to refer to him as "the best of the New Deal type." The Roosevelt-Wallace ticket swept to victory, defeating Willkie and his running mate by five million votes nationwide. In the Electoral College, the Democrats gave the Republicans a 449–83 thumping.

Wallace would be the new vice president. But the other new man of 1940, Willkie, would have his own role, as a frequent ally of the New Dealers. Before the war was done, Willkie and

Wallace would be appearing together as champions of a strikingly parallel vision for the postwar era. They even joined up to address the topic in a December 1943 national broadcast that was part of the radio series *Beyond Victory*, sponsored by the Carnegie Endowment for International Peace. Willkie called for an end to colonialism while Wallace proposed a global New Deal designed to raise the people of the world out of poverty. The former rivals were singing now from the same hymnal about laying the foundation for a postwar era that would not repeat the mistakes of the past. That same year, Wallace and Willkie both contributed to a popular book, *Prefaces for Peace*, on the need for a new international order dedicated to economic, social and racial justice.

There could be no greater measure of the extraordinary moment that developed during the course of World War II than the shared efforts of Willkie and Wallace on behalf of the Four Freedoms vision that FDR had outlined. While Wallace entered the 1940s as a progressive of long standing, stretching back to his support of Robert La Follette's groundbreaking 1924 independent presidential bid, Willkie evolved toward the ardent liberalism that would frequently align him with the administration.

Barely two months after the 1940 election, Willkie was telling Republican groups to abandon isolationism and embrace the global struggle against fascism. "Whether we like it or not America cannot remove itself from the world," he warned in a January 1941 speech to New York Republicans. "I take issue with all who say we can survive with freedom in a totalitarian world. I want to say to you even though some of you may disagree with me, and I say it to you with all the emphasis of my being, that if Britain falls before the onslaught of Hitlerism, it will be impossible over a period of time to preserve the free way of life in America."

Historian Howard Jones asserts that Willkie "had more influence on causing the American people and government to turn away from isolationism in the years from 1940 to 1944 than anyone other than President Franklin D. Roosevelt." Roosevelt, impressed by Willkie's sincerity, made him a roving ambassador to the allied countries that FDR had begun to refer to as "the united nations," a group that included the Soviet Union. Willkie did much more than merely carry messages to Winston Churchill, Joseph Stalin and Chiang Kai-shek, however. He began to formulate arguments for "winning the peace" that were more radical than those advanced by any other prominent figure, save Wallace.

Willkie argued that Americans would need "to accept the most challenging opportunity of all history—the chance to create a new society in which men and women the world around can live and grow invigorated by independence and freedom."

Willkie made that appeal at the close of *One World*, the book he wrote after making a seven-week, 31,000-mile journey through war zones and national capitals in the summer and fall of 1942. The trek allowed him, he wrote, "to see and talk to hundreds of people in more than a dozen nations, and to talk intimately with many of the world's leaders. It was an experience which few private citizens and none of those leaders have had. It gave me some new and urgent convictions and strengthened some of my old ones. These convictions are not mere humanitarian hopes; they are not just idealistic and vague. They are based on things I saw and learned at first hand and upon the views of men and women, important and anonymous, whose heroism and sacrifices give meaning and life to their beliefs."

One World, which topped the *New York Times* best-seller lists for four months in 1943 and sold more than 1.5 million copies during the period, was many things. A travelogue. A report from the front. An assessment of leaders and their ambitions. But above all, it was a manifesto that outlined a plan for avoiding the mistakes of the past. "I live in constant dread that this war may end before the people of the world have come to a common understanding of what they fight for and what they hope for after the war is over," wrote Willkie, a veteran of World War I. "I was a soldier in the last war and after that war was over I saw our bright dreams disappear, our stirring slogans become the jests of the cynical, and all because the fighting peoples did not arrive at any common postwar purposes while they fought. It must be our resolve that this does not happen again."

Willkie called for "a council of the United Nations—a common council in which all plan together, not a council of a few, who direct or merely aid others as they think wise." And that council, he argued, must be serious about the work of "the freeing of the conquered nations." This was a specific reference to Willkie's belief that "a war of liberation" must be about more than ending the occupation of countries overrun by the Nazis and the Japanese. It must be about ending colonialism and "giving to all peoples freedom to govern themselves as soon as they are able, and the economic freedom on which all lasting self-government inevitably rests."

Denouncing Western imperialism, Willkie explained that the people of other regions "may not want our type of democracy ... but they are determined to work out their own destiny under governments selected by themselves." He accepted that among the United Nations there would be governments with which the United States disagreed ideologically and practically, including the Soviet Union. Willkie was a capitalist in good standing, yet he refused to bow to Red Scare hysteria at home. He even went so far as to personally represent former Communist Party organizer William Schneiderman before the U.S. Supreme Court, pro bono, in a 1943 case that wound up overturning a deportation order based on Schneiderman's views. "Of all the times when civil liberties should be defended, it is now," Willkie told the court. And he was ardent in arguing during the war that "it is possible for Russia and America, perhaps the most powerful countries in the world, to work together for the economic welfare and peace of the world." To those who fretted about cooperation with Stalin and the "Reds," Willkie replied: "No one could be more opposed to the Communist doctrine than I am, for I am completely opposed to any system of absolutism. But I have never understood why it should be assumed that in any possible contact between Communism and democracy, democracy should go down."

Willkie's *One World* vision featured a sharp rebuke of British prime minister Winston Churchill, an old-school imperialist who announced in the midst of the war, "I did not become His Majesty's first minister in order to preside over the liquidation of the British Empire." Willkie's objection, however, was not confined to foreign leaders who mouthed the language of "freedom" and "liberation" while scheming to maintain the violent arrangements of suppression and discrimination. The people of the United States, he argued in the language of one of his chapter titles, would need to address "Our Imperialisms at Home":

> A true world outlook is incompatible with a foreign imperialism, no matter how high-minded the governing country. It is equally incompatible with the kind of imperialism which can develop inside any nation. Freedom is an indivisible word. If we want to enjoy it, and fight for it, we must be prepared to extend it to everyone, whether they are rich or poor, whether they agree with us or not, no matter what their race or the color of their skin. We cannot, with good conscience, expect the British to set up an orderly schedule for the liberation of India before we have decided for ourselves to make all who live in America free.

Willkie wrote that at a time when the United States Congress refused to condemn lynching, when Northern cities were rigidly segregated and when Southern states maintained an American apartheid.

Willkie, the Republican, rejected the compromises that Roosevelt accepted in order to hold together the Democratic Party. "We have practiced within our own boundaries something that amounts to race imperialism," Willkie declared. "The attitude of the white citizens of this country toward the Negroes has undeniably had some of the unlovely characteristics of an alien imperialism—a smug racial superiority, a willingness to exploit an unprotected people. We have justified it by telling ourselves that its end is benevolent. And sometimes it has been. But so sometimes have been the ends of imperialism. And the moral atmosphere in which it has existed is identical with that in which men—well-meaning men—talk of 'the white man's burden.'"

He added: "Today it is becoming increasingly apparent to thoughtful Americans that we cannot fight the forces and ideas of imperialism abroad and maintain any form of imperialism at home. The war has done this to our thinking. Emancipation came to the colored race in America as a war measure. It was an act of military necessity. Manifestly it would have come without war, in the slower process of humanitarian reform and social enlightenment. But it required a disastrous, internecine war to bring this question of human freedom to a crisis, and the process of striking the shackles from the slave was accomplished in a single hour. We are finding under the pressures of this present conflict that long-standing barriers and prejudices are breaking down. The defense of our democracy against the forces that threaten it from without has made some of its failures to function at home glaringly apparent."

Willkie maintained that there could be no return to the "normalcy" of the prewar era. Normalcy, he argued, had not served America well, historically or in the current fight. "Our very proclamations of what we are fighting for have rendered our own inequities self-evident," he said. "When we talk of freedom and opportunity for all nations, the mocking paradoxes in our own society become so clear they can no longer be ignored. If we want to talk about freedom, we must mean freedom for others as well as ourselves, and we must mean freedom for everyone inside our frontiers as well as outside."

This was the language of radical hope, of a belief that immense sacrifice could generate immense progress. Yet, despite his best efforts, Willkie had no real hope of advancing this agenda within a Republican Party that rejected his 1944 presidential candidacy unceremoniously and unequivocally. Rather, the last great hope that the postwar era might "begin the world over again" rested with another man: the vice president of the United States.

So it was that Henry Wallace opened the fight against American fascism.

3

"You Drew Blood from the Cave Dwellers"

Wrestling with Demagoguery and the Wealthy Men Who Finance Authoritarianism

Those who write the peace must think of the whole world. There can be no privileged peoples. We ourselves in the United States are no more a master race than the Nazis. And we cannot perpetuate economic warfare without planting the seeds of military warfare. We must use our power at the peace table to build an economic peace that is charitable and enduring.
> —Henry Wallace, "The Price of Free World Victory," speech given in New York before the Free World Association, May 8, 1942

[Henry Wallace] is a human being who has become a statesman … driving into the minds of the American people certain truths made clear as no other statesman in this period has done.
> —Eleanor Roosevelt, "Henry Wallace's Democracy," *New Republic*, August 7, 1944

What began as a battle between one Henry and another evolved into the most revealing American debate of the World War II era. One Henry, magazine publisher Henry Luce, was in the words of his able biographer Robert E. Herzstein, "the most influential private citizen in America of his day." He used his bully pulpits, *Time* and *Life* magazines, to make himself, in the words of historian of journalism James Baughman, "America's single most powerful and innovative mass communicator." In this capacity, he advanced the agenda of empire-building capitalism favored by the class warriors of the Grand Old Party. The other Henry, Vice President Henry Wallace, was the second most influential *public* citizen of his day. Their clash began in early 1941, as the United States was being drawn into World War II. It would define the battle lines of American politics across the decades, to this very day.

Luce and Wallace both rejected isolationism. The publisher's oft-stated allegiance to "God, the Republican Party and free enterprise" was that of the multinational capitalist—not that of the right-wing zealots who were spinning conspiracy theories about FDR's strategies for getting the U.S. into the war. The vice president, meanwhile, was a stalwart internationalist. Yet, these were very different men with very different values.

In the February 17, 1941, issue of his enormously popular *Life* magazine, Luce published his famous essay "The American Century." He argued that the United States was already in the war informally, as part of a "collaboration" with Winston Churchill's embattled Britain, and all but certain to be formally engaged before the fighting was done. "Almost every expert will agree that Britain cannot win complete victory—cannot even, in the common saying, 'stop Hitler'—without American help," Luce wrote. Now, he argued, "in any sort of partnership with the British Empire, Great Britain is perfectly willing that the United States of America should assume the role of senior partner. This has been true for a long time. Among serious Englishmen, the chief complaint against America (and incidentally their best alibi for themselves) has really amounted to this: that America has refused to rise to the opportunities of leadership in the world."

Luce proposed to rise to the occasion with a Pax Americana, a worldview that historian John Morton Blum would suggest "contemplated a political, economic and religious imperialism indistinguishable, except by nationality, from the doctrines of Kipling and Churchill." In the field of national policy, Luce explained,

> the fundamental trouble with America has been, and is, that whereas their nation became in the 20th century the most powerful and the most vital nation in the world, nevertheless Americans were unable to accommodate themselves spiritually and practically to that fact. Hence they have failed to play their part as a world power—a failure which has had disastrous consequences for themselves and for all mankind. And the cure is this: to accept wholeheartedly our duty and our opportunity as the most powerful and vital nation in the world and in consequence to exert upon the world the full impact of our influence, for such purposes as we see fit and by such means as we see fit.

Denouncing "this virus of isolationist sterility [that] has so deeply infected an influential section of the Republican Party," Luce advocated interventionism with a purpose: to make himself and people like him richer. Dropped amid his rumination on the language to be employed in discussing the role of the United States—"if we cannot state war aims in terms of vastly distant geography, shall we use some big words like Democracy and Freedom and Justice? Yes, we can use the big words"—were pronouncements that left little doubt regarding his own aims and those of his class. The United States had "a golden opportunity, an opportunity unprecedented in all history, to assume the leadership of the world—a golden opportunity handed to us on the proverbial silver platter. ... America as the dynamic center of ever-widening spheres of enterprise ... America as the principal guarantor of the freedom of the seas ... America as the dynamic leader of world trade." Reflecting on how, "throughout the 17th century and the 18th century and the 19th century, this continent teemed with manifold projects and magnificent purposes," Luce now proposed Manifest Destiny for the world.

He offered an expanded calculus in which other nations might be considered based on what they "will be worth to us." He ended by declaring "the world of the 20th century, if it is to come to life in any nobility of health and vigor, must be to a significant degree an American Century."

Luce's article would prove to be highly popular with and influential for the powers-that-be. But Sidney Hillman, president of Amalgamated Clothing Workers of America, saw it as little more than a proposal that "American big business exploit the rest of the world."

The publisher devoted much of his article to attacking FDR and the New Deal, and haughtily dismissed the Roosevelt-Wallace landslide of just three months earlier by asserting that Roosevelt "owes his continuation in office today largely to the coming of the war." Luce adopted the language of FDR's right-wing critics, claiming that the administration had saddled the country with "huge Government debt, a vast bureaucracy and a whole generation of young people trained to look to the Government as the source of all life. The party in power is the one which for long years has been most sympathetic to all manner of socialist doctrines and collectivist trends."

Nothing about Luce's "American Century" sat well with Henry Wallace. As a counter, the vice president proposed "the Century of the Common Man."

A Long-Drawn-Out People's Revolution

Wallace traveled to New York on May 8, 1942, to address the Free World Association, having cleared the agenda-setting speech he was about to deliver with Roosevelt, who despised Luce. The Free World Association stood at the forefront of international "Stop Hitler Now" campaigning, promoting active resistance to Nazism, working with American Jewish groups to reveal the horrors of the Holocaust and arguing that the authoritarian threat must be answered first by winning the war and then by developing a global democratic federation.

Wallace titled his speech "The Price of Free World Victory," and it was in it that he addressed the future circumstance of the common man.

"Some have spoken of the 'American Century,' " he said, referring directly to Luce. "I say that the century on which we are entering—the century which will come into being after this war—can be and must be the century of the common man. ... No nation will have the God-given right to exploit other nations. Older nations will have the privilege to help younger nations get started on the path to industrialization, but there must be neither military nor economic imperialism."

Wallace described World War II in Biblical terms that spoke directly to millions of Americans and people around the world listening in via radio. (He personally translated the speech into Spanish and repeated its essential themes in a separate broadcast to Latin America.)

Satan is now trying to lead the common man of the whole world back into slavery and darkness. For the stark truth is that the violence preached by the Nazis is the devil's own religion of darkness. So also is the doctrine that one race or one class is by heredity superior and that all other races or classes are supposed to be slaves. The belief in one Satan-inspired Fuhrer, with his Quislings, his Lavals, his Mussolinis—his "gauleiters" in every nation in the world—is the last and ultimate darkness. Is there any hell hotter than that of being a Quisling, unless it is that of being a Laval or a Mussolini? In a twisted sense, there is something almost great in the figure of the Supreme Devil operating through a human form, in a Hitler who has the daring to spit straight into the eye of God and man. But the Nazi system has a heroic position for only one leader. By definition only one person is allowed to retain full sovereignty over his own soul. All the rest are stooges. They are stooges who have been mentally and politically degraded, and who feel that they can get square with the world only by mentally and politically degrading other people. These stooges are really psychopathic cases. Satan has turned loose upon us the insane.

Rallied against Satan and his stooges, suggested Wallace, were veterans of "a long-drawn-out people's revolution."

"In this Great Revolution of the people," he explained, "there were the American Revolution of 1775, the French Revolution of 1792, the Latin American revolutions of the Bolivarian era, the German Revolution of 1848, and the Russian Revolution of [1917]. Each spoke for the common man in terms of blood on the battlefield. Some went to excess. But the significant thing is that the people groped their way to the light. More of them learned to think and work together."

The applause from the crowd in the Grand Ballroom of New York's Commodore Hotel, which included refugees from Nazi-occupied lands and their liberal allies, built with each line.

Wallace continued: "No compromise with Satan is possible. We shall not rest until the victims under the Nazi and Japanese yoke are freed. We shall fight for a complete peace as well as a complete victory." The vice president defined "complete peace" in starkly anti-imperialist terms. "Yes, and when the time of peace comes, the citizen will again have a duty; the consumer will have a duty—the supreme duty of sacrificing the lesser interest for the greater interest of the general welfare," he said. "Those who write the peace must think of the whole world. There can be no privileged peoples. We ourselves in the United States are no more a master race than the Nazis. And we cannot perpetuate economic warfare without planting the seeds of military warfare. We must use our power at the peace table to build an economic peace that is charitable and enduring."

Wallace finished his speech with a plea for expanding literacy in a largely illiterate world, which was still susceptible to the appeals of double-talking tyrants.

In those countries where the ability has been recently acquired or where the people have had no long experience in governing themselves on the basis of their own thinking, it is easy for demagogues to arise and prostitute the mind of the common man to their own base ends. Such a demagogue may get financial help from some person of wealth who is unaware of what the end result will be. Herr Thyssen, the wealthy German steel man, little realized what he was doing when he gave Hitler enough money to enable him to play on the minds of the German people. The demagogue is the curse of the modern world, and of all the demagogues, the worst are those financed by well-meaning wealthy men who sincerely believe that their wealth is likely to be safer if they can hire men with political "it" to change the signposts and lure the people back into slavery of the most degraded kind.

"Not even William Jennings Bryan had employed such a combustible mixture of radical and religious rhetoric," *New Yorker* magazine writer Alex Ross would muse decades later. This argument that the fight against fascism required opposition not merely to the distant demagogues of Europe and Asia but to the financiers who might enable American demagogues would frame Wallace's message going forward, along with the call for massive investment in domestic and international job creation, education, social services and peacemaking to combat the threat. It was rooted in Christian faith and the unapologetically liberal and vaguely social-democratic economic theories of reformers such as British economist William Beveridge, who in 1942 issued his groundbreaking report on how the war-ravaged country might address the "Giant Evils" that afflicted society: Want, Disease, Ignorance, Squalor and Idleness.

A young Edward R. Murrow suggested that the postwar era would be defined by whether the vice president's program would become "the forerunner of the American policy of tomorrow." Eleanor Roosevelt's biographer, Blanche Wiesen Cook, wrote that "Wallace's speech complemented ER's vision, and she never tired of quoting his words," and pointing out that "she vigorously opposed Henry Luce's notion of an American Century and rejected completely his call for 'the Americanization of the world.'" Walter Lippmann, a frequent critic of the vice president, told Wallace that the speech was "the most moving and effective thing produced by us during the war" and, indeed, that he thought it "perfect, and you need have no qualms about letting it be circulated not only all over the country but all over the world."

Wallace's New York speech was translated into twenty languages and featured in books and pamphlets that were distributed to workers in defense plants, sailors, and soldiers. Recordings of the speech were issued as phonograph albums, sometimes with musical accompaniment. *The Price of Victory*, a short film based on the speech and narrated by Wallace, was produced by Paramount Pictures and the U.S. Office of War Information. It was even nominated for an Academy Award for Best Documentary Feature in 1943.

Aaron Copland was so inspired by the address that he wrote a short musical piece based on it for the Cincinnati Symphony Orchestra. "It was the common man, after all, who was doing all the dirty work in the war and the army; he deserved a fanfare," explained Copland, the son of Jewish immigrants who had made common cause with the "popular front" leftists of the 1930s. His *Fanfare for the Common Man*, as a 2018 National Public Radio tribute noted, would eventually be "performed for presidents, played to honor victims at the opening of the National September 11 Memorial & Museum and [used to lend] a sense of gravity to television sports and news programs" and "has even been heard in space: in 2008, NASA pilot Eric Boe chose it as wake-up music for his crew of astronauts on the space shuttle Endeavor."

Along with all the accolades it received, however, Wallace's speech was denounced by those who heard it as a threat to their politics and to their powers. As Wallace continued to speak, and to expand upon his themes, the denunciations grew louder. Luce's wife, Clare Boothe Luce, a newly elected Republican member of the House of Representatives from a wealthy district in Connecticut, took to describing the vice president's internationalism as "globaloney," while Secretary of State Adolf Berle, who was already fretting about the "reds" who might be on the State Department payroll, joked that he had to station policemen around his home when Wallace visited "because of your talk about revolutions." Sharper reactions came from the *Wall Street Journal* and the *New York Times*, which would soon be devoting editorial after editorial to calling out Wallace's rhetoric. British prime minister Winston Churchill was reportedly "enraged" by Wallace's talk of uprooting imperialism and ending empires. Like Churchill, nascent Cold Warriors at home grumbled about Wallace's inclusion of the Russian Revolution on his list of long-drawn-out people's revolutions, citing it alongside their complaints about Roosevelt's willingness to work closely with Soviet premier Joseph Stalin.

But Roosevelt was determined to promote cooperation. "Never before have the major Allies been more closely united—not only in their war aims but also in their peace aims," he would say before the war was done, as he predicted "the end of the system of unilateral action, the exclusive alliances, the spheres of influence, the balances of power, and all the other expedients that have been tried for centuries—and have always failed." Such pronouncements unsettled people like Whittaker Chambers, the former Communist who had become a red-baiting editor of Luce's *Time* magazine, and who would eventually make a name for himself by portraying the Roosevelt administration, including the Department of Agriculture that Wallace ran for FDR's first two terms, as a hotbed of left-wing skullduggery.

Though Luce and Wallace exchanged passive-aggressive compliments after the vice president parried the "America Century" with the "People's Revolution," political battle lines were being drawn. Wallace began to argue within the White House for a pushback against what he referred to as "the *Time-Fortune-Life* crowd" and its allies within the administration. He saw the wartime debate in stark terms, as he explained in a December 28, 1942, diary entry recalling an end-of-the-year meeting with Roosevelt.

"I said there was one group of people in the United States at the present time definitely moving toward producing a postwar situation which would eventually bring us into war with Russia; and another group moving into a situation that would eventually bring us into war with England," Wallace wrote. "I said the time had come when we must begin to organize skillfully and aggressively for peace. He said he was going to go a long way in his speech to Congress on [January] 7th, that he was going to appeal particularly to the soldier boys, saying that he knew what kind of world they were fighting for; they were fighting for a world in which there would be no more war and in which they as individuals could be sure of a job. He said he was going to put in his speech that he had been advised that it was bad politics to say what he had said, but he felt it was the thing to do anyway."

Wallace's personal interactions with Roosevelt were as important as his public pronouncements because, as in all consequential presidential administrations, FDR's inner circle was both a team of rivals and an ideological battleground. The New Deal coalition that produced four landslide victories for Roosevelt was enormous. It included every region and just about every partisanship. There were Southern Democrats who stood far to the right of most Republicans. There were Northern and Western Democrats who stood to the left of some Socialists. Roosevelt was elected in 1932 on something of a unity ticket, with a Northeastern liberal at the top, paired with Southern conservative John Nance Garner, a wily Texan and former Speaker of the House who was never fully onboard for the New Deal. FDR had a high tolerance for internal conflict and heard his aides out before making decisions. He also followed the news obsessively, taking note of the rise of militant trade unions, political parties like the Wisconsin Progressives and the Minnesota Farmer Laborites and other popular movements that were staking out positions to the left of the Democrats. There is no question that he moved left during the course of his presidency, but it was not a steady process. He would lurch left and then edge back; he would welcome the hatred of the bankers and plutocrats and then meet the investors and business owners whose buy-in he needed to retool the economy, especially as it became clear that the United States would be drawn into World War II. The decision to move Wallace from the Department of Agriculture to the vice presidency was a reflection of the president's desire to have one of the more left-wing members of his administration at his side, in position as a potential successor. He valued Wallace's advice and counsel. Yet he also listened to those who warned that Wallace was too idealistic, too mystical, too radical. It was a constant balancing act.

When Wallace was with the president in the same room, the two men maintained a working relationship that was intellectually adventurous and passionate. Wallace often brought reports from a labor rally or a meeting with African-American, Latino or Jewish activists to the Oval Office. Like Eleanor Roosevelt, Wallace was an advocate for those whose voices were rarely heard in the corridors of power. The first lady and the vice president served as a counterbalance to those who assumed that the country was comfortably united in a time of war. No, they warned, there were tensions, and they needed to be addressed. When Wallace counseled that the administration needed to provide clarity regarding the purpose of the sacrifices it was demanding from Americans and the shape of its postwar vision, FDR listened. So it was that the president was soon sounding many of the themes Wallace had raised in his New York address.

"The Axis powers knew that they must win the war in 1942—or eventually lose everything," Roosevelt said on January 7, 1943, in his State of the Union address. "I do not need to tell you that our enemies did not win the war in 1942." He followed that mordant line by surveying the map of global conflict and vowing to take the war to the enemy. "I cannot tell you when or where the United Nations are going to strike next in Europe. ... But I can tell you that no matter where and when we strike by land, we and the British and the Russians will hit them from the air heavily and relentlessly. ... Yes, the Nazis and the Fascists have asked for it—and they are going to get it. ... Yes, 1943 will not be an easy year for us on the home front. We shall feel in many ways in our daily lives the sharp pinch of total war," the president warned. But he said the tide was turning in the right direction and, keeping a promise he had made to Wallace two weeks earlier, Roosevelt detailed a vision of the postwar era:

> We, and all the United Nations, want a decent peace and a durable peace. In the years between the end of the First World War and the beginning of the Second World War, we were not living under a decent or a durable peace.
>
> I have reason to know that our boys at the front are concerned with two broad aims beyond the winning of the war; and their thinking and their opinion coincide with what most Americans here back home are mulling over. They know, and we know, that it would be inconceivable—it would, indeed, be sacrilegious—if this nation and the world did not attain some real, lasting good out of all these efforts and sufferings and bloodshed and death.

Referencing his Four Freedoms speech from two years earlier, he told the Congress that

> the people at home, and the people at the front, are wondering a little about the third freedom—freedom from want. To them it means that when they are mustered out, when war production is converted to the economy of peace, they will have the right to expect full employment—full employment for themselves and for all able-bodied men and women in America who want to work.

They expect the opportunity to work, to run their farms, their stores, to earn decent wages. They are eager to face the risks inherent in our system of free enterprise.

They do not want a postwar America which suffers from undernourishment or slums or the dole. They want no get-rich-quick era of bogus "prosperity" which will end for them in selling apples on a street corner, as happened after the bursting of the boom in 1929.

When you talk with our young men and our young women, you will find they want to work for themselves and for their families; they consider that they have the right to work; and they know that after the last war their fathers did not gain that right.

When you talk with our young men and women, you will find that with the opportunity for employment they want assurance against the evils of all major economic hazards, assurance that will extend from the cradle to the grave. And this great Government can and must provide this assurance.

I have been told that this is no time to speak of a better America after the war. I am told it is a grave error on my part.

I dissent.

And if the security of the individual citizen, or the family, should become a subject of national debate, the country knows where I stand.

FDR closed with a rejection of isolationism and imperialism that mirrored much of what Wallace had been saying. "Hitlerism, like any other form of crime or disease, can grow from the evil seeds of economic as well as military feudalism," the president declared. "Victory in this war is the first and greatest goal before us. Victory in the peace is the next. That means striving toward the enlargement of the security of man here and throughout the world—and, finally, striving for the fourth freedom—freedom from fear." To that end, FDR proposed a worldview, like that of Wallace, that rejected heavy-handed empire building in favor of diplomacy and cooperation. "The very philosophy of the Axis powers is based on a profound contempt for the human race," he said. "If, in the formation of our future policy, we were guided by the same cynical contempt, then we should be surrendering to the philosophy of our enemies, and our victory would turn to defeat."

The War within a War

Franklin Roosevelt's words echoed those of Henry Wallace on that January day. But as 1943 progressed, it became painfully evident that the administration was deeply divided on the practical questions of how to pursue the war, and the peace.

During the course of 1942 and 1943, Wallace fought inside the Roosevelt administration to advance his views, often with the president's support but sometimes without it. The bitterest battle—the "war within a war," as historian Bascom Timmons put it—was with Secretary of Commerce Jesse Holman Jones, a real-estate mogul from Texas whose power inside and outside government was such that FDR sometimes referred to him as "Jesus H. Jones." In what Wallace biographers Culver and Hyde would describe as "the most celebrated intragovernmental squabble of the era," Wallace was pitted against a sixty-eight-year-old "fiscal and social conservative with no interest in politics as a vehicle for change."

Jones had come to Washington as an appointee of a Republican president, Herbert Hoover, yet he had remained to chair the powerful Reconstruction Finance Corporation through Roosevelt's first two terms. During the war years, he served not only at Commerce but as Federal Loan Administrator, which gave him responsibility over all federal investment agencies. Jones was so used to calling so many of the shots regarding federal finances and priorities that he was sometimes referred to as the head of "the fourth branch of government." He bristled at FDR's assignment of key responsibilities to Wallace, who signaled from the start of his term as vice president that he intended to maintain the activist role he had established as head of Agriculture.

Before he was sworn in on January 20, 1941, Wallace had studied the office of the vice presidency, including a 1920 essay titled "Can the Vice President Be Useful?" penned by a failed contender for the job named Franklin D. Roosevelt. As FDR began his third term in the White House, he moved to expand the scope and character of the No. 2 job—which Wallace's predecessor, Garner, had suggested was "not worth a bucket of warm spit"—by issuing Executive Order 8839 shortly before the U.S. entry into World War II. That order established the Economic Defense Board, which Wallace would chair. After Pearl Harbor, it was renamed the Board of Economic Warfare.

Culver and Hyde note that the position gave the vice president a role in "dealing with a wide range of international economic issues including exports, imports, 'preclusive buying' (the purchase of strategic materials in order to keep them out of the enemies' hands), foreign exchange transactions, international credit and transportation, the control of foreign-owned properties, and patents and all other matters related to foreign economics." Less than two months after he issued the executive order empowering the new vice president, FDR issued another, creating the Supply Priorities and Allocations Board, where Wallace, again as the chair, would be in charge of speeding the delivery of arms and other materials to allies in Europe. The Des Moines Register described the vice president as the "American minister of economic defense, and the chief planner of the new world order when the war is over." In short order, Culver and Hyde recount: "Wallace had become the most powerful vice president in the nation's history. No vice president had ever wielded such administrative authority, much less a policy voice of consequence. Roosevelt 'used me in a way which made the office for a time a very great office,' Wallace later observed."

The operative words were "for a time." The vice president was determined to go all out to defeat fascism on the battlefield and in the postwar era—so determined that lines of division quickly developed within the administration.

At every turn, Wallace emphasized the importance of making a win-the-war-and-win-the-peace connection. In an essay he wrote for the *Atlantic* magazine just weeks before the United States entered World War II, Wallace had argued: "The overthrow of Hitler is only half the battle; we must build a world in which our human and material resources are used to the utmost if we are to win complete victory. This principle should be fundamental as the world moves to reorganize its affairs. Ways must be found by which the potential abundance of the world can be translated into real wealth and a higher standard of living. Certain minimum standards of food, clothing and shelter ought to be established, and arrangements ought to be made to guarantee that no one should fall below those standards."

That made sense to some key figures in the White House, including Eleanor Roosevelt, who in her 1942 essay "What We Are Fighting For" described the war in the context of "the world struggle of ordinary people for a better way of life" in which "the human beings of the world, regardless of race or creed or color, are to be looked upon with respect and treated as equals."

There was good reason to believe that Franklin was sympathetic with the message. But FDR's administration really was that team of rivals, and within it were clear factions that the president welcomed and encouraged as he kept building out a Democratic coalition far broader than any the party had seen before. Wallace positioned himself at one pole in FDR's big tent. Jesse Jones held up the other pole.

Jones thought of himself as a businessman, not an idealist, and he had nothing but disdain for Wallace personally and politically. He decried "the socialist-minded uplifters and uppity underlings" of the Board of Economic Warfare, and he steadfastly resisted efforts by the vice president and his staff to include "labor clauses" in BEW contracts that called for foreign producers to "maintain such conditions of labor as will maximize production ... adequate shelter, water and safety appliances" and fair wage rates. Wallace explained that "greater stimulus" would boost production. The BEW's blunt-spoken executive director, Milo Perkins, argued, "It isn't radical to believe that you can get as much in return by increasing the food to a human being as by increasing the food to a mule."

This emphasis on the condition of workers was indeed seen as radical by the administration's conservative critics. Ohio Republican senator Robert A. Taft warned about the danger of "setting up an international WPA," referring to the New Deal's Depression-era jobs program. Taft and his fellow congressional conservatives found a willing ally in Jones, who, according to Culver and Hyde, "opposed anything that changed the customary relationship between capital and labor."

As the vice president accumulated more authority during 1942 and early 1943, the *St. Louis Post-Dispatch* reported on "the crumbling empire of Jesse H. Jones." But Jones was not about to stand down. He held a trump card: as the *Wall Street Journal* noted, "Jones still must sign the checks." This he did slowly—so slowly that Wallace and Perkins began to raise concerns about delays in the acquisition of raw materials needed for the war effort. As Wallace was literally traveling to the jungles of Latin America in search of better sources of everything from rubber to quinine, and as Perkins was identifying cheaper and faster methods for processing and distributing supplies, the pair grew increasingly agitated with Jones. In June 1943, they sent a 28-page complaint to the Senate Committee on Appropriations, which detailed "obstructionist tactics ... delay of the war effort ... hamstringing bureaucracy and backdoor complaining" by Jones. Wallace warned, "We are helpless when Jesse Jones, as our banker, refuses to sign checks in accordance with our directives" and suggested that the bureaucratic barriers the BEW was running up against were "utterly inexcusable in a nation at war."

"These," Jones biographer Steven Fenberg observed, "were fighting words." Jones accused Wallace of "malice, innuendos and half-truths." At that point Perkins, always a hotter head than Wallace, let rip. He accused Jones of holding up the acquisition of quinine, used to treat malaria, and adopting a "Rip Van Winkle approach to a commodity that means life or death to our soldiers." The clash became national news. Jones roused his allies on Wall Street and in the war industries and appealed to conservative Republicans and Democrats in Congress, especially fellow Texas Democrats like House Speaker Sam Rayburn and Senate Foreign Relations Committee Chair Tom Connally, to support his efforts to rein in the liberals. Jones found willing allies at the State Department, where there were worries that alliances with "old order" leaders like Winston Churchill were being jeopardized by talk of "labor clauses" and Wallace's assertion that "the new democracy by definition abhors imperialism."

As the wrangling between Jones and Wallace grew more intense and more public, the president grew more agitated. Roosevelt did not want the differences of opinion within his White House to go public—especially at a critical point in a war that was far from won. So, on July 15, 1943, he issued Executive Order 9361 abolishing the Board of Economic Warfare and transferring its work to a new Office of Economic Warfare, which would consolidate projects previously overseen by Wallace and Jones under FDR's "fix-it" man, Leo Crowley.

Crowley would soon be heading a powerful agency dubbed the Foreign Economic Administration. A fiercely anti-Soviet banker aligned with Wall Street, Crowley was seen as much more of a Jones man than a Wallace man. So it was fair to say that the decision went to Jones. Indeed, as journalist I.F. Stone observed, "Behind Jones is the State Department, and behind the State Department are those forces, clerical and capitalist, which have no intention of letting this era become, in Wallace's phrase, the Century of the Common Man."

Henry Wallace understood now that he was in a fight not just for his own political future but for that of the Democratic Party and, by extension, for the nation in the postwar era.

Wallace did not fear for his relationship with Roosevelt. Even as the dust from the BEW punch-up was settling, FDR assured his vice president, "It is needless for me to tell you that the incident has not lessened my personal affection for you." Within days, the two men were consulting on what would today be described as "messaging," framing out the bold themes that Wallace would take on the road as a roving champion of the administration.

Still, there was no denying that Wallace's authority had been diminished, and within the upper echelons of the Democratic Party there was now open speculation that he would be bumped from the 1944 ticket. In a July 20, 1943, diary entry, the vice president offered a clear-eyed assessment of his relationship with FDR. He had no doubt that the president was "really fond of me except when stimulated by the palace guard to move in other directions."

So Wallace chose to go around that palace guard. With FDR's encouragement, he began speaking out against American fascism. Wallace devoted hours, even days, to constructing speeches and articles on the subject. From the start, he distinguished the fascist threat at home from the threat posed by Hitler and Mussolini. He expected to stir controversy. That was the point. Privately, however, Wallace speculated to Secretary of the Interior Harold Ickes that he and his ideas might be swept aside by a rising tide of "bipartisan American fascism."

Wallace had already suggested, in a March 8, 1943, address at Ohio Wesleyan University, that "we shall decide sometime in 1943 or 1944 whether to plant the seeds for World War No. 3. That war will be certain if we allow Prussia to rearm either materially or psychologically. That war will be probable in case we double-cross Russia. That war will be probable if we fail to demonstrate that we can furnish full employment after this war comes to an end and Fascist interests, motivated largely by anti-Russian bias, get control of our government." Though he did not make specific reference to "American fascism" in the speech, Wallace warned, "Those who preach isolationism and hate of other nations are preaching a modified form of Prussian Nazism, and the only outcome of such preaching will be war."

The Last New Dealer?

By mid-July, Wallace had resolved to get specific. On July 24, 1943, he arrived in Detroit to deliver the speech that would formally introduce the idea of homegrown fascism (as recounted in Chapter 1). He had chosen to come to Detroit, in consultation with union allies and with a text already vetted by Roosevelt, to call out racial hatred and division as a threat to the war effort. Appearing in one of a number of cities that had experienced race riots that summer, Wallace would make the link between racism at home and the hatred preached by Hitler and his followers.

It was here that Wallace inserted the term "American fascism" into the wartime debate. At a press conference shortly after his arrival in Detroit, Wallace said that "certain American fascists claim I'm an idealist." These homegrown authoritarians disdained him, he asserted, because he threatened their dreams of reclaiming the outsize power and privilege they had enjoyed before the New Deal began to reposition government on the side of the great mass of Americans. "Old-fashioned Americanism is the last refuge of the fascists," Wallace told the reporters. "But by old-fashioned Americanism they do not mean what is implied by the term, but mean the situation that existed when great corporations rose to power economically and politically. The reason Mr. Roosevelt is so hated by many businessmen is the fact that he stopped making Washington a way-station on the road to Wall Street."

Roosevelt had said much the same thing in the past, when he closed his campaign for a second term with a rally at Madison Square Garden on October 31, 1936. "We have not come this far without a struggle, and I assure you we cannot go further without a struggle," FDR said back then.

> For twelve years this nation was afflicted with hear-nothing, see-nothing, do-nothing Government. The nation looked to government but the government looked away. Nine mocking years with the golden calf and three long years of the scourge! Nine crazy years at the ticker and three long years in the bread-lines! Nine mad years of mirage and three long years of despair! Powerful influences strive today to restore that kind of government with its doctrine that that government is best which is most indifferent.
>
> For nearly four years you have had an administration which instead of twirling its thumbs has rolled up its sleeves. We will keep our sleeves rolled up.
>
> We had to struggle with the old enemies of peace—business and financial monopoly, speculation, reckless banking, class antagonism, sectionalism, war profiteering.
>
> They had begun to consider the government of the United States as a mere appendage to their own affairs. We know now that government by organized money is just as dangerous as government by organized mob.
>
> Never before in all our history have these forces been so united against one candidate as they stand today. They are unanimous in their hate for me—and I welcome their hatred.

At the press conference the day before his 1943 Detroit speech, Wallace was asked whether he was "the last New Dealer." In response, he argued that what was really playing out was the old fight between "men and corporations who put money rights above human rights" and progressives who "put human rights above money rights." Within the Democratic Party, he acknowledged, "each group is conscious of the existence and the need of the other. It's just a question of which is going to dominate. I'm confident the people will take care of that."

The following day Wallace delivered his speech referencing "Americanized fascism."

> We will not be satisfied with a peace which will merely lead us from the concentration camps and mass murder of Fascism into an international jungle of gangster governments operated behind the scenes by power-crazed, money-mad imperialists. Our choice is not between a Hitler slave-world and an out-of-date holiday of "normalcy." The defeatists who talk about going back to the good old days of Americanism mean the time when there was plenty for the few and scarcity for the many, when Washington was a way-station in the suburbs of Wall Street ... Nor is our choice between an Americanized fascism and the restoration of prewar scarcity and unemployment. Too many millions of our people have come out of the dark cellars and squalor of unemployment ever to go back. Our choice is between democracy for everybody or for the few—between the spreading of social safeguards and economic opportunity to all the people—or the concentration of our abundant resources in the hands of selfishness and greed.

The initial reaction to Wallace's speech was rapturous. The crowd in Detroit cheered the vice president on, and African-American newspapers across the country praised him for recognizing that homegrown racial hatred existed on a continuum with Hitler's vile doctrines. The July 26, 1943, *New York Times* placed the story of Wallace's Detroit speech high on Page 1 and reproduced the entire address inside.

By the next day, however, the newspaper's influential editorial page was denouncing it. "Vice President Wallace has done a poor service to the American people with his reckless talk about 'American Fascists,' " the editorial stated. "If he had used this phrase to describe the handful of native or alien crackpots (some of them now in jail) who have gone about this country trying unsuccessfully to organize feeble imitations of Mussolini's Black Shirts no one could object. But he did not use the phrase this way. Instead, he borrowed it for a sweeping denunciation of opponents of Mr. Roosevelt's domestic policies—the 'powerful groups,' in his language, 'who hope to take advantage of the president's concentration on the war effort to destroy everything that he has accomplished on the domestic front over the last 10 years.' "

The *Times* was appalled at what it described as Wallace's demagoguery. "The people who belong to these 'powerful groups'—presumably anyone with a shred of conservative opinions on any phase of the whole domestic situation—may be mistaken in their point of view. They may be shortsighted and behind the times and not as well advanced in their social thinking as is Mr. Wallace. But they are not 'Fascists,' and to call them 'Fascists' is dangerous nonsense."

Never mind that Southern Democrats would double down on Jim Crow in the aftermath of World War II, as returning veterans would be attacked by local officials because they demanded the right to vote. Never mind that civil liberties denied to Americans like the Japanese of California during the war years would continue to be denied in the postwar era. Never mind that, in less than a decade, Senator Joe McCarthy of Wisconsin would be organizing a Red Scare that would lead to blacklisting, jail terms, financial ruin and worse for Americans accused of joining a Communist Party that was not only legal but was campaigning in and sometimes winning elections during the 1930s and 1940s. Never mind that conservative Democrats and their right-wing Republican allies enacted a Taft-Hartley law written to thwart the multiracial and multiethnic unions being organized in the Deep South by the CIO's "Operation Dixie" campaign and in the southwest by the left-wing International Union of Mine, Mill and Smelter Workers. Despite what would unfold in the coming years, the *Times* editors reassured their readers, "Not at any point in their thinking or their actions do these more conservative people with whom Mr. Wallace disagrees correspond to the Fascist pattern."

The *Times* editorial got one thing right, however, when it speculated, "It is unlikely that Mr. Wallace's remarks will draw from the president a rebuke." Indeed, Roosevelt was impressed with the speech. On July 28, three days after Wallace's appearance in Detroit and one day after the *Times* editorial appeared, FDR wrote the vice president. "Your speech was splendid," he declared.

"P.S.," the president added. "You drew blood from the Cave Dwellers!"

4

The Fight against American Fascism

Henry Wallace and the Consequences of Speaking Truth to Power

The American fascist would prefer not to use violence. His method is to poison the channels of public information. With a fascist the problem is never how best to present the truth to the public but how best to use the news to deceive the public into giving the fascist and his group more money or more power.
　　　　—Henry Wallace, *New York Times*, April 9, 1944

I know personally from experience that there is a certain zone which when a man has walked through it, he has got to be careful. Maybe Time was the scissors that Delilah used for shearing Samson! After which, "Samson wist not that God had departed him!" I am afraid—deeply and mortally afraid—because I love my country and want it to go right, that I can hear Delilah's scissors clicking.
　　　　—William Allen White to Henry Wallace, August 10, 1943

Amid all the perfervid debate about whether Trump or Trumpism was ushering in homegrown fascism during the first year of the 45th presidency, a social-media meme started making the rounds. It purported to quote Henry Wallace defining an American fascist as "one whose lust for money or power is combined with such an intensity of intolerance toward those of other races, parties, classes, religions, cultures, regions or nations as to make him ruthless in his use of deceit or violence to attain his ends." That read like *too* perfect a prediction of Trump and Trumpism. People were skeptical, as they often are of online memes. The fact-checking website Snopes.com took up the question: "Did FDR's Vice-President Write an Op-Ed About 'American Fascism'?" The website recognized why people would doubt that a sitting vice president might have made so bold a statement. But Snopes certified that the quote had been "correctly attributed."

It is a measure of how time and bias unwind our history that Wallace's engagement with the threat of American fascism was forgotten. Seventy-five years earlier, however, what Wallace was doing went to the very heart of the struggle for the soul of the Democratic Party and the country. For the better part of a year, from the summer of 1943 to the summer of 1944, everyone who was paying attention knew that Wallace was defining fascism in an American context, as he wrote in the *New York Times*: "Every Jew-baiter, every Catholic hater, is a fascist at heart. The hoodlums who have been desecrating churches, cathedrals and synagogues in some of our larger cities are ripe material for fascist leadership." They knew that, even as American leaders denounced the crimes of German and Italian fascists, the vice president was charging that the United States harbored millions of "patriotic Americans" who were "willing at all times to engage in any degree of deceit and violence necessary to place his culture and race astride the world."

Wallace was expanding the definition of American fascism. He was not just talking about Fritz Julius Kuhn's Nazi-inspired German American Bund and the Fascist League of North America that Mussolini's agent, Paolo Ignazio Maria Thaon di Revel, had organized in New York and Boston. This was about more than the fear that there lingered in the United States remnants of the crowds that packed arenas for the Bund's prewar rallies, like the 1939 "Mass Demonstration for True Americanism" that filled Madison Square Garden with 20,000 self-identified "American patriots" who mingled chants of "Sieg

Heil!" with the recitation of the Pledge of Allegiance, cheered speakers who mocked the Roosevelt administration's "Jew Deal" and unfurled banners that read "Wake Up America. Smash Jewish Communism." This was about more than the incidents like those in which young men dressed in the SS-inspired uniforms of the American Ordnungsdienst marched into Milwaukee public meetings and beat up anyone who dared to object when the jagged thunderbolt symbol of the SS was raised beside the stars and stripes. About more than the assassination in January 1943 of the antifascist campaigner Carlo Tresca, which took place at the corner of Fifth Avenue at 15th Street in New York City.

"The dangerous American fascist is the man who wants to do in the United States in an American way what Hitler did in Germany in a Prussian way," argued Wallace in his landmark essay "The Danger of American Fascism," published in the *New York Times* Sunday magazine on April 9, 1944. He charged that those who sought to divide the United States along lines of race, religion and class could be "encountered in Wall Street, Main Street or Tobacco Road."

"Some even suspect," Wallace wrote, "that they can detect incipient traces of it along the Potomac."

That was a politically risky line for a candidate for re-election, especially at a time when the New Deal Coalition included a Southern contingent that defended segregation and threatened to withhold support for initiatives that challenged racism. The Southerners, and the Northern business interests that often aligned with them, were not going to appreciate it when a Democratic vice president said, "It may be shocking to some people in this country to realize that, without meaning to do so, they hold views in common with Hitler when they preach discrimination against other religious, racial or economic groups."

It was certainly not unheard of during World War II for critics of racism and anti-Semitism to compare hatred at home with hatred abroad, especially African Americans like Asa Philip

Randolph and C.L. Dellums of the Brotherhood of Sleeping Car Porters, actor and singer Paul Robeson and New York City councilman Adam Clayton Powell Jr. (who in 1944 would be elected to Congress). But with the publication of "American Fascism," Wallace made himself the highest-profile partisan in a very real fight against hatred on the home front. Histories of the war years often default to Greatest Generation tropes and the carefully manufactured image of a nation united in a fight for the future. While it is true that many among that generation of Americans felt a unity of purpose when it came to fighting the Axis powers, nevertheless there were deep divisions over what that fight was really about, how victory could be achieved and what that victory would mean.

At least some of the roots of the civil rights movement can be traced to a time when Randolph and his allies mounted their March on Washington Movement to integrate the war industries. Randolph traveled the country to appear at rallies—drawing 15,000 in St. Louis, 20,000 in Chicago, 23,500 in New York—as it became clear in 1941 that the U.S. would enter the war. The message of the movement was bold for the time—"Free from Want! Free from Fear! Free from Jim Crow!"—but not too bold for the circumstances that African Americans faced in a country where skilled workers and technicians were denied employment because of racist policies. One company, A.O. Smith, an auto parts firm in Milwaukee that played a major role in World War II tank production, announced that it "never did and does not intend to employ Negroes." In the burgeoning aircraft industry, which by 1940 had production facilities in large cities across the country with substantial African-American populations, blacks made up less than 2 percent of employees. "Management officials in that industry often stated overtly their determination to keep blacks out," according to historian Joe William Trotter Jr. The need for a government response was made clear after the president of the North American Aviation conglomerate declared: "While we are in complete sympathy with the Negro, it is against company policy to employ them as aircraft workers or mechanics. We use none except white workers in the plant."

The response came in the form of FDR's Executive Order 8802 of June 1941, which prohibited racial and ethnic discrimination in the defense industry, and was further expanded by Executive Order 9346 in May 1943. These were dramatic victories achieved by challenging the false patriotism that demanded silent acquiescence to a narrow definition of what the war was about. Randolph rejected descriptions of the American mission that failed to understand it as a fight against "a vile and hateful racism," as he put it at a 1942 rally in Detroit, "and a manifestation of the tragic and utter collapse of an old, decadent democratic political liberalism which worshipped at the shrine of a world-conquering monopoly capitalism."

Randolph's language at that rally was emphatic and radical. "Unless this war sounds the death knell to the old Anglo-American empire systems, the hapless story of which is one of exploitation for the profit and power of a monopoly-capitalist economy, it will have been fought in vain," he said. "Our aim then must not only be to defeat Nazism, fascism and militarism on the battlefield but to win the peace, for democracy, for freedom and the Brotherhood of Man without regard to his pigmentation, land of his birth or the God of his fathers."

There were risks in using such boldly antiracist language, as even a young Frank Sinatra learned within the far safer context of acting in a short Hollywood film. Sinatra, thirty, starred in *The House I Live In*, a 1945 short in which he confronted a pack of young hooligans who were chasing a Jewish boy. "You must be a bunch of those Nazi werewolves I've been readin' about," shouted Sinatra. "Mister, are you screwy?" asked one of the boys. "Not me," declared the singer, "I'm an American." "Well," another boy demanded to know, "whaddaya think we are?" "Nazis," replied Sinatra, who then explained: "Look, fellas: Religion makes no difference. Except maybe to a Nazi—or somebody as stupid. Why, people all over the world worship God in many different ways. God created everybody. He didn't create one people better than another. Your blood's the same as mine; mine's the same as his [gesturing to the Jewish boy]. Do you know what this wonderful country is made of? It's made up of a hundred different kinds of people. And a hundred different ways of talking. And a hundred different ways of goin' to church. But they're all American ways. Wouldn't we be silly if we went around hating people because they combed their hair different than ours? Wouldn't we be a lot of dopes?"

Sinatra was merely playing a role in a film that won an Honorary Academy Award and a special Golden Globe. Yet in the postwar era, that role and Sinatra's mild activism on the left drew the scrutiny of the House Un-American Activities Committee, and charges by Hearst newspapers gossip columnist Lee Mortimer that Sinatra was one of the Hollywood "fellow travelers" who engaged in "the promotion of class struggle or foreign isms posing as entertainment." Such was the level of anti-Communist hysteria that bubbled just beneath the surface in America, erupting spectacularly in the years that followed World War II.

Sinatra got off easy compared with songwriter Earl Robinson, who wrote the music for "The House I Live In," the film's title song and a hit in its own right. One of the finest songwriters of his time, Robinson wrote tunes that were performed by Sinatra, Bing Crosby and other stars (along with campaign songs for FDR and Wallace) and had a thriving career until he was blacklisted and ended up running a high school music program. The lyrics for "The House I Live In" were written by "Lewis Allan," who in 1937 also wrote the lyrics for "Strange Fruit," the anti-lynching song that was made famous by Billie Holiday and Nina Simone and that in 1999 would be named the "song of the century" by *Time* magazine. "Lewis Allan" was a pen name adopted by New York City schoolteacher Abel Meeropol, who in 1950 was called before a New York State committee investigating Communist Party influence in the schools and faced more than his share of harassment for his ardent advocacy on behalf of racial justice. After the U.S. government executed Ethel and Julius Rosenberg, Meeropol and his wife, Anne, adopted the Rosenbergs' young sons, Michael and Robert.

This was a time when Congress refused to entertain the anti-lynching and anti–poll tax legislation proposed at the opening of each new session by U.S. Representative Vito Marcantonio, a New Yorker who was elected on the Republican and American Labor Party ballot lines and worked closely with left-wing unions, militant antifascist groups and New York City's Communist Party. Many of the most powerful congressional Democrats were virulent racists and anti-Semites, like Senate Military Affairs Committee chairman Robert Reynolds, a wealthy North Carolinian who preached an isolationist "Fortress America" doctrine and responded to the plight of Jewish refugees with a proposal for an outright ban on immigration that would "save America for Americans." Reynolds said he wanted to "build a wall about the United States so high and so secure that not a single alien or foreign refugee from any country upon the face of this earth could possibly scale or ascend it."

If Wallace had limited his critique of American fascism to the overt racists and anti-Semites that Willkie and others decried, he would have had less trouble. What distinguished Wallace's critique of American fascism was his determination to go deeper, to talk about the enablers of the racists and anti-Semites.

"The obvious types of American fascists are dealt with on the air and in the press," Wallace wrote in the *Times*. "These demagogues and stooges are fronts for others. The really dangerous American fascists are not those who are hooked up directly or indirectly with the Axis. ... American fascism will not be really dangerous until there is a purposeful coalition among the cartelists, the deliberate poisoners of public information and those who stand for the KKK type of demagoguery."

This was a definition of fascism that brought the issues of

authoritarianism and totalitarianism, of media manipulation and political machination, home to America.

"If we define an American fascist as one who in case of conflict puts money and power ahead of human beings, then there are undoubtedly several million fascists in the United States," Wallace charged. "There are probably several hundred thousand if we narrow the definition to include only those who in their search for money and power are ruthless and deceitful. Most American fascists are enthusiastically supporting the war effort. They are doing this even in those cases where they hope to have profitable connections with German chemical firms after the war ends. They are patriotic in time of war because it is to their interest to be so, but in time of peace they follow power and the dollar wherever they may lead."

Wallace saw the prospects of an American fascism in the predictable machinations of big business. "We all know the part that the cartels played in bringing Hitler to power, and the rule the giant German trusts have played in Nazi conquests," he explained. "Monopolists who fear competition and who distrust democracy because it stands for equal opportunity would like to secure their position against small and energetic enterprise. In an effort to eliminate the possibility of any rival growing up, some monopolists would sacrifice democracy itself."

This was all too much for the editorial page of the *Times,* which took the extraordinary step of denouncing Wallace's essay on the very Sunday it was published in the newspaper's magazine. Decrying what it referred to as the "shrill cries of 'Fascist'" that foster "an atmosphere charged with emotion, suspicion and bitterness," the *Times* editorial accused Wallace of going too far in his denunciations of monopolies and cartels. "It is astonishing that Mr. Wallace cannot see that in going to such lengths he approaches the very intolerance that he condemns," the editorial said.

The *Times* was effectively arguing that "it can't happen here." But in doing so, the paper missed Wallace's point. The vice president was inviting consideration of the threat posed by "a native brand of fascism," as novelist Philip Roth would do in his 2004 alternative history *The Plot against America*. In that novel, Roth tried to show how the past "might have been different and how fascism might have happened here"— imagining the election of America Firster Charles Lindbergh over Roosevelt in 1940; alliance with Germany, Italy and Japan; and the implementation in America of anti-Semitic laws. In Roth's dystopia, Americans assured themselves that it wasn't fascism because Lindbergh and his congressional allies were "bound to follow the law as set down by the constitution. ... They were Republican, they were isolationist, and among them, yes, there were anti-Semites—as indeed there were among the southerners in FDR's own party—but that was a long way from their being Nazis." Roth's fictional Americans did not see the fascism happening right in front of them.

Wallace was sounding that same warning, in reality, and in real time. Had he been more cautious in his approach, he might well have earned the praise of the *New York Times*, the grudging embrace of his fellow Democrats, a second term as vice president and, with the death of Franklin Roosevelt less than three months after his fourth inauguration day, almost a full term as president.

But Wallace felt a sense of urgency for his party, for his country, and for the world, that would cost him almost everything—except the bully pulpit from which he came close to writing his own alternative history.

Wrestling with Churchill

A full year passed between the day Henry Wallace visited Detroit and put the issue of American fascism on the agenda, and the day he faced the delegates of the 1944 Democratic National Convention. Wallace filled many roles during this time, including that of Franklin Roosevelt's roving ambassador. He spoke in dozens of cities across the United States. He also traveled around the world at FDR's behest, logging 27,132 miles and 135 hours of flight time in one extended trek to the Soviet Union and China.

In a remarkable 56-page pamphlet, *Our Job in the Pacific*, which was published by the American Council of the Institute of Pacific Relations in 1944 and widely distributed at the price of 25 cents, the vice president asserted that Japan had "disrupted the old imperial-colonial pattern in Asia and the Pacific and we must choose whether to aid in restoring the old pattern or to aid in creating a new one." As far as Wallace was concerned, the U.S. should support the "emancipation of [the British Empire's] colonial subjects in India, Burma and Malaya as part of a general postwar push to upend colonialism and promote the development of impoverished lands."

After the pamphlet was published, Wallace asked a wealthy friend who maintained close relations with British diplomats, Texas publisher Charles Marsh, "if he had had any repercussions from his British friends on the pamphlet." Marsh laughed, Wallace recalled in a diary entry, "and said that Flight Commander Dahl (who is now with the British Secret Service) had been very much excited. Apparently while I was gone, the entire British Secret Service was shaking with indignation as well as the British Foreign Office. Dahl said to Marsh at the height of the indignation, 'This is very serious. You know Churchill is likely to ask Roosevelt to get a new vice president.'"

Flight Commander Dahl was Roald Dahl, who would achieve fame as the author of a stack of best-selling books for children, including *James and the Giant Peach*, *Charlie and the Chocolate Factory*, *Matilda*, *The Witches*, *Fantastic Mr. Fox* and *The BFG*. But at that time he was a dapper young intelligence officer who had been dispatched to wartime Washington to gather information for Churchill. "Of particular concern to the British," noted author Christopher Klein in an essay on Dahl's spycraft, "were the anti-imperialist views of Vice President Henry Wallace, with whom Dahl socialized and played tennis."

Author Jennet Conant recounted the machinations surrounding *Our Job in the Pacific* in her book *The Irregulars: Roald Dahl and the British Spy Ring in Wartime Washington*. "All the time, Dahl had been biding his time at the embassy, doing as he was told like a good boy, when a 'lucky break' came his way," Conant explained. "It was an ordinary night in June, and he was dining at Marsh's R Street mansion, as was his custom. When he arrived, Marsh tossed a sheaf of papers into his lap and said '... what do you think of that?' " *That* was a draft of the pamphlet Wallace had written. Dahl quickly determined that it "would make them rock back at home." He excused himself, quietly called another British agent who raced over, grabbed the document, had it copied and returned while Marsh was attending to other guests. In short order, it was shipped off to London, where Churchill "could hardly believe what he was reading." According to Conant, Wallace's proposal "for the liquidation of the British Empire inspired Churchill to 'cataclysms of wrath.' "

It was not the first time that Wallace's anti-imperialism had offended Churchill. A year earlier, in May 1943, the men clashed during a meeting in which Wallace's talk of a postwar "century of the common man" unsettled the old imperialist.

Churchill "made it more clear," recalled Wallace in his diary, "that he expected England and the United States to run the world, and he expected the staff organizations which had been set up for winning the war to continue when the peace came, that these staff organizations would by mutual understanding really run the world even though there was a supreme council and three regional councils. I said bluntly that I thought the notion of Anglo-Saxon superiority, inherent in Churchill's approach, would be offensive to many of the nations of the world as well as to a number of people in the United States. Churchill had had quite a bit of whiskey, which, however, did not affect the clarity of his thinking process but did perhaps increase his frankness. He said why be apologetic about Anglo-Saxon superiority, that we were superior, that we had the common heritage which had been worked out over the centuries in England and had been perfected by our constitution. He himself was half American, he felt that he was called on as a result to serve the function of uniting the two great Anglo-Saxon civilizations in order to confer the benefit of freedom on the rest of the world."

When Wallace proposed bringing the people of Latin America into Churchill's postwar scheme "so that the citizens of the New World and the British Empire could all travel freely without passports," the vice president recalled, "Churchill did not like this. He said if we took all the colors on the painter's palette and mix them up together, we get just a smudgy grayish brown. I interjected, 'And so you believe in the pure Anglo-Saxon race or Anglo-Saxondom über Alles.'" That earned a rebuke from the prime minister, which was fine by the vice president. "Apparently my frank talking with Churchill at the Saturday and Monday luncheons has caused the British to reach the conclusion that I am not playing their game of arranging matters so that the Anglo-Saxons will rule the world," he wrote a few days later. "Frankly I am glad to know where they stand and they know where I stand. I am sure that 200 million Anglo-Saxons in the United States, England, Canada, Australia, New Zealand, and South Africa are not enough to run the world and that if they try it in the spirit which seems to be animating Churchill, there will be serious trouble ahead."

Wallace began to integrate a critique of "Anglo-Saxondom über Alles" imperialism into his speaking and writing. In "The Danger of American Fascism," he warned that "fascism in the postwar inevitably will push steadily for Anglo-Saxon imperialism and eventually for war with Russia. Already American fascists are talking and writing about this conflict and using it as an excuse for their internal hatreds and intolerances toward certain races, creeds and classes."

A Grand and Glorious Fight

As Wallace turned the volume up, the columnist Max Lerner declared, "There is not a man in the country, or anywhere in the world, who is saying the things Wallace is saying." Wallace was making the biggest play of his career. He well understood the risks, and he embraced them. "Time will not wait," he declared at a September rally organized by the Chicago United Nations Committee to win the peace. "The breath of the future is on us as it has never been before."

Wallace was not just fighting against the president's right-wing critics. He was fighting to renew the favor of FDR, who still regarded his vice president highly but perhaps not highly enough to expend the political capital needed to keep him on the ticket in 1944. He was fighting, as well, for the future of a Democratic Party where a conservative bloc was organizing to take the apparatus back from the New Dealers. FDR had struggled for more than a decade against elements of the party that had never really embraced the New Deal, William Allen White wrote in an August 1943 letter to Wallace. White, a liberal Republican editor from Kansas, believed that the president wavered in the internal wrangling between Jesse Jones and the vice president. Now Wallace was fighting back, and White hailed him for it. But White warned Wallace to be careful: "Maybe Time was the scissors that Delilah used for shearing Samson! ... I am afraid—deeply and mortally afraid—because I love my country and want it to go right, that I can hear Delilah's scissors clicking."

Perhaps Wallace heard the clicking as well. The vice president explained in response to White that he had "no illusions" about "the rascals ... who work behind the scenes to try and control each party." Yet, he concluded, "I think it is much easier to get rid of a certain type of reactionary influence in the Democratic Party than it is to get rid of it in the Republican Party." But he would not fight in the traditional way, in the smoke-filled rooms. "Practical politics of this kind simply did not appeal to me," he told an ally who proposed a conventional campaign. Instead, as Culver and Hyde recounted: "Wallace concluded that his future as a public figure rested with the people, not with the nexus of political-bureaucratic-journalistic power brokers in Washington. If he was to marshal the forces of progressivism in the cause of a just and lasting peace, he would have to do it in public view."

Wallace began with a radical embrace of the New Deal. FDR had joked at a December 28, 1943, press conference that "Dr. New Deal"—the Depression-era battler against poverty and monopoly—had not been prepared to respond to the damage done on December 7, 1941, so "Dr. Win-the-War" had been called in. That sounded right to Henry Luce's *Time* magazine, which neglected Roosevelt's reference to the two physicians as partners and included a death notice for the New Deal in its obituary column. Wallace pushed back at a January 1944 Democratic gathering:

> The New Deal is not dead. If it were dead the Democratic Party would be dead, and well dead. But the New Deal is not dead, and the New Deal has yet to attain its full strength. The New Deal is as old as the wants of man. The New Deal is Amos proclaiming the needs of the poor in the land of Israel. The New Deal is New England citizens dumping tea in Boston Harbor. The New Deal is Abraham Lincoln preaching freedom for the oppressed ... The New Deal is Franklin Roosevelt.

"In point of fact," the *Washington Post* observed, "the New Deal today is Henry Wallace." Raymond Moley, a former economic adviser to the president who had moved to the right and clearly hoped FDR would do the same, suggested, "What we really have then is a left-wing New Deal whose spokesman is Henry Wallace, attacking what many in the inner circle of Washington regard as the appeasement of business by the president."

The internal struggle was more complicated than that. As he so frequently did during the longest presidency in American history, Roosevelt was exploring his options. He was trying to keep on good terms with big business—even the CEOs and bankers whose hatred he once welcomed—but also with the unions and the social activists who saw Wallace and Eleanor Roosevelt as their champions. He wanted to get along with both Churchill and Stalin. As he prepared to seek a new term, he was trying to maintain a balance between Southern segregationists, who objected to FDR's executive order prohibiting racial discrimination in the defense industries, and a rising generation of African Americans who wanted a permanent ban on discrimination in all industries. Throughout this period, the president met with Wallace, vetted his speeches, sent approving notes after they were delivered, and dispatched him on missions inside and outside the country. But he also met with Democratic Party stalwarts who wanted to dump Wallace from the ticket.

Wallace understood this dynamic. Wallace had many rivals, but he also had allies. Eleanor Roosevelt would come by the vice president's apartment for long conversations. Wallace would play Russian and Spanish music on the record player. She would knit. They talked politics. "She agreed completely that the Democratic Party must be a liberal party," he wrote in a diary entry from the fall of 1943. In another entry he recalled, "I told her that I felt the only way any liberalism could express on a national basis was through the Democratic Party." But would it?

Through the long wartime winter of 1943 into 1944, Wallace traveled the country at his own expense, speaking in union halls and on factory floors, on waterfronts and in hotel ballrooms, in farm country and big cities, about what was at stake. He rallied with African Americans against racism, with Jews against anti-Semitism, with women for an Equal Rights Amendment, with returning soldiers about what the country owed them for their sacrifices. He did not limit himself to Democratic audiences.

"Those who fight for us in this war belong to many parties, many creeds and many races," he said. "This is a people's war. The peace must be a people's peace."

Historian Peter Dreier has referred to Wallace as "the New Deal's evangelist," and never was the vice president's missionary zeal so ardent as in February 1944, when he embarked on a speaking tour that focused on the theme "America Tomorrow." It took him to Los Angeles; San Diego; San Francisco; Portland, Oregon; Seattle; Milwaukee; Chicago; Springfield, Illinois; St. Louis; and Minneapolis, where a young professor of political science at Macalester College, Hubert Humphrey, would introduce him to a crowd of 10,000 at the Minneapolis Armory and tell the vice president "progressive forces look to you for inspiration and leadership."

Historian John Morton Blum observed that the tour put Wallace "unequivocally on his party's left," with speeches in which he "called for a 'general welfare economy' and predicted 'a profound revolution' after the war that would be 'gradual and bloodless' if the press, politicians and men of wealth used their influence 'on behalf of the public good.' " Their cooperation was not assured, however, as Wallace explained in the opening address of the tour to a crowd of 5,000 gathered in Los Angeles. "Big business must not have such control of Congress and the executive branch as to make it easy for them to write the rules of the postwar game," he warned.

"The Big Three—Big Business, Big Labor and Big Agriculture —in the struggle to grab federal power for monopolistic purposes, are certain to come into serious conflict unless they recognize the superior claims of the general welfare of the common man," he said. "Each of the Big Three has unprecedented power at the present time. Each is faced with serious postwar worries. Each can save itself only if it learns to work with the other two and with government in terms of the general welfare. To work together without slipping into an American fascism will be the central problem of postwar democracy."

The next day, after meeting with African-American, Mexican-American and Jewish groups to strategize about making sure that the transition from defense production to peacetime production did not see a return of workplace discrimination, Wallace spoke to thousands of workers at L.A.'s Wilmington shipyard and then rallied Teamsters to oppose the threat of fascism in the postwar era. "It is so easy in government to put the dollar and the plant before the man," he said. "This is a fascistic idea. Yet, unless labor makes itself heard among the congressional and governmental committees which have so much to do with problems of reconversion of industry and postwar activity, we shall see a tendency for property rights to be placed ahead of human rights."

Again and again he returned to the theme that a domestic variation on fascism, characterized by corporate overreach and deference on the part of government to the demands of monopolists and segregationists, posed a genuine threat to the postwar era. Upon his return to Washington, Wallace was hailed by FDR, who opened a mid-February cabinet meeting by announcing, "Well, the vice president has just returned from a great trip."

The *New York Times* was not so impressed. In an editorial published a week after the America Tomorrow tour began, the editors asked of Wallace, "Who are the 'stooges' who put Wall Street first and the country second?" Accusing the vice president of endangering the war effort with reckless charges and suggesting he had disregarded "the tolerance and good temper that must lie at the heart of any democracy that is to work," the editors entertained the notion that "Mr. Wallace, it may be, does not expect to be taken literally. Perhaps he is merely throwing the most abusive word in his vocabulary at people whose political or economic views differ from his own. Perhaps he thinks it fashionable now to accuse people of fascism where formerly one might have accused them only of being narrowly selfish, or lacking in public spirit, or being reactionary, or merely conservative." The *Times* complained that Wallace was tossing around deeply charged epithets indiscriminately.

"Who are these American Fascists?" the editorial asked. The paper wanted evidence that the men about whom Wallace spoke met the narrowest definition of a "fascist," as believers in "one-party totalitarian government," "the abolition of the free secret ballot" and "the suppression of all opposition, and by any means," using violence so extreme that "those who disagree with them [are] either to be shot or thrown into concentration camps."

This narrow definition of fascism had already drawn criticism from the paper's own readers. "Mr. Wallace knows his 'American Fascists,' because he knows that this war is basically a war between special privilege and human rights," the prominent academic and author H.A. Overstreet wrote in a letter to the editor published the previous summer. "In every nation the line has been drawn between those who set special privilege first and those who set human rights first. France fell apart not because of a 'handful of native crackpots' but because there were thousands of 'patriotic' Frenchmen in high economic and governmental positions who preferred the strong rule of fascism over the people than a rule of the people that would threaten their special privileges."

Another writer, Ashley Miller, hailed Wallace for alerting the nation "to a very real, though little understood, menace to its future—and to a lasting peace." Even the United States Department of War made many of the same connections that Wallace was making, in a short film the department produced in 1943 called *Don't Be a Sucker*. In it, a young American businessman is listening to a racist speaker at an outdoor meeting, who complains that: "I see negroes holding jobs that belong to me and you. Now I ask you, if we allow this thing to go on, what's going to happen to us real Americans?" An aging immigrant with an Eastern European accent approaches the young man and says: "I've heard this kind of talk before, but

I never expected to hear it in America. I was born in Hungary but now I am an American citizen. And I have seen what this kind of talk can do—I saw it in Berlin. I was a professor at the university. I heard the same words we have heard today." Amid images portraying the rise of Nazism in Germany, the Hungarian immigrant recalls his own German experience and says: "I was a fool then. I thought Nazis were crazy people, stupid fanatics. Unfortunately, it was not so. They knew they were not strong enough to conquer a unified country, so they split Germany into small groups. They used prejudice as a practical weapon to cripple the nation."

Why was the War Department delivering this message? Because, though the military itself remained segregated, defense industries were integrating thanks to the campaigning of Randolph and his allies in a burgeoning civil rights movement. (Notably, it was in 1943, at the height of the war, that the newly founded Congress of Racial Equality began using nonviolent direct action to integrate restaurants, and that the NAACP opened its Washington office to begin aggressively lobbying the U.S. Congress and the White House.) By 1944, the Southern Regional Office of the National Urban League reported that thousands of African Americans were working in the aircraft industry plants of the South: 2,274 at the North American Aviation plant in Dallas, 730 at the Convair plant in Fort Worth, 1,502 at the Bell bomber plant in Atlanta. The War Department had a vested interest in keeping people working together in vital industries, and in dialing down tensions. But there were tensions. Violent race riots broke out in Harlem, Detroit and elsewhere across the country.

The internment of Japanese Americans revealed the vulnerability of the American promise of equal protection. Many knew that what their government was doing was wrong, yet few spoke up in opposition to that wrong. Henry Wallace failed to object publicly to what the administration in which he served was doing. Nor did most liberals and progressives during the war years, even though it was an unconscionable choice that revealed FDR and his aides at their worst. Shortly after the war ended, Wallace called for reparations for those who had been interned. He also used the Japanese internment as an example of the ways in which presidents of both parties have not just trammeled civil liberties but erred against human decency.

One of the lonely critics of the removal of tens of thousands of Japanese-American families from the homes and communities where they had long resided was Rev. Emery Andrews, the pastor of Seattle's Japanese Baptist Church. In 1943 Andrews said that "future historians will record this evacuation—this violation of citizenship rights—as one of the blackest spots on American history; as the time that democracy came the nearest to being wrecked." When asked if the shameful chapter in American history would be repeated, Andrews responded that it could happen again—if not to the Japanese, then to some other group.

In the War Relocation Authority (WRA) camps to which Japanese Americans were sent, and from which some of the bravest soldiers of World War II were recruited and drafted, groups formed such as the Heart Mountain Fair Play Committee, which, in the words of the *Los Angeles Times*, "dared to ask how they could be ordered to fight for freedom and democracy abroad when they were denied it at home."

This concern that the United States, while fighting fascism abroad, was allowing fascistic practices at home was frequently raised on the floor of the House of Representatives by its most radical member. Vito Marcantonio of New York argued in 1944 that the discriminatory employment practices of Southern railroad companies were undermining the war effort, saying, "Your railroads were not delivering the goods on time, not delivering men on time because of lack of manpower, and yet they refused to upgrade highly skilled Negroes who are so essential to the delivery of goods and soldiers to their destinations." Such behavior, he said, attacked the ideals "for which men are fighting and dying everywhere in the world." Marcantonio also criticized the House Un-American Activities Committee on the House floor during a debate about funding the committee, which was chaired by Martin Dies, a conservative Texas Democrat. Dies had a penchant for claiming that socialists, communists and assorted "reds" were driving U.S. policy. "There will be rejoicing in Berlin," Marcantonio said, "which will congratulate itself on the fact that it will continue to have the opportunity of making use of the statements and words of the Dies Committee, its chairman and its investigators." Marcantonio was a student of the rise of fascism in Italy, and had for years worked to counter the influence of Mussolini's allies among American Italians. He warned that European fascists had used "the anti-Communist cry" to divide opponents. "The anti-Communist slogan was and is Hitler's technique of conquest, conceived from the very inception of his plan for world conquest," he declared. "To adopt that same line within our own country now, while Hitler and his anti-Comintern Axis partners use it as a weapon of war against us, would be suicidal."

Roosevelt himself had argued in a 1938 message to Congress that the United States must guard against consolidations of economic power that might mimic those seen in Germany or Italy. "Unhappy events abroad have retaught us two simple truths about the liberty of a democratic people," he said. "The first truth is that the liberty of a democracy is not safe if the people tolerate the growth of private power to a point where it becomes stronger than their democratic state itself. That, in its essence, is fascism—ownership of government by an individual, by a group, or by any other controlling private power."

FDR could be blunt, but Wallace was blunter. He suggested that some of the unworthy men were wealthy Americans, captains of industry, who would exploit racial prejudice and ethnic divisions in order to enrich themselves and secure their power. This did not sit well with the powerful, or with the newspapers they read—especially the *New York Times*. Wallace initially ignored the *Times* editorials in February that demanded he explain what he meant when he spoke of the "American fascist" on his "America Tomorrow" tour. But he eventually wrote his reply to the *Times*, the famous essay that filled three pages of its April 9, 1944, Sunday magazine under the headline: "Wallace Defines 'American Fascism': The Vice President Says It Pollutes Public Opinion, Encourages Intolerance and Presents a Challenge to Our Democratic Way of Life."

"The American fascists are most easily recognized by their deliberate perversion of truth and fact," Wallace wrote. "Their newspapers and propaganda carefully cultivate every fissure of disunity, every crack in the common front against fascism. They use every opportunity to impugn democracy. They use isolationism as a slogan to conceal their own selfish imperialism. They cultivate hate and distrust of both Britain and Russia. They claim to be super-patriots, but they would destroy every liberty guaranteed by the Constitution. They demand free enterprise, but are the spokesmen for monopoly and vested interest. Their final objective toward which all their deceit is directed is to capture political power so that, using the power of the state and the power of the market simultaneously, they may keep the common man in eternal subjection."

The fight against American fascism would not be waged by pointed fingers of blame at this industrialist or that editor, Wallace wrote, but rather by remaining on "guard against intolerance, bigotry and the pretension of invidious distinction."

Even today there are still debates about how to define fascism, but we recognize now that it cannot be identified by a single rigid set of characteristics. "Fascism takes on the colors and textures of the nation it infects," author Adam Gopnik observed in 2016. "In Italy, it is bombastic and neo-classical. In Spain, it is Catholic and religious. In Germany, it is violent and romantic. In England, its form was paternalistic and aristocratic, through Oswald Mosley. So it's no surprise that the American face of fascism would take on the form of celebrity television." And Henry Giroux, a cultural critic who has written extensively on authoritarianism, says: "Fascism looks different in different cultures, depending on that culture. In fact, it is the essence of fascism to have no single, fixed form."

The fight that Henry Wallace waged against American fascism was a fight *for* democracy. A vital American democracy, he argued, was the antidote to American fascism.

> Democracy to crush fascism internally must demonstrate its capacity to "make the trains run on time." It must develop the ability to keep people fully employed and at the same time balance the budget. It must put human beings first and dollars second. It must appeal to reason and decency and not to violence and deceit. We must not tolerate oppressive government or industrial oligarchy in the form of monopolies and cartels. As long as scientific research and inventive ingenuity outrun our ability to devise social mechanisms to raise the living standards of the people, we may expect the liberal potential of the United States to increase. If this liberal potential is properly channeled, we may expect the area of freedom of the United States to increase. The problem is to spend up our rate of social invention in the service of the welfare of all the people.

If that read like a political appeal, it was. At the very opening of his essay for the *Times*, Wallace wrote, "The supreme god of a fascist, to which his ends are directed, may be money or power; may be a race or a class; may be a military, clique or an economic group; or may be a culture, religion, *or a political party*." (Emphasis added.)

The exchange with his friend White about both major political parties continued as Wallace readied his battle for a second nomination. "Well," Wallace concluded in a final note to the progressive Republican editor, "we shall each keep fighting in our own way and perhaps between us we can produce results." That was a knowing wink to the broader struggle, and to Wallace's own circumstance as he prepared to wrestle for the soul of the Democratic Party.

5

July 20, 1944, 10:55 P.M.

When Democrats Began to Abandon the New Deal

Issues that will be with us for a generation—perhaps even for a hundred years—will take form at this convention and at the November election.

— Henry Wallace addressing the Democratic
National Convention, July 20, 1944

What I understood was that, for better or worse, history was turned topsy-turvy that night in Chicago.

— Florida senator Claude Pepper, recalling
the events of July 20, 1944

There truly are critical junctures, pivot points, when everything is decided. Often, they involve bombs or assassinations. Sometimes, however, the fall of a gavel is all it takes.

Claude Pepper knew what was at stake. He understood that if he could get to the rostrum of the 1944 Democratic National Convention before the gavel fell on the night of July 20, 1944, the Democratic Party might carry the New Deal forward, and with it the promise of the Four Freedoms and the possibility of an Economic Bill of Rights. So Pepper rushed the stage.

"After President Roosevelt had accepted the nomination and the audience was uplifted by his stirring words, a group of us decided to start a parade for the nomination of Henry Wallace for vice president," the senator from Florida, a lonely Southern liberal, recalled many years later.

"Pretty soon the aisles were filled with the marching enthusiasts. After we had been around three times, as I recall, I stepped up on my chair by the middle aisle where I sat as the chair of the Florida delegation and looked over the parade to see the strength of it," he said. "I was surprised by the number of state standards and Wallace placards in the parade, as well as the evident enthusiasm, not only of the marchers, but of many other delegates and of the galleries."

As he surveyed the Chicago Stadium, it occurred to Pepper that "if Wallace were to be nominated vice president at all, it would have to be then." The senator determined that he would try "to get the convention to proceed to the nomination of a vice president at that time."

Pepper knew that the bosses had scheduled the vice-presidential vote for the next day, when the last pieces of their plan to block Wallace would be pulled into place. But Pepper also knew that the delegates could set their own rules, and that he could move a motion to renominate Wallace. "I began to wave my banner and to shout for recognition from the chairman. However, struggle as I might, I could not get his recognition. I was confident, however, that he had seen me and no doubt divined what I had in mind.

"Finally," Pepper recalled, "I pushed my way up the middle aisle to the gate leading to the platform. Fortunately this was manned by an old friend of mine who readily let me on the stairway leading to the platform."

Curtis D. MacDougall, chronicler of Wallace's campaigns, was in the hall that evening. He contended that "if a vote—an honest, un-bossed vote—had been taken of the entire house that night, Henry A. Wallace would have been renominated in a landslide."

David Lawrence, the burly chairman of the Allegheny County Democratic Party and close associate of banker Richard Mellon, had attended every Democratic convention since 1912 (and would, as the eventual mayor of Pittsburgh and governor of Pennsylvania, attend every convention through 1964). On this night, he gave the signal from the bosses. Shut it down. The hapless convention chair, Indiana senator Samuel Dillon Jackson, pleaded with Democratic National Committee chairman Robert Hannegan that the crowd was too riled up, "too hot" to stop. But with Pepper within feet of the microphone, Hannegan, who for months had schemed to prevent Wallace's renomination, screamed at Jackson to entertain a motion to adjourn the meeting. "Motion made," shouted Jackson. "As many as favor will signify by saying 'aye.' Contrary 'nay.'"

Cries of "No!" roared around him. Georgia governor Ellis Arnall, a Wallace ally, said Lawrence's motion to adjourn was "overwhelmingly defeated."

Yet Senator Jackson was taking his orders from the bosses, not those who hoped to toss aside Jim Crow.

"The ayes have it," he shouted, as the gavel came crashing down.

The minutes of the convention recorded that "the meeting recessed at 10:55 p.m."

"All that most of us who were there knew was that suddenly the chairman banged the gavel and walked off the platform, followed by his entourage, leaving it vacant," MacDougall recalled. "Slowly the tumult died down and we all started home."

As the report published in the British weekly *New Statesman and Nation* concluded, "The machine managed to get it delayed, and in the interval used all its arts to secure the victory for its own choice, Senator Truman."

Truman would become president nine months later, authorize the bombing of Hiroshima and Nagasaki, embrace the Cold War, dispatch the military to Korea and authorize an "acceleration in the furnishing of military assistance to the forces of France and the Associated States in Indochina" (the first U.S. troops sent to Vietnam), lose control of Congress to conservative Republicans and Southern Democrats who gutted the New Deal's labor protections with the Taft-Hartley Act, and permit the Smith Act trials of American Communist Party leaders, editors and elected officials. Truman was not a conservative. As president he raised the minimum wage and integrated the U.S. military. He criticized the worst excesses of McCarthy. He kept the Democratic Party sufficiently together to win re-election in 1948, beating Republican Tom Dewey (along with States Rights Democrat Strom Thurmond and Progressive Wallace). But he never really gained traction as president, as evidenced by his failure to overturn the Taft-Hartley law and the collapse of his effort to establish a national health-care program. Truman entered the last year of his tenure in the Oval Office with an all-time-low approval rating of 22 percent, and his hopes of winning a full second term in 1952 were dashed after Democratic voters rejected him in the New Hampshire primary in favor of populist Tennessee senator Estes Kefauver.

Truman's legacy was a Democratic Party that oversaw rather than extended the New Deal. The party's sense of mission faded. Over time, it would become a party that, in the words of author William Greider, chose leaders who "see their role as managerial rather than big reform." Democrats, Greider held, devolved over time into a party gripped by the "fear that even talking about ideology will stick them with the right's demon label: 'liberal.'"

Truman was made of stronger stuff than the Adlai Stevensons, Hubert Humphreys and Michael Dukakises who followed him, and of better stuff than the Bill Clintons and Joe Liebermans who steered the party down the course of "Third Way" centrism. But Truman lacked FDR's vision and strategic sense. His triumph in 1948 was achieved not by mobilizing an expanded electorate but by finding a narrow path to victory with less than 50 percent of an overall turnout that had dropped by 3 percent from 1944. Truman may have been a man of many good intentions. But he set the stage for the devolution of the Democratic Party.

Henry Wallace's champions argued that everything would have been better had he kept the vice presidency and succeeded Roosevelt. But even Wallace had his doubts about that. If Wallace had maintained his close relationship with Eleanor Roosevelt and many of the strategically savvy New Dealers, he would almost certainly have been better at mobilizing the Democratic base in the 1946 congressional elections that proved disastrous for the party, and from there might have extended domestic successes. Had Willkie lived, and had he aligned with Wallace, they might have forged a postwar foreign policy built around FDR's Four Freedoms rather than Cold War dogmas.

However, the mess that Wallace made of his 1948 presidential bid, with a third-party campaign that relied too heavily on bumbling Communist Party hangers-on and Hollywood celebrities and too little on New Dealers like Pepper and the leaders of the CIO, will always color the conversation. So be it. The point is, Wallace was on point in 1944. He and his allies worried that the compromising of the Democratic Party would eliminate defenses against a resurgent right and the looming threat of American fascism. Even if the full realization of the danger would not be recognized until decades later, their immediate fear was of a party that, in Wallace's words, tried "to play the Republican game." They were right to worry.

By the time that the vice president arrived at the 1944 convention, his wrangling with Jesse Jones over the war effort during the spring and early summer of 1943 had already revealed the extent of his own political vulnerability, and that of the left in general. Jones, FDR's conservative secretary of commerce, had not gotten everything he had wanted, but he would soon be boasting about shutting down the prospect of a Wallace presidency. Secretary of the Interior Harold Ickes confided to Wallace, "We have already lost the peace."

Campaigning for a New Deal Party

In November 1943, Associated Press political writer Jack Bell visited the vice president in his office. Wallace recalled in his diary that Bell "wanted to know if I thought the president was running for a fourth term. I said I didn't know any more than he did but that I assumed the president would be nominated for a fourth term. He said he wanted to know, point blank, if I was running for vice president. I told him that I was interested in getting my ideas over. He said, 'Well, you could get your ideas over much better if you were vice president than you could if you were out of public life.' He continued, 'I suppose you know that some of the men around the White House are against you being nominated again.' I said I didn't know that, but that I had understood from general conversation that some of the men around the White House had been quite active in the Jesse Jones affair."

A few days later, newspapers across the country carried an article in which Bell provided a succinct assessment of the power struggle within the White House. "Henry Wallace is carrying on a unique campaign for renomination as vice president on the personal assumption that President Roosevelt will be a candidate for a fourth term," Bell reported. "Although he reputedly has been scratched from the race by administration insiders who feel he would be of little vote-getting value in 1944, he is out to prove to the president that he represents labor and liberal elements in the Democratic Party that must be reckoned with at the next national convention."

Wallace would have welcomed a decision by FDR to again place his thumb on the scale, but he recognized the likelihood that the president's signal would be subtler this time. FDR faced new and more complicated political demands, as Wallace noted in a diary entry following a November conversation with Eleanor Roosevelt. "The president has told her that so far as he personally had been concerned, it had been necessary for him to

87

refrain from furnishing liberal leadership until the Democratic primaries were over in the Southern states," he wrote. "He did not want a third party put in the field in the South."

As the 1944 convention approached, Roosevelt and his aides feared a party split. Conservative Democrats like 1924 presidential nominee John Davis, who would eventually appear before the Supreme Court as a defender of the "separate but equal" doctrine in a companion case to *Brown v. Board of Education*, had already broken with the party to back FDR's Republican opponents. And Dixiecrats entertained the fantasy of replacing Roosevelt on the 1944 ticket with one of their own, Virginia senator Harry Byrd. (Byrd did not mount a formal challenge to the president, but he did secure a little under 10 percent of the first-ballot votes when the roll call of convention delegates was conducted.) As the same time, former secretary of war Harry Woodring, who had served in FDR's cabinet until 1940, was busy organizing conservative Democrats across the country into an organization designed to oppose a fourth term for the president, and to retake the party from "socially minded, so-called intellectuals" and "the mavericks, fellow travelers and European ideologists" who sought to steer the party to the left. Woodring and his allies demanded "a reunited Democratic Party under the leadership of 1932"—the year before the New Deal began.

Wallace's first task was to prove to Roosevelt, and to the delegates to the convention, that the Democratic Party would be stronger as a New Deal party. As veteran White House reporter Charles Hurd explained it, "Mr. Wallace is giving the United States today its first view of a vice president forsaking the traditional anonymity and silence of his office to stump the hustings in debate over issues that his president has endeavored to submerge."

Wallace wrote and spoke constantly over the next several months about "what America wants ... what America can have and how America can get it." In the postwar era, he argued, soldiers and defense-industry workers, farmers and shopkeepers, men and women, people of all races and ethnicities would demand more work, more income, more security and more freedom. And rightly so. Against those demands, he said, the monopolists, the corporatists and their political cronies would play every card in their hands. He imagined a struggle between the advocates of "a true general welfare democracy" and "a new kind of fascism."

As 1943 gave way to 1944, Americans began to explore the notion of a postwar period in which the outlines of the future would quickly take shape. After a decade and a half of depression and then war, there was reason to be hopeful. America had successfully converted itself into the "arsenal of democracy." Government planning, in the form of wartime industrial and social policies, seemed for the most part to be working. Of course, there were tensions. The barons of industry objected to being told how to run their factories. People bristled at rationing and, in some cases, at the changing character of workplaces where women and people of color were finally being given employment opportunities that had for so long been denied them.

But the headlines told the story of a war effort that would prevail. In the first weeks of 1944, Allied forces landed at Anzio and American troops began securing victory after victory. The 872-day siege of Leningrad was finally lifted and Soviet forces began winning critical battles on the Eastern Front. Sixth months later, in a single week, Rome was taken by the Allies, the D-Day invasion was launched and the Red Army put the final touches on plans for Operation Bagration, the Belorussian offensive that by August would shatter the German frontline.

Victory was imaginable, even foreseeable, and factions were digging in for the struggle to shape postwar America. The U.S. Chamber of Commerce, which had grudgingly cooperated with the Roosevelt administration during the war years, was already preparing to renew its historic mission of opposing what it called "an increasingly powerful federal government and the labor movement." The Chamber had allies in government, including the powerful chairman of the Senate Commerce Committee, North Carolina Democrat Josiah Bailey. Before the war Bailey had worked with business allies to co-author a "Conservative Manifesto" that called for cutting corporate taxes, deregulating business, weakening labor laws and maintaining the rigid "states' rights" agenda favored by Southern politicians. They were already talking about raising money to lobby for the agenda as war gave way to peace.

Labor leaders saw what was coming and planned to counter it with new organizing drives, such as the CIO's ambitious "Operation Dixie" plan to organize the South. "The CIO Political Action Committee has done the initial spadework in recent months ... and 14 regional offices are planned throughout the country to help organize labor's mighty political arm for the crucial issues that lie before us," National Maritime Union leader Joe Curran said in December 1943. "At home and abroad, labor's role has grown tremendously in line with the tremendous problems that must be solved. It is up to labor to do the same job to win the peace that it is doing to win the war."

FDR sometimes echoed the "win the peace" themes Wallace and others were advancing as a blend of New Deal economics and Four Freedoms foreign policies. In January 1944, FDR preached the gospel of economic democracy in his State of the Union address: "It is our duty now to begin to lay the plans and determine the strategy for the winning of a lasting peace and the establishment of an American standard of living higher than ever before known. ... A new basis of security and prosperity can be established for all—regardless of station, race or creed." If that pledge sounded a lot like Wallace, so, too, did the president's warning that "people who are hungry and out of a job are the stuff of which dictatorships are made."

Henry Wallace and his allies, it seemed, were shaping the debate. "Wallace Keeps New Deal Alive as a Political Issue," announced a *New York Times* headline from March 5, 1944;

its subhead read, "The Vice President, It Is Now Believed, Has a Good Chance to Be Renominated."

Underneath, *New York Times* writer Charles Hurd observed: "In this campaign for what is believed to be the vice-presidential nomination, it may be assumed [Wallace] is endeavoring to hold Mr. Roosevelt to New Dealism and at the same time demonstrate his indispensability as spokesman for the masses who originally gave Mr. Roosevelt his overwhelming majorities." Hurd wrote that whether Wallace's transcontinental speeches are "those of a crusader for postwar continuance of the New Deal prewar arguments and programs, or those of an active candidate for the vice presidency is not really material. Both roles seem to be present. A year ago it seemed most unlikely that Mr. Wallace could win nomination for a second term as vice president. Today political observers believe he has an even chance of proving his indispensability to a fourth-term ticket."

Pollster George Gallup on the same day released a new survey indicating that "if popularity with the rank and file of a political party were the controlling factor in the choice of vice presidents, Henry A. Wallace would have, as of today, a commanding lead over other possibilities mentioned for the vice presidency." Gallup noted that Wallace was attracting 46 percent support nationally—more than twice that of any other prospect—and was now "ahead in every section of the country." What was striking, the pollster noted, was the vice president's strength in the Southern states where his critics had suggested Wallace's talk of racial justice would weaken the ticket. "Although a number of Southern political leaders have been highly critical of Mr. Wallace, their revolt against him has apparently not extended to the rank and file," wrote Gallup. Indeed, Wallace was leading the next closest candidate, Secretary of State Cordell Hull, by a margin of better than 2–1.

Gallup mentioned just one cloud on the horizon for Wallace— the fact that "actual political practice" did not give the authority over vice-presidential nominations to the rank and file. If the president did not dictate a choice, the pick would be made by "party leaders in the traditional 'smoke-filled room.'"

Working in uncomfortable alliance with the Dixiecrats, prominent donors with corporate and Wall Street ties (like Edwin Pauley, the California oil man who served as party treasurer in the 1940s and would eventually become a close ally of Ronald Reagan) and big-city bosses (Chicago mayor Ed Kelly, former Memphis mayor Edward Crump, Edward Flynn from the Bronx, and Frank Hague from Jersey City), were doing their best to wire the machinery of the convention against the vice president.

Wallace had allies as well, like Philip Murray, the Scottish-born steelworker who headed the CIO, and Sidney Hillman, the socialist immigrant from Lithuania who headed the CIO's powerful Political Action Committee. Liberal senators like Pepper and Pennsylvania's Joe Guffey were backing him, as were Southern progressives like Georgia governor Ellis Gibbs Arnall. Actress and California congressional candidate Helen Gahagan Douglas told a reporter that Wallace was her certain choice for vice president.

Had Roosevelt said the same thing, the matter would almost certainly have been settled. But FDR worried that forcing Wallace on the convention a second time would stir resentment among the Southerners and the bosses at a point where he could not afford to lose them. The president took counsel from top Democrats and speculated about various prospects, including James Byrnes, the influential director of the Office of War Mobilization, and Supreme Court Justice William O. Douglas.

The weeks before the convention was to open on July 19 were a time of high intrigue in and around the White House. Labor leaders met with the president to argue on Wallace's behalf, while the bosses argued for anyone else. Roosevelt took it all in, sending mixed signals and creating confusion. There may have been moments, Wallace presumed, when the president determined to "ditch me as noiselessly as possible." But just as quickly Roosevelt changed his view, when confronted with indications that, as Wallace put it, "he had been lied to by his advisers."

The advisers were themselves conflicted. They agreed that they wanted Wallace booted off the ticket. But they could not agree about why. The money men, like Ed Pauley, wanted Wallace gone because he was talking about breaking up monopolies and suggesting that there was something wrong with CEOs running not just corporations but the government. Some of the big-city bosses were anti-Wallace because they feared he would remake the party nationally and jeopardize their fiefdoms. (Edward Flynn fretted that he "seemed to have become the candidate of the radicals of the country.") Others were angling on behalf of cronies, none more so than DNC chair Bob Hannegan. A Missourian who owed his rapid rise in Democratic circles to the sponsorship of Senator Harry Truman, he was constantly maneuvering to move his patron closer to the presidency. Manipulating the nominating process was something Hannegan could do with relative ease at a time when open primaries were uncommon and delegations consisted of the beneficiaries of the potent patronage systems. "The handsome, gregarious Hannegan—Mr. Busyman Bob, as he would be remembered—was playing an extremely deceitful game at this, his first national convention," wrote historian David McCullough. As McCullough noted, it was often difficult to determine when the party chair was doing the president's bidding and when he was doing his own.

With the opening of the convention barely a week away, FDR conceded during one late-night session at the White House that William O. Douglas and Truman would be solid contenders for the vice presidency. In a story told many times and in many different ways, Hannegan obtained a note from the president suggesting that he would be satisfied to run with either man. Some versions of the story suggest that the president named Douglas as a first preference but that the party chair then schemed to obtain a second note, or asked a secretary to type one with the Douglas-Truman order reversed. What is certain, however, is that Hannegan tried after a July 11 meeting with Roosevelt to convince Byrnes and Wallace that the president wanted them out of the running.

Byrnes, an old political hand who had served in the Senate before joining Roosevelt's White House team, wasn't buying it. According to McCullough, Byrnes "determined to settle the matter, returned to his White House office and put through a call to Roosevelt, who by this time was at his home in Hyde Park, New York. Byrnes, who had once been a court stenographer, took down their conversation in shorthand. Roosevelt said again he was not favoring anybody: 'I told them so [he said of Hannegan and his associates]. When we all went over the list I did not say I preferred anybody or that anybody would cost me votes, but they all agreed that Truman would cost fewer votes than anybody and probably Douglas second."

Byrnes pressed him. "If Hannegan and his friends were to release any kind of statement saying the President preferred Truman and Douglas, that could make things very difficult," Byrnes said. "'We have to be damn careful about language,' Roosevelt answered. 'They asked if I would object to Truman and Douglas, and I said no. That is different from using the word prefer. That is not expressing a preference, because you know I told you I would have no preference.'"

Roosevelt asked Byrnes if he planned on seeking the vice-presidential nomination, according to McCullough. No fool, Byrnes asked his boss what *he* thought. "After all, Jimmy," replied Roosevelt, "you are close to me personally and Henry is close to me. I hardly know Truman."

Wallace was, indeed, close to the president. So when Hannegan came calling, the vice president turned him away. "We might as well understand each other," Wallace said. "I will not withdraw as long as the president prefers me."

Wallace was offended by Hannegan's intrigues. If this was the game he had to play, Wallace figured he could put a few of his own pieces in place. So he made one last move.

"I hope it will be the same old team"

When Wallace returned in mid-July from a strenuous trip across Siberia and China, he met several times with the president. Though he had been out of the country for weeks, Wallace's popularity was on the rise; the press had given the tour widely favorable coverage. "In Washington movie audiences erupted in cheers when newsreels showed footage of Wallace in China," according to Culver and Hyde. And a new Gallup poll showed Wallace with a large nationwide lead among Democratic voters: 65 percent to 17 percent for Kentucky senator Alben W. Barkley, 5 percent for House Speaker Sam Rayburn, 4 percent for Senator Harry Byrd of Virginia and so on.

With the convention just days away, Wallace noted in his diary that he offered again to withdraw if Roosevelt wanted to choose someone else. No, said Roosevelt. "While I cannot put it just this way in public, I hope it will be the same old team," the president said. Roosevelt and Wallace agreed that while FDR would not dictate a choice as he had done in 1940, he would send a note regarding his preference to the convention.

Dispatched the next day, on July 14, it read:

My dear Senator Jackson: In light of the possibility that you will be chosen as permanent chairman of the convention, and because I am wholly willing to give you my own personal thought in regard to the selection of a candidate for vice president. I do this at this time because I expect to be away from Washington.

The easiest way of putting it is this: I have been associated with Henry Wallace during the past four years as Vice President, for eight years earlier while he was Secretary of Agriculture, and well before that. I like him and I respect him, and he is my personal friend. For these reasons, I personally would vote for him for renomination if I were a delegate to the convention.

At the same time, I do not wish to appear in any way as dictating to the convention. Obviously, the convention must do the dictating. And it should—and I am sure it will—give great consideration to the pros and cons of its choice.

Wallace understood that the letter would be read for what it was: an expression of sympathy that fell short of an endorsement. With conflicting signals from the White House, Wallace was well aware that Hannegan and his cronies would seize the opening to argue that FDR really did want a new face on the ticket. He did not have to wait for *Time* to explain, after the nomination fight was settled, that Roosevelt remained "the undisputed master of the Democratic Party," and that "with his support Henry Wallace might again have won the vice-presidential nomination. But the president chose to buy party unity instead." Wallace did not, however, believe that his fate was sealed.

When his train arrived at Chicago's 63rd Street Station on Wednesday, July 19, Wallace recognized that the president's stance had given him an opening—nothing more, but also nothing less—and he was prepared to exploit that opening with an appeal to the hearts and souls of the convention delegates. At dinner that night, a friend asked why he was so calm. "There is only one issue in my nomination and that is the existence of liberal government in the United States," Wallace replied.

"I happen to be the symbol of that issue," he explained. "It is the cause of liberalism which is at issue and not my own fortunes."

A year of struggle, in which Wallace had positioned himself as the St. George of the New Deal standing at the ready to slay the dragon of American Fascism, would culminate in one last speech. With the encouragement of the White House and the grudging approval of convention organizers, Wallace was permitted on the afternoon of July 20 to second the nomination of Roosevelt. As the vice president strode to the podium, the thousands of young people, union members and grassroots campaigners who filled the galleries of the great hall began to cheer. Then the delegates joined in. Announcing himself not as the vice president of the United States but as the chairman of the Iowa delegation, Wallace declared: "Now we have come to the most extraordinary election in the history of our country. Three times the Democratic Party has been led to victory by the greatest liberal in the history of the United States." Of course, Roosevelt must be nominated anew, he said, because "the Democratic party can win only if and when it is the liberal party."

> The future belongs to those who go down the line unswervingly for the liberal principles of both political democracy and economic democracy regardless of race, color or religion. In a political, educational and economic sense there must be no inferior races. The poll tax must go. Equal educational opportunities must come. The future must bring equal wages for equal work regardless of sex or race. Roosevelt stands for all this. That is why certain people hate him so. That also is one of the outstanding reasons why Roosevelt will be elected for a fourth time."
>
> The Democratic Party cannot long survive as a conservative party. The Republican Party has a monopoly on the conservative brains and the conservative dollars. Democrats who try to play the Republican game inside the Democratic Party always find that it just can't work on a national scale.

In essence, Wallace argued, the convention was not choosing its nominees but its future. "Our problem is not to sell Roosevelt to the Democratic convention but to sell the Democratic Party and the Democratic convention to the people of the United States," he explained. "There is no question about the renomination of President Roosevelt by this convention. The only question is whether the convention and the party workers believe wholeheartedly in the liberal policies for which Roosevelt has always stood."

MacDougall described the scene: "There was bedlam in the Chicago Stadium. Wallace signs were everywhere."

Because of Roosevelt's rapidly declining health, there was a morbid sense that delegates to the 1944 convention were

97

nominating two presidents. Historian of American political parties Wilfred Binkley noted that impression in his account of the proceedings: "Every element in the convention reminiscent of the Jacksonian Democratic tradition—the interest of the common man—shouted for Wallace. So irresistible were they that the will of the delegates had to be overwhelmed by intrigue, manipulation and main force on the part of the interests that could not tolerate the idea of Wallace as president."

Wallace had tried to make the fight to define the post war era the issue. The United States and its allies would prevail on the battlefield, he said. Indeed, on the day that Wallace arrived in Chicago, July 19, the U.S. Army secured the French city of Saint-Lô and began a critical pivot in the invasion of Normandy, while other Army elements entered Livorno in Italy and U.S. Marines prepared to land on Guam. Word came from Japan that, after a series of stinging defeats for his country's forces, General Hideki Tojo had resigned as the head of government. On the day Wallace spoke, July 20, as the Red Army was sweeping into Poland and resistance forces prepared to launch the Lwów Uprising against the Nazi occupiers, German colonel Claus von Stauffenberg attempted to assassinate Hitler inside the Führer's Wolf's Lair field headquarters near the Eastern Front.

What mattered, Wallace told the delegates, was that after the war "the voice of our new world liberalism must carry on."

"The convention is in the hands of the enemy"

Former Nebraska senator George Norris, the aging champion of old-school Midwestern progressivism who, like Wallace, had abandoned the Republican Party to align with Roosevelt, told the vice president that the speech he delivered to the 1944 convention was "one of the most courageous exhibitions ever seen at a political convention in this country." But Norris, who two years earlier had lost his seat when Nebraska Democrats refused to help him secure re-election, added a sobering political note. "If you had been trying to appease somebody you made a mistake," he said, reminding his friend that "you were talking straight into the faces of your enemies who were trying to defeat you."

Henry Luce's *Time* offered a similar assessment. "Whether conservatives squirmed or Southerners saw red or New Dealers cheered, Henry Wallace's speech was the first that riveted the delegates' attention," the magazine reported. "It was blunt, grave, tactless. It easily explained why Henry Wallace was the best loved and most hated man in the stadium."

Unfortunately, the haters had the upper hand. On the night of July 20, after shutting down the convention with Wallace on the verge of victory, Hannegan and his crew pulled out all the stops to make sure July 21 would be different. "The Wallace movement would advance no further," Culver and Hyde wrote. "Overnight the bosses worked feverishly to secure Truman's nomination. Ambassadorships were offered. Postmaster positions were handed out. Cold cash changed hands." Frank Comerford Walker, the immediate former DNC chair and current postmaster general, "was said to have called every state chairman that night, assuring each one that Roosevelt wanted the Missourian as his running mate." No one really knew if this was the president's wish. But even if it was not, few argued with the man who sat at the intersection of party politics and patronage.

MacDougall, who had cheered for Wallace the night before, and who, as a Democratic congressional candidate in Illinois, had a pass to attend the July 21 session, suddenly realized that he would not get back into the stadium. "Radio announcers revealed that it had been decided to keep the convention in continuous session without recess," he recalled. "Otherwise, those holding tickets for the afternoon session alone would be ineligible and those with tickets for the evening would be able to take their places. Those evening ticketholders were the same

Democratic Party rank and file who had defied their bosses the night before to join the Wallace claque. They had to be kept out at all cost." According to Wallace biographer Russell Lord, "Returning for the evening session, Wallace supporters, even some of the mightiest, found their places taken by minions of Boss Kelly [the mayor and local party boss] and their badges or credentials challenged or rejected at this doors." Secretary of the Interior Harold Ickes tried to reach Roosevelt in California, hoping for intervention, but he could not get through to the president. Harold Young, the politically savvy Texan who for many years served as Wallace's ablest aide, surveyed the hall and declared, "This convention is in the hands of the enemy!"

The Wallace forces fought against all odds. Claude Pepper seconded the vice president's nomination with a speech in which he speculated about how shameful it would be for Democrats if Henry Wallace proved to be "too democratic for the Democratic National Convention." Georgia governor Arnall, who had battled his own party to allow African-American voters to participate in Democratic primaries, told the convention that it was vital to renominate Wallace as a "reassurance that the Democratic Party remains true to the ideals of progressive liberalism."

The first ballot provided a measure of that reassurance. Wallace won 429.5 of the 589 votes that he needed to remain on the ticket. Truman was behind with 319.5. The rest of the votes were scattered among Alabama senator John Hollis Bankhead II, a segregationist born on his family's plantation just seven years after the end of the Civil War, and the better part of a dozen "favorite sons" and also-rans. On the second ballot, Wallace's total rose to almost 480. Before the roll call was finished, however, most of Bankhead's Southern backers had flipped to Truman. Then the arm-twisting accelerated. Bosses began to switch the votes of their delegations, often without consulting the delegates themselves. By the time the voting formally closed, Harry Truman had 1,031 votes and the nomination.

In its review of the convention, the *New Republic* argued that "with a little more skill, a little more preliminary work, the liberals might have won on their most important issue, the renomination of Henry Wallace." And, added Mark Sullivan of the *New York Post*, then a liberal paper, the "defeat of Henry A. Wallace was more than just the defeat of a candidate. It was the interruption of the New Deal as, so to speak, an ideological dynasty."

Wallace accepted the outcome, vaguely amused by the fact that "Democratic leaders had to work many times as hard to stop me in 1944 as they had to put me over in 1940." Ickes told Wallace that he had come out of the convention far better regarded "than the man who was nominated in your place," and that "next only to the president you are the strongest man in the Democratic Party." Mark Ethridge, the liberal newspaper editor from Louisville tapped by FDR to lead the Fair Employment Practices Committee's investigation into racial discrimination in the workplace, told Roosevelt that the Truman pick had backfired. "Truman may have improved the ticket had he not become, unfairly, I believe, the symbol of duplicity and the fair-haired child of Southern racists and Northern city bosses," he wrote in a letter to the president.

Wallace, meanwhile, eschewed the vitriol. Rather, he hit the campaign trail. He even appeared with Truman at a huge rally in Madison Square Garden, where the crowd was clearly more favorable to the man the party bosses had shunned than the man they nominated. To make sure there was no booing on the eve of the election, Wallace embraced Truman and delivered a unifying message: "This has been and is a people's war. The peace must be a people's peace. The way to get it is to re-elect Roosevelt and then make the Democratic Party into a truly liberal party."

It sounded to the crowd that night, and to most of the reporters who were present, like a repeat of Wallace's mantra. But there was a subtle difference. Wallace believed that FDR was "the greatest liberal in the history of the United States," but he saw more clearly than ever that the Democratic Party had within it a cabal that would resist the New Deal and the Second Bill of Rights. This confederacy was very powerful. And the compromises it demanded could, he worried, provide an opening to American fascism.

Reflecting on the convention that denied him the vice-presidential nomination and, almost certainly, the presidency, Henry Wallace concluded that "the internal foulness of the Democratic Party has not yet reached the point of lancing the boil."

6

Into the Wilderness

Birth of the Not-as-Bad-as-the-Republicans Democratic Party

It looked like the United States was getting ready to embark on an era of power politics and imperialism in international affairs.
— Henry Wallace, diary, May 10, 1945

As a leader of a third party [Henry Wallace] will accomplish nothing. He will merely destroy the very things he wishes to achieve.
— Eleanor Roosevelt, "My Day," December 31, 1947

Writing a few days after the close of the 1944 Democratic National Convention for *PM*, the great liberal daily newspaper of New York City, Max Lerner mused: "The heartening thing to me is how close a man like Wallace came to sweeping a hard-boiled convention. Don't forget that some pretty powerful forces were arrayed against Wallace. Don't forget that he had expressed the most candidly progressive ideas of any man in high public life. No fight is lost which can afford either that daring or that integrity. The fight over Wallace was not a rear-guard action, but a language action in which we fought for something new in a new spirit and didn't quite make it. Some day we will."

Lerner's optimism was shared by millions of American liberals, progressives and radicals in the fall of 1944. They imagined that the Democratic Party Wallace had proposed in his address to the delegates in Chicago was still within reach. Much of their faith rested with Franklin Roosevelt, who finished the 1944 campaign sounding like he embraced "the thesis that the Democratic Party can win only if and when it is the liberal party," as Wallace had put it at the convention. "Roosevelt, finally roused, began to sound like the liberal warrior of old," Russell Lord wrote of the last days of the campaign, describing how the president hit Chicago on October 28 in full form, calling for "a peacetime economy of 60 million jobs, incentive taxation, new conservation and crop insurance programs, free collective bargaining, decent health care and housing."

Arriving by train at 6 p.m. in a city where the temperature had dropped to 14 degrees and the wind was whipping off Lake Michigan, FDR proceeded to an outdoor rally where 110,000 stalwarts packed Soldier Field and 125,000 more surrounded the stadium to listen to the speech via loudspeakers. Framing his remarks as a discussion of the future of America, the president announced, "When our men and women return home from this war, they shall come back to the best possible place on the face of the earth—they will come back to a place where all persons, regardless of race, color, creed or place of birth, can live in peace and honor and human dignity—free to speak, free to pray as they wish—free from want—and free from fear."

Recounting the Second Bill of Rights he had read out in his State of the Union address the previous January—and referring to it now as an "Economic Bill of Rights"—FDR rejected the dismissal of his program by critics as "the dreams of starry-eyed New Dealers." He knew, he said, that Americans "agree with these objectives—that they demand them—and that they are determined to get them—and that they are going to get them."

Helen Keller, reading from a Braille text at a rally with Wallace three days later, spoke of "the thunder of waking conscience," and Wallace clearly felt it. Promised a major post in the new administration by Roosevelt, he was in regular communication with the president through the fall campaign. On the morning after FDR spoke at Soldier Field, Wallace telegraphed praise for a "magnificent" speech. "Your goal of sixty million jobs is perhaps high but I glory in your daring and as you say, Americans can do the seemingly impossible," he wrote from a campaign stop in Michigan. "We are predicting that you will carry thirty-six states, have a three million popular majority and a hundred Electoral College majority." Roosevelt wired back: "I promise to make good on the sixty million jobs if you will do the same on your predictions regarding 36 states, the popular vote and Electoral College majorities."

Roosevelt wound up carrying exactly thirty-six states, his popular-vote margin was 3.5 million and he won the Electoral College tally by a lopsided 432–99 over the hapless ticket of moderate Republican Thomas Dewey and red-baiting conservative John Bricker. Democrats picked up twenty House seats, for a fifty-one-seat advantage in that chamber, and maintained their overwhelming 57–36 majority in the Senate.

"Bipartisan isolationism has been destroyed," Wallace declared on election night. "Full steam ahead for a people's peace and jobs for all has been ordered."

The 1944 election results provided Democrats with their best overall finish for the next seventy-five years, with the exception of former New Dealer Lyndon Johnson's thumping of Barry Goldwater in 1964. After Roosevelt, only one Democratic nominee for president would win two consecutive elections for the presidency with more than 50 percent of the vote: Barack Obama in 2008 and 2012. And for most of his presidency, Obama's agenda was thwarted by a Republican-controlled House and obstructionist Republicans in the Senate. The only other two-term Democratic president in the period from 1944 until 2008, Bill Clinton, never secured 50 percent of the vote nationally in either of the three-way elections he won, and saw control of the House and the Senate flip to the Republicans two years into his first term.

Back in the Cabinet

Roosevelt kept his promise to make a place for Wallace in the next administration. Wallace was given his pick of domestic cabinet posts and chose the job of commerce secretary. The papers called it "poetic justice," because FDR had to remove Wallace's old nemesis, Jesse Jones, from the post. Wallace wrote an extended memorandum in which he proposed "a new Department of Commerce and a new concept of its work," one that would meet and perhaps exceed the president's 60 million jobs promise. The plan was to work in cooperation with other agencies to make investments that would help the U.S. economy while empowering impoverished and disenfranchised peoples around the world. Wallace's agenda raised the prospect of clashes with State Department conservatives who were already veering toward Cold War politics. This seemed to suit Roosevelt, who began his fourth term with a January 20 inaugural address in which he announced, "We have learned that we cannot live alone, at peace; that our own well-being is dependent on the well-being of other nations far away."

Segregationist Democrats and right-wing Republicans in the Senate moved immediately to block Wallace's nomination. They portrayed the fight as nothing less than a struggle between capitalism and socialism. Wallace, meanwhile, used the period between the end of his vice-presidential term and his confirmation as commerce secretary to write a short book, *Sixty Million Jobs*. The book was packed with facts and figures, but it did not read as a policy manual. Like the pamphlets of Tom Paine, this was Wallace rallying Americans to a cause.

The *Times of London* described the debate over Wallace's nomination as "pregnant with significance for the future" and reported that "it involves all those mighty issues which agitate men's minds when they look forward to the world after war— the true function of government in a democratic state; the yearning to be rid of the scourge of unemployment; the conflict between social conscience and the nostalgia for the old ways." Wallace had emerged, the paper explained, "as the apostle of full employment at home and of an expansionist trade policy abroad. He believes that if, by the cooperation of the State and private industry, 60,000,000 Americans can be found jobs, not only the United States but the whole world will benefit. He is convinced that if the standard of living in such countries as India and China can be raised even slightly, there will be such an abundance as to keep the wheels turning in all the industrial communities of the West. Whatever his limitations, Mr. Wallace's conception of a world set free from hunger, want and fear through a deliberately fostered policy of expansion is one that commends itself to the sympathies of many people outside the United States."

Wallace was finally confirmed with a 56–32 Senate vote on March 1, 1945. He did not get all the powers he had hoped for, but he was powerful nevertheless. During frequent meetings in the winter of 1944–1945, Roosevelt and Wallace talked about what the Commerce Department could do as a beachhead for the New Deal. They also discussed what could be done to counter Churchill's imperialism, create a United Nations and maintain good relations with the Soviet Union.

The wrangling over the vice-presidential nomination in 1944 had temporarily strained relations between Roosevelt and Wallace. But as Wallace moved to the Department of Commerce, their relationship became stronger. Both men spoke of the pleasure they took from working together. It was not 1933 again, but the prospect that great things might yet be accomplished animated their discussions.

The enthusiasm was real. But it was not the full story. Wallace could see that FDR had lost a great deal of weight and that his body shook, sometimes violently, as he spoke. "He was a gallant figure," Wallace wrote, "but also pitiable—as he summed up his precious strength." As winter turned to spring, Roosevelt headed south to his Little White House retreat at Warm Springs,

Georgia, where he had swum in the healing waters since 1924. It would be his last journey.

The news of FDR's death, on April 12, 1945, shook the nation as no passing of a president had since that of Abraham Lincoln. A generation of young men and women, many of them dispatched to distant battlefields or working in the defense industries of a war that was not yet finished, had known no other president. "The ordinary people of the United States had, to an extraordinary degree, accepted the president's acts as a measure of the country's advancement and consigned to his hands their interests and hopes," wrote Freda Kirchwey, editor of the *Nation*, in an April 21, 1945, commentary aptly titled "End of an Era." "They did not trust the Democratic Party or the administration as a whole; they trusted Roosevelt."

Kirchwey continued: "Even when he seemed to compromise or retreat they were content to wait until he found it expedient to swing back to his own basic line. To millions of Americans, he was the New Deal, all it gave or promised them personally. The political consequences of this sense of identification between the leader who has gone and the people who followed him will be felt in every part of our society. Men fighting in the mountains of northern Italy, workers on assembly lines in Detroit or Los Angeles will be inclined to new ways of thinking and acting because he is dead. Heads of state will orient their policies differently. Businessmen will make new plans."

Roosevelt's name had appeared on five of the Democratic Party's seven national tickets since 1920. Under his leadership the last four of those elections had been won, up and down the ticket: the presidency, the House, the Senate, overwhelming numbers of state and local offices. He had reimagined the party, rebranded it, repositioned it. He had not made it everything that liberals wanted it to be, as the 1944 convention made clear—but he had held out the promise of a continually evolving New Deal. For many of his political supporters, it seemed as if they lost not just a leader of their party but its reason for being. "To many," historian David McCullough observed, in a reflection on the beginning of Truman's presidency, "it was not just that the greatest of men had fallen, but that the least of men—or at any rate the least likely of men—had assumed his place."

What of the Economic Bill of Rights? The Four Freedoms? The People's Peace? Wallace updated the manuscript for *Sixty Million Jobs* to include a poignant new section: "[After] the Soldier Field address, as I continued campaigning on into the East, I noted the immediate encouragement given by Franklin Roosevelt's words. He had given his pledge that government would not shirk its responsibility to all the people. And that pledge, alone, was sufficient to give people a new faith in the future. The man who made the pledge is dead. But we must justify his faith. We must do this not for the sake of redeeming the pledge of Franklin Roosevelt. We must do this to justify our faith in ourselves and our country."

Even as he wrote those words, however, Wallace knew that what Roosevelt created was unraveling. On the train that carried FDR's body from Washington to the Hudson River village of Hyde Park, where the president would be interred, Wallace kept a journal. He considered the members of the administration with whom he was traveling and concluded, "The cord which had bound the Cabinet had snapped."

Out with the New Dealers, in with the Wall Streeters

Truman ushered out the old New Dealers. Secretary of Labor Frances Perkins, the first woman appointed to a presidential cabinet and a liberal sociologist who had been FDR's champion of worker rights since the administration was inaugurated on March 4, 1933, was gone barely two months after Roosevelt's burial. Secretary of the Interior Harold Ickes, the old progressive who had also taken office on March 4, 1933, and who had helped to define the New Deal as head of the Public Works Administration, was gone ten months to the day after FDR died. By the spring of 1946, only Wallace, who had taken charge of the Department of Agriculture on March 4, 1933, retained a cabinet post as a true New Dealer. The conservative *Chicago Tribune* delighted in noting that "the New Dealers are out and the Wall Streeters are in."

The new president and the new secretary of commerce were on a collision course. On May 10, 1945, a month into Truman's tenure, Wallace confided in his diary that "it looked like the United States was getting ready to embark on an era of power politics and imperialism in international affairs."

During their long meetings at the White House in the winter of 1944–1945, Wallace had warned FDR "that there were some senators who felt that the president was appeasing Russia." He noted in his diary that the president "vigorously" defended cooperation with the Soviet Union over the more belligerent course proposed by Winston Churchill.

In the 1930s, Wallace argued against diplomatic recognition for Moscow because he objected to restrictions on religious freedom in the Soviet Union. But as World War II wound down, he held to the view that "it is much safer for the peace of the world if Russia is a member of the family of nations." This was FDR's calculus as well. In February 1945, Roosevelt traveled to Crimea for the Yalta Conference with Churchill and Stalin at which Roosevelt obtained Stalin's commitment to participate in the United Nations. Speaking to Congress on March 1, 1945, the president declared, "I come from the Crimean conference, my fellow Americans, with a firm belief that we have made a start on the road to a world of peace."

The Soviet Union's disregard for the agreement's commitment to allow the people of Europe "to create democratic institutions of their own choice" led to immediate tensions, which were further stoked by Churchill. At the same time, division and distrust were fostered by an Anglo-American disregard for the partisans who led left-wing, Communist or Trotskyist move-ments that competed for power in postwar governments; the French Communist Party was one such movement, finishing first in the 1945 and 1946 legislative elections in that country. FDR recognized the challenges of the moment but sought to avoid conflict by maintaining lines of communication with Moscow. Wallace, who had for several years warned of the prospect that "fascist interests motivated by anti-Russian bias" might after the end of World War II steer the United States in a direction "where World War III will be inevitable," agreed that maintain-ing the dialogue had to be the priority. Both men were accused of being too deferential to Stalin, too willing to overlook Soviet totalitarianism and too absorbed with Roosevelt's faith that a Big Three agreement and cooperation represented "the best pledge for a secure and peaceful world."

There is no telling precisely how FDR's views might have evolved in the postwar era. To the end, he maintained a complex, cajoling, complimentary and castigatory relationship with Stalin and the Soviets. Historian Thomas Fleming observes that "Wallace would stubbornly pursue Franklin D. Roosevelt's naïve view of Soviet Russia unto his own political destruction." But there are arguments to this day disputing the notion that FDR and Wallace were as naïve as their critics suggested. In the notes he wrote in 1973 to go with the Wallace diaries that he edited, the historian John Morton Blum maintained that at least until the time Truman literally and rhetorically applauded Churchill's 1946 "Iron Curtain" speech at Fulton, Missouri, "the possibility existed of a practical accommodation between the United States and the Soviet Union, of a temporary coexist-ence of mutually suspicious spheres of influence, of a gradual lessening of hostility and a gradual movement, as Wallace rec-ommended, first toward commercial and scientific cooperation, all within the framework of the United Nations."

Blum concluded that "even after the Fulton speech, the United States could have assisted the countries of the Southern

Hemisphere more on an altruistic and less on a political basis. American records, easy to access, disclose that Truman never expected a rapprochement with the Soviet Union. Wallace had reason to disagree. He had the prescience to realize that the hard line abroad would generate hysterical reactions to dissent at home, lead to the postponement of urgent domestic reforms and encourage military adventures costly alike of men and morale. He had the foresight to propose alternatives to which the United States government turned only after a quarter century of terrible waste had made accommodation more attractive to most of the American people."

Truman grew increasingly frustrated with his commerce secretary's criticism of the administration's Cold War brinksmanship, bloated military budgets, power politics and imperialism. Wallace's popularity was acknowledged, grudgingly, and he was frequently dispatched to address rallies organized by liberal and left-wing groups. Truman and Wallace would consult on the content of the speeches, but their relationship was decaying rapidly. In a September 12, 1946, speech to a labor rally for New York State Democratic candidates at Madison Square Garden, Wallace said:

> Tonight, above everything else, I want to talk about peace—and how to get peace. Never have the common people of all lands so longed for peace. And yet, never in a time of comparative peace have the common people so greatly feared war.
>
> During the past year or so, the significance of peace has been increased immeasurably by the atom bomb, guided missiles and airplanes which soon will travel as fast as sound. Make no mistake about it—another war would hurt the United States many times as much as the last war. We cannot rest in the assurance that we invented the atom bomb—and therefore that this agent of destruction will work best for us. He who trusts in the atom bomb will sooner or later perish by the atom bomb—or something worse.

We must realize that modern inventions have now made peace the most exciting thing in the world—and we should be willing to pay a just price for peace. If modern war can cost us four hundred billion dollars, we should be willing and happy to pay much more for peace.

The price of peace—for us and for every nation in the world—is the price of giving up prejudice, hatred, fear, and ignorance.

Wallace continued: "The Republican Party is the party of economic nationalism and political isolation—and as such is as anachronistic as the dodo and as certain to disappear. The danger is that before it disappears it may enjoy a brief period of power during which it can do irreparable damage to the United States and the cause of world peace." As for Democrats, a recent mass lynching in Georgia was an "illustration of the kind of prejudice that makes war inevitable." Wallace told the crowd that Democrats needed to break with Democrats on the issue.

"If we are to work for peace in the rest of the world," he said, "we here in the United States must eliminate racism from our unions, our business organizations, our educational institutions and our employment practices." Wallace also objected to the renewed influence of Wall Street with regard to economic policy, and, he pointed out: "We are still arming to the hilt. Our excessive expenses for military purposes are the chief cause of our unbalanced budget. If taxes are to be lightened we must have the basis of a real peace with Russia—a peace that cannot be broken by extremist propagandists … Russian ideas of social-economic justice are going to govern nearly a third of the world. Our ideas of free-enterprise democracy will govern much of the rest. The two ideas will endeavor to prove which can deliver the most satisfaction to the common man in their respective areas of political dominance. But by mutual agreement, this competition should be put on a friendly basis. Let the results of the two systems speak for themselves."

Wallace explained that he was delivering remarks that had been vetted "page by page" just two days earlier by Truman. Unfortunately, Truman could not be counted on. A career politician whose primary motivations had little to do with ideology and much to do with self-preservation, the president was inclined to defer to party elites and the media.

Seizing on an opening to finally boot Wallace from the cabinet, the old guard aligned with key Republicans and conservative media to stir up an outcry over the Madison Square Garden speech. A reporter asked Truman whether he thought the speech conflicted with State Department policy. "I do not," Truman replied. But Secretary of State James F. Byrnes was furious, as Lawrence Lader recounted in a 1976 article in *American Heritage* magazine. "When Byrnes threatened to resign, the president fired Wallace on September 20," Lader wrote. "That same day Truman wrote his mother and sister: 'Well, now he's out, and the crackpots are having conniption fits.'"

Truman did not merely elbow Wallace aside just eight days after Wallace's speech; the new president embarked upon what Lader characterized as a "drastic reversal of Roosevelt's policy, pushed by White House advisers like Navy Secretary James V. Forrestal." Forrestal wanted a showdown with the Soviet Union "now rather than later," Lader wrote. "Truman agreed: 'We have got to get tough with the Russians.'"

The stated objection by the hawks who now had Truman's ear was Wallace's call for the independent pursuit of peace by the United States, and his denunciation of imperialism. "Make no mistake about it," Wallace had said, "the British imperialistic policy in the Near East alone, combined with Russian retaliation, would lead the United States straight to war unless we have a clearly defined and realistic policy of our own." For good measure, he clarified, "I am neither anti-British nor pro-British, neither anti-Russian nor pro-Russian."

But there was more to the objection by Truman's advisers to Wallace's remarks than a disagreement over foreign policy.

The commerce secretary's greatest sin, at least in the eyes of his critics, was his suggestion that a mixed economy similar to those being developed in Scandinavian social democracies, and even in the post-Churchill United Kingdom, might ultimately develop in the United States. "Under friendly peaceful competition the Russian world and the American world will gradually become more alike," Wallace said. "The Russians will be forced to grant more and more of the personal freedom, and we shall become more and more absorbed with the problems of social-economic justice."

Wallace felt the need to clarify more than his feeling toward the British and Russians. He was making a point about how to think about and engage with competing ideologies. "I am not a Communist, or a Socialist, or Marxist of any description," he declared, "but I find nothing criminal in the advocacy of different economic and social ideas." This might have been an acceptable idea in the FDR era, but it was a tougher sell now that Truman was in charge.

The New Deal coalition was always a balancing act. It included independent radicals who aligned with the successful third parties of the upper Midwest: Wisconsin's Progressives, Minnesota's Farmer-Laborites, North Dakota's Non-Partisan Leaguers. FDR was strongly supported by New York's American Labor Party, which maintained a popular front sensibility that welcomed Communists into its ranks. Toward the end of Roosevelt's presidency, the coalition also included New York's Liberal Party, which was initially organized by Socialists and others on the left but rejected alliances with the Communists. Even some Republicans, such as Willkie and New York mayor La Guardia, joined in an embrace of economic and social and racial justice, and proposed what was described as "enlightened internationalism."

The politics of the 1930s and early 1940s had been nightmarish for the oligarchs and plutocrats, the corporatists and monopolists, the segregationists and xenophobes who had imagined the United States as their personal preserve. They knew that the Democratic Party would remain a little bit liberal. But they were determined to do whatever was necessary to prevent Wallace and his supporters from reconstituting radical politics within its fold. As the former vice president warned, the "money power" of Wall Street was reasserting itself.

Out of office, Wallace tried to forge a different future. Lader was not the only eyewitness to the era who would suggest that Wallace's 1948 presidential bid began on that September 1946 evening in New York City. That was certainly what Truman and his aides feared at the time, with some justification. "Within two months of the September 12, 1946, attack on administration foreign policy, Wallace had cut deeply into Truman's strength," Lader contended. "Although 48 percent of registered Democrats supported Truman as their next presidential candidate, according to the Gallup poll, 24 percent now backed Wallace. His blueprint for Soviet-American unity drew unprecedented crowds in his speaking tour that spring. Yet Wallace continued to insist that he and all 'progressive forces' must work within the Democratic Party."

Inside or Outside the Democratic Party?

Wallace was hardly on a straight trajectory from his ejection from the Truman administration to his doomed 1948 Progressive Party run. He certainly knew, as the *Chicago Sun* editorial page observed, that with his firing, "the New Deal as a driving force is dead within the Truman administration." But he continued to believe it was alive within the Democratic Party. As he campaigned across the country for Democratic candidates in the 1946 congressional and state elections, Wallace accepted an invitation from California's state Democratic Party chair, James Roosevelt, the late president's son. Appearing before a rally organized by progressive groups along with AFL and CIO trade unionists, Wallace announced, "I am still a Democrat" and that "more than ever I am a progressive." He said that he wanted to do "everything I can to elect progressive Democrats to Congress," and that "if the Democrats fail to control the 80th Congress there is only one way in which we get control again and that is by becoming more progressive."

Wallace's foreboding about the 1946 election was grounded in an understanding that weak Democrats could not mobilize their base in sufficient numbers to beat the Republicans. The first midterm election of Harry Truman's presidency was a disaster, with Democrats losing control of both the House and Senate for the first time since Herbert Hoover's presidency. The new Republicans were not in the mold of Wendell Willkie. Wisconsin ended the era of the progressive Republican La Follettes and sent Joseph McCarthy to the U.S. Senate. California replaced New Dealer Jerry Voorhis with a young Republican lawyer who had already figured out how to use red-baiting as a political tool. His name was Richard Nixon.

Truman would wrestle with the new Congress on some issues and work with it on others, but it soon became clear that the reactionaries had the upper hand. In part this was because of the incoherence of the Truman administration in the face of the GOP's portrayal of the election as a battle not of Democrats v. Republicans, but of Communism v. Republicanism. Carroll Reece, the Republican National Committee chairman, claimed the federal bureaucracy was filled with "pink puppets."

Segregationist Democrats gleefully joined in on the red-baiting rhetoric. Mississippi senator Theodore Bilbo, a Klansman who had filibustered to block anti-lynching legislation, portrayed multiracial labor unions' advocacy for civil rights protections as the work of "Northern Communists." Representative John Elliott Rankin, a fiercely racist and anti-Semitic Mississippi Democrat who helped establish the House Un-American Activities Committee as a standing congressional committee, ripped the CIO's Southern organizing campaign as "a

Communist plot" and launched into a racist diatribe about how it could lead to African-American voting rights. "We're all asleep at the switch," Rankin said. "They're taking over the country; we've got to stop them if we want this country."

While Truman was no Bilbo or Rankin, in the immediate postwar years he traveled rather too comfortably in the circles of Southern and border-state segregationists, and he failed to embrace many of the recommendations of his own Commission on Civil Rights because he did not want to offend the party's large Southern bloc. Yet, pressured by Wallace and civil rights leaders like A. Philip Randolph and conscious of the need to mobilize African-American voters in the industrial North, the president would eventually bend to the demands of civil rights campaigners for the integration of the military. It was, however, a soft bend.

Truman was all too willing to assume a managerial role in order to maintain his status as the party's default choice in 1948. New York union leader Louis Hollander complained of "the weakness displayed by the Truman administration in giving way to the monopolists and the reactionaries." United Auto Workers union president Walter Reuther griped that the Democratic election setbacks of 1946 resulted from frustration with the "indecision, bungling and appeasement" of the reactionaries by Democrats in Congress and "the great capacity of the Truman administration to conform to those policies."

Red-Scare Democrats

Less than two months after the new Republican Congress was seated at the beginning of 1947, Truman bent to the mounting anti-Communist hysteria at precisely the time it was being used to undo New Deal programs. First, the president outlined his Truman Doctrine, with its ever-expanding military budgets and Cold War interventionist policies. Then, on March 21, 1947,

Truman signed Executive Order 9835, the "Loyalty Order" that ushered in a new era of background investigations and loyalty oaths for federal employees and signaled to state and local governments, colleges and universities and the private sector that the Red Scare had become fully bipartisan.

With the creation of the Attorney General's List of Subversive Organizations under Truman, the federal government practiced McCarthyism some three years before McCarthy. A top Truman aide, Clark Clifford, would admit in an interview with journalist Carl Bernstein three decades later that it was all a political ploy. "The President didn't attach fundamental importance to the so-called Communist scare," Clifford said. "He thought it was a lot of baloney." He also acknowledged that "I felt the whole thing was being manufactured."

Clifford remembered Truman's acquiescence as a "political problem." The president, he said, "had to recognize the political realities. He'd gotten a terrible clobbering in 1946 in the congressional elections. We gave a good deal of thought to how to respond. We had a presidential campaign ahead of us and here was a great issue, so we set up this whole kind of machinery." Bernstein, whose parents were Communist Party members whose lives were dramatically disrupted by the Red Scare, wrote a memoir in which he reviewed Clifford's comments and concluded that Truman and his aides "made the whole goddamn thing up." Historian Eric Foner, whose own family members were blacklisted during the 1940s and 1950s, gave Bernstein's book examining the issue, *Loyalties: A Son's Memoir*, a somewhat mixed review. But Foner recognized that "Bernstein's real discovery" was that "the president knew that no threat to internal security existed; the boards were established in 1947 to fend off Republican charges of being 'soft' on communism."

Foner recounted Bernstein's trajectory to the truth. "Eventually," he writes, "Carl realizes that his father is right about the witch hunts—the Communists' 'crime' was not membership in a disloyal

party but union organizing, civil rights work and other political activities. The target of McCarthyism was not a conspiracy
to overthrow the government, but the legacy of the New Deal.
... For all its flaws, *Loyalties* does drive home a truly subversive idea: Rather than a nest of spies, the Communist Party
was an integral and honorable part of the American radical
tradition."

As early as December 1946 at the founding convention of
the Progressive Citizens of America, Wallace saw the outlines
of the Red Scare to come.

> We shall not allow the enemy to stampede us into foolish red-
> baiting. As we work to fight off the enemy, as his stooges try to
> stir up jealousies and get us fighting among ourselves, we shall
> never be against anything simply because Russia is for it. Neither
> shall we ever be for anything simply because Russia is for it.
> We shall hold firmly to the American theme of peace, prosper-
> ity and freedom, and shall repel all the attacks of the plutocrats
> and monopolists who will brand us as Reds. If it is traitorous to
> believe in peace—we are traitors. If it is communistic to believe
> in prosperity for all—we are Communists. If it is un-American
> to believe in freedom from monopolistic dictation—we are un-
> American. I say that we are more American than the neo-Fascists
> who attack us. The more we are attacked the more likely we are
> to succeed, provided we are ready and willing to counterattack.
> On with the fight!

Wallace was strikingly well positioned to lead a movement
that might have pulled the Democratic Party back toward the
New Deal and the Four Freedoms. That is what many of his
supporters wanted him to do. Wallace's political adviser, Harold
Young, argued that a primary challenge to Truman would move
the president to the left while at the same time forging a base
within the party for future campaigns. California Representative
Helen Gahagan Douglas pleaded with Wallace to remain inside
the Democratic Party, where he could build upon the efforts of

progressives across the country to maintain New Deal coalitions. And former California attorney general Robert Kenny, a leader of the left-wing National Lawyers Guild and a national co-chair of Progressive Citizens of America, mounted a "Democrats for Wallace" campaign that sought to get the former vice president on primary ballots. "Wall Street is counting happily on a race between Dewey and Truman," Kenny told the California State Democratic Central Committee in the summer of 1947. "They would rather have Dewey win, as they expect he will—but the stock exchange would shudder only slightly if a miracle came to pass and Truman were elected."

Kenny argued against starting a third party. "We are here as Democrats fighting for a live and progressive Democratic Party," he told that California party meeting. "A Democratic Party which will unite behind the ideals of Henry Wallace will find a third party not an enemy but an ally. If liberals, fearing a third party, decide to back Truman, they suffer nothing but defeat—win, lose or draw."

Many critics of a third-party run by Wallace, including Kenny, well understood the value of a multiparty politics that reflected the broad range of ideas in the United States. Progressives were fully aware of the narrow nature of the Democratic Party leadership. But those who, like Kenny, had been battling for decades to build the left also knew that the political processes were arranged to protect the duopoly. In the early days of the New Deal, robust left-wing third parties in Minnesota (Farmer-Labor) and Wisconsin (Progressive) actually beat the Democrats and Republicans in races for governorships and Senate and House seats. Socialists, Communists and union-backed parties were competitive in particular regions and cities across the country. FDR often cooperated with parties that stood to the left of the Democrats; he effectively endorsed the Wisconsin Progressives over the Democrats in the 1930s and early 1940s, and he ran in New York as a "fusion" candidate on both the Democratic and American Labor Party lines.

By the time Roosevelt finished his presidency, however, the Minnesota Farmer-Laborites had merged with the Democrats in that state and the Wisconsin Progressives were in the process of atomizing into oblivion. The Socialists had seen their support collapse to one-tenth of what it once was, and the Communists, having adopted a Popular Front "Communism is twentieth-century Americanism" strategy, briefly converted from a political party into the Communist Political Association. FDR's personal appeal was a crucial factor in many of the realignments of the era, as the popular president made it easier for voters who had not previously considered themselves Democrats to vote the party line. At the same time, a nationalizing media tended to blur regional political distinctions, and Democratic and Republican party leaders worked to game the rules in their favor. Only a handful of states—notably New York and to a lesser extent California—made third-party and independent politics easy. And even in those states, media and political elites had mastered the art of scaring voters away from alternatives to the Democrats and Republicans.

In *Gideon's Army*, his 1965 book on the 1948 campaign, Curtis MacDougall recalled that Robert Kenny "thought then and still thinks that there was an excellent chance to capture the California and possibly the Oregon and Washington delegations, and that their placing Wallace's name in nomination at the 1948 Democratic convention would have been wise." It is notable that the calculus did not speak of winning the nomination or the presidency, and it is true that working within the Democratic Party, with all the barriers and constraints that involved, would have been difficult. Yet it offered liberals and progressives more options than the third-party route. By the fall of 1947, the labor federation that had been closest to Wallace, the Congress of Industrial Organizations, was warning against a third-party bid. (The CIO included many of the progressive unions that had launched the "Operation Dixie" Southern organizing drive and had also battled hardest against the destructive

Taft-Hartley law and the dismantling of the infrastructure of the New Deal. Its leaders had many gripes with Truman. But they feared the election of a Republican president who might, with a Republican Congress, further erode FDR's legacy.) One of Wallace's closest associates during the period, Michael Straight, the publisher of the *New Republic* who had hired Wallace as the magazine's editor, warned in the summer of 1947 against a third-party bid. "I doubt if we have the strength to start a third party," he reckoned. "Yet, it may be started anyway under auspices and with ambitions that will make it a hopeless adventure, a children's crusade."

But Wallace was not listening to the wisest of his old allies. Even as the prospect of a presidential bid by the former vice president caused Truman and his aides to temper the bombastic Truman Doctrine in favor of the more cooperative Marshall Plan in Europe, Wallace continued to despair at the failure of the administration to adopt progressive policies and its compromises with the Red Scare.

At a May 19, 1947, rally in Los Angeles, Wallace, joined by Katharine Hepburn, denounced the House Un-American Activities Committee and the use of anti-Communist fervor to undermine campaigning for racial justice, economic democracy and peace. "We burned an innocent woman on a charge of witchcraft," Wallace said. "We earned the scorn of the world for lynching Negroes. We hounded labor leaders and socialists at the turn of the century. We drove 100,000 innocent men and women from their homes in California because they were of Japanese ancestry. We branded ourselves forever in the eyes of the world for the murder by the state of two humble and glorious immigrants: Sacco and Vanzetti. These acts today fill us with burning shame. Now other men seek to fasten new shame on America." Wallace proceeded to name-check successive HUAC chairs. "I mean the group of bigots first known as the Dies Committee, then the Rankin Committee, now the Thomas Committee—three names for fascists the world over to roll on their tongues with pride."

Wallace believed that Truman's loyalty boards and the development of lists of subversives threatened an "American inquisition" that would tear apart the country, silence reformers and thwart social progress for decades to come. Disparaging the president's approach as a threat to "everything in America that is worth fighting for," Wallace rose to new rhetorical heights at a Madison Square Garden rally on March 31, 1947, with a prescient speech in which he foresaw what would come to be known as the McCarthy era taking shape.

> Intolerance is aroused. Suspicion is engendered. Men of the highest integrity in public life are besmirched. The president's executive order creates a master list of public servants. From the janitor in the village post office to the Cabinet member, they are to be sifted and tested and watched and appraised. Their past and present, the tattle and prattle of their neighbors, are all to be recorded.
>
> Whom will its inquisition condemn if this drive continues? Every American who reads the wrong books; every American who thinks the wrong thoughts; every American who means liberty when he says liberty; every American who stands up for civil rights; every American who speaks out for one world; every American who believed in Willkie; every American who supported Roosevelt. Only they who say shibboleth shall pass by the gate.

Wallace also saw the dark clouds of the Cold War gathering. "When President Truman proclaims the worldwide conflict between East and West, he is telling the Soviet leaders that we are preparing for eventual war," he said in an NBC radio address that spring. "They will reply by measures to strengthen their position in the event of war. Then the task of keeping the world at peace will pass beyond the power of the common people everywhere who want peace. Certainly it will not be freedom that will be victorious in this struggle. Psychological and spiritual preparation for war will follow financial preparation; civil liberties will be restricted; standards of living will be forced downward; families will be divided against each other; none of the values that we hold worth fighting for will be secure."

Rejecting "the outworn ideas of imperialism and power politics," Wallace argued that Truman was simply wrong. "The way to handle communism is by what William James called the replacing power of the higher affection. In other words, we give the common man all over the world something better than communism. I believe we have something better than communism here in America. But President Truman has not spoken for the American ideal. It is now the turn of the American people to speak."

The New Party

Wallace announced his "New Party" campaign for the 1948 election on December 29, 1947. In doing so, he boxed himself in for the remainder of the campaign. As his former aide Gardner Jackson observed, Wallace seemed like "a person answering calls the rest of us don't hear." Even the Americans who agreed with Wallace, millions of liberals who had seen him as their champion, were unprepared to risk the Republican presidency that might result from his third-party run. Wallace's words were stirring: "By God's grace," he declared, "the people's peace will usher in the century of the common man." But they never really connected with the Americans he proposed to rally.

Wallace framed his quixotic campaign as a bid for peace. "The bigger the peace vote in 1948," he argued, "the more definitely the world will know that the United States is not behind the bipartisan reactionary war policy which is dividing the world into two armed camps and making inevitable the day when American soldiers will be lying in their arctic suits in the Russian snow." That message did have an appeal to a war-weary electorate. It extended far beyond the cadres of the American Communist Party, which endorsed and worked for

Wallace's independent candidacy. But as the campaign progressed, the idea that what came to be known as the Progressive Party was "Communist dominated" took hold on the pages of right-wing newspapers and in the smoke-filled rooms where Democratic bosses gathered, and even among the leadership of CIO unions that had once provided Wallace an essential support. The label became a central theme of attacks on the new party by conservatives, as well as by the emerging bloc of Cold War liberals who believed that Wallace's vote-diverting campaign had to be crushed in order for Truman to have any chance of winning. Thus Wallace came under immense pressure from non-Communist backers of the Progressive Party to make a clearer break with the Communists.

Members of the Communist Party played a significant role in Wallace's 1948 campaign, especially when it came to drafting the new party's platform—to the immense frustration of prominent New Dealers who were aligned with Wallace, such as economist Rexford Tugwell. As many of Wallace's liberal allies drifted away from the campaign in the summer and early fall of 1948, the influence of Communist Party retainers on the strategies and messages of the party increased to a point where, as the editors of the *Nation* suggested, Wallace was inspiring "at once the despair of his friends and the jest of his enemies." Tugwell took to describing himself as "an uneasy member of the Progressive Party" and said Wallace needed to be much firmer in denouncing not just "aggressive foreign policy on our part" but also "Russian imperialist interests." Wallace spoke and wrote frequently about his disagreements with the Communist Party and the Soviet Union, yet his strong opposition to the Red Scare politics of the moment led him to reject suggestions by Tugwell and others that he take formal steps to distance his candidacy from the CP.

Wallace stood on principle against the notion that a new politics should be built by adopting the tactics of the Democrats and Republicans he criticized. "For Wallace and his constituency," explained historian Norman Markowitz in his 1973 book *The Rise and Fall of the People's Century*, "the practical effects of red-baiting on American society continued to be far more important than flesh-and-blood American Communists. While making the standard New Deal argument that American Communism was insignificant and could succeed only in times of massive depression, Wallace defended the civil liberties of Communists as essential to the defense of all Americans and to the maintenance of the atmosphere in which the New Deal could continue to expand." This stance, historian Thomas Devine would suggest many years later in another assessment of the 1948 campaign, "weakened his party, though the Communists themselves played an even more significant role. For all their self-deluding rhetoric regarding the 'great people's movement,' the Communists undermined at every turn any chance that Progressives would become the kind of 'third force' that Wallace, Tugwell and others envisioned. Their sectarian behavior destroyed the fledgling Progressive Party at the local, state and national levels, leaving those who expressed views that dissented from the Cold War consensus with no organized forum to do so. Such men and women found themselves silenced and marginalized—not only by 'red-baiters,' as many scholarly accounts have emphasized, but by the Communists who paid them little respect, caused them endless anguish, and cost them their credibility."

The Doomed Crusade

It is common for contemporary historians to embrace the view that decisions made in the fall of 1948 provided the truest measures of Wallace as a politically impractical dreamer. In fact, the greater evidence of his impracticality came a year earlier, with his determination that it was possible to build and sustain a new party at a time when there were so many structural, political and historic barriers to doing so. By the fall of

1948, there was little Wallace could do to improve his political fortunes. Yes, an argument can be made that taking less advice from the Communist Party tacticians who hung around the Progressive Party headquarters in New York might have made for more strategically sound choices in the 1948 campaign. But a parallel argument can be made that many of the ablest grassroots campaigners for Wallace in the campaign's closing days were Communists, fellow travelers or independent leftists from unions and social movements in places like Tampa and Detroit and Fargo who shared their candidate's determination to reject red-baiting, no matter the political cost.

In the late 1940s, there were still many believers in a Popular Front approach that rejected the dictates of the CP, even while they worked with the CP on behalf of peace and social justice. This is a detail of the fast-moving and complex politics of the postwar era glossed over by those who imagine that Wallace's 1948 campaign was nothing more than a Communist project. It is fair to suggest that the vast majority of Wallace's backers were, like the candidate himself, critical of Soviet Communism.

But that opposition did not preclude them from working with Communists, Socialists and radicals of many stripes. Decades later, a World War II bomber pilot who had earned the Distinguished Flying Cross, George McGovern, summed up the sentiments of the thousands of young people who were attracted to Wallace's 1948 campaign.

"The Russians had 27 million people killed in World War II; the whole country was laid to waste—I mean the physical country as well as the people—and it seemed to me they would probably be the last country in the world that wanted to start World War III," McGovern said. "And so, when Henry Wallace, who had been secretary of agriculture, and later vice president, when he started saying what I thought, I swung over to him. And there were probably some radicals in the party way out in left field, but it didn't include me. I was that ex-Republican who was looking for somebody who would lift the banner of peace."

Wallace's challenge to racism also inspired many voters. Wallace and his Progressive Party running mate, Idaho Democratic senator Glen Taylor, insisted on appearing before integrated audiences in the segregated South. Their campaigning was praised and endorsed by W.E.B. Du Bois, Paul Robeson and a young Harry Belafonte. The civil rights strategist Jack O'Dell, who was active with the Seamen for Wallace Committee that organized in New Orleans, would write of how those integrated rallies in the South "electrified and inspired" a new generation of campaigners for civil rights. It mattered, O'Dell argued, that Wallace faced down angry mobs in places like Greensboro, North Carolina, and that Taylor chose to be arrested by Birmingham police commissioner Bull Connor's officers rather than follow orders to enter an integrated rally through a door marked "whites only."

In September 1948, Wallace spoke on NBC radio after a seven-state journey through the South.

> You read the press accounts of my trip. The papers told you eggs were thrown at me; they told you I was booed. You read that in some cities local authorities would not permit me to talk to free American meetings, to unsegregated audiences. All of this is true but it is not the real headline. The real headline is that it is possible to do what some said was impossible—to hold unsegregated meetings in every Southern state and to hold them without incident. ...
>
> I came out of the South with the utter conviction that segregation, racial prejudice and Jim Crow, can cost America its life. For these evils are not simply problems of the South. No, the lynchings and knifings of Negroes in the South have their counterparts in every part of our country. A mob wrecks a Negro's home in Detroit; police run down citizens of Harlem; Mexican-Americans are railroaded to jail in Los Angeles. In Northern restaurants, in Western schools, in Midwestern hospitals, it is the same and even the children's genes are infected. In the nation's capital, the marble

tournament to determine who is the best player in Washington does not allow competition between Negro and white children. This is an issue above politics, for whatever denies the freedom of the Negro, destroys the freedom of the whites. It is a cancer that eats into the very moral fiber of the American people. ...

I used to think that time, long-drawn-out time, would handle these evils. But since World War II, I know that time is far, far shorter than it used to be. I know that today we are in desperate need of a solution which respects the dignity of the human soul. And the old parties cannot give us this solution even if they would. For Mr. Dewey's party is the party of corporations whose profits are rooted in discrimination, the party of wage differentials. And Mr. Truman's party is held together with the cement of discrimination. Both are parties of profit—and they have found prejudice a profitable business.

Wallace's assertion that the major parties were indistinguishable resonated with millions of Americans at the start of the 1948 campaign. But the energy and enthusiasm of the mass rallies of the late winter and early spring faded as Election Day approached. Key backers, especially in the labor movement, distanced themselves from the campaign. In addition, Truman moved marginally to the left on civil rights and developed his "Give 'em Hell, Harry" persona. The president was conscious of the threat Wallace's candidacy posed in states like California and New York, especially after the stunning February victory of a Wallace-backed American Labor Party candidate, Leo Isacson, in a special election for a New York City congressional seat. Truman's leftward shift gave onetime Wallace allies like Claude Pepper a rationale to explain their desertion from Gideon's Army.

Pepper had organized a "Dump Truman" effort in the spring and summer of 1948; but once it failed, he grudgingly traveled to Brooklyn, to the very precincts that most favored Wallace, a month before the election to say that voting for the Democratic nominee was "the last best hope of a progressive democracy in the United States." Leaders of the United Auto Workers, who just five years earlier had invited Wallace to Detroit to help them challenge racism as "American fascism," struck a darker note. Leading the charge against Wallace and the Progressive Party, the union warned ominously that "people who are not sympathetic with democracy in America are influencing him," even as rank-and-file UAW members campaigned for Wallace in Detroit, Milwaukee and other blue-collar towns.

By November, Wallace was doing his best to hold the Progressive Party together in its stronghold of New York City with an open-car tour of Brooklyn. Newspapers and magazine that had once covered the former vice president's every move, and that in some cases had championed his claim on FDR's legacy, now dusted off lurid tales of the former secretary of commerce exchanging "guru letters" with the Russian painter and philosopher Nicholas Roerich, being duped by the Soviets during his wartime travels in Siberia, and, amazingly, being just a bit too athletic. At sixty, Wallace remained remarkably fit; he played tennis, boxed, arm-wrestled and tossed boomerangs with considerable skill. Somehow, as the press piled on, even this was seen as suspect—a sign of immaturity in a man who would be president. He was, by the fall, consigned to also-ran status and treated accordingly. The major papers and radio networks dismissed him as a barely worthy of attention—except as a target for a final round of red-baiting. Truman gave them fodder. "I hate communism," he declared toward the end of the campaign. "I deplore what it does to the dignity and freedom of the individual. I detest the godless creed it teaches. I have fought it at home. I have fought it abroad, and I shall continue to fight it with all my strength. This is one issue on which I shall never surrender. Now, my friends, the truth of the matter is, the communists are doing all they can to defeat me and help my Republican opponent. Just take a look at the facts. The Communist Party of the United States is today supporting a third-party candidate in an effort to defeat me."

Wallace and many of his strongest supporters would eventually conclude that the Communists did their Progressive Party insurgency more harm than good. Wallace had asserted on the campaign trail: "I'm never going to say anything in the nature of red-baiting. But I must say this: If the Communists would run a ticket of their own this year, we might lose 100,000 votes but we would gain 3 million. I know if the Communists really wanted to help us, they would run their own ticket this year and let us get those extra votes." With the passage of time, he and others would make a compelling case that many of the Communist Party functionaries who were associated with the Wallace campaign were more focused on their own sectarian projects than on organizing a viable candidacy. But it is also easy to get lost in the weeds of old arguments of the left and miss an essential detail of the 1948 campaign: the last message that most Americans got from the press before they went to the polls on November 2 was do not, under any circumstances, vote for Henry Wallace.

The influential editorial pages of the nation's newspapers were adamant in their denunciations of the former vice president. The *Pittsburgh Press* helpfully advised Pennsylvanians not to physically assault the candidate when he came to town, because "the way to beat Mr. Wallace is to vote against him—not toss eggs." In a nation where 1,750 daily general circulation newspapers still provided the steadiest flow of information and advice to voters, only one local paper, the York, Pennsylvania, *Gazette and Daily*, backed Wallace.

Published from 1915 to 1970 in the Pennsylvania Dutch country by Josiah W. Gitt, whose family had resided in the region for 250 years, the *Gazette and Daily* was one of the last of the country's iconoclastic daily papers. "J.W. Gitt was raised in the shadows of the Gettysburg Battlefield, and he grew up with a lifelong aversion to war and killing," recalled McKinley Olson, the paper's last editor. "He also read Charles Dickens's novels when he was young, which gave him a passion for fair play and social justice—which were among the attributes of his newspaper." Asked by a newly hired writer for guidelines in crafting editorials, Gitt replied that "the fundamentals on which my editorial policy is based" were found in the Declaration of Independence, the Bill of Rights and the Sermon on the Mount. In a 1947 column headlined "What Progressives Can Do," Gitt argued that the defenders of the New Deal had to "refuse to be diverted or divided by the enemy drawing a Red herring across the trail." In addition, he advised them to

> stand for and fight for a more equitable distribution of the products of the soil and the factory; a foreign policy which will encourage peace and goodwill and not act as a partner of reaction in protecting itself against a better distribution of wealth and income abroad; protect labor in its right to bargain on equal terms with capital and toward that end preserve and continue the Wagner Labor Relations Act without amendment or emasculation; put into practice the American ideal of the equality of man; destroy monopoly and put an end to restraint of trade and the maintenance of high prices by either open or tacit agreement; secure full employment and make it a national policy; do the planning necessary to make full employment continuous, with minimum wages high enough to enable those who labor to secure for themselves and their families a high standard of living; provide at government expense an education for everyone who desires it in proportion to the individual's capacity to absorb and not in accord with ability to pay; provide old age pensions high enough to enable those too old to work to live a happy life in their declining years; and see to it that unemployables for physical reasons have enough to maintain them in good circumstances.

Gitt called himself an anti-monopolist and asserted: "I believe in progressive capitalism. I am not a materialist and in no sense am I a Marxist. I start from a different premise. I am a sentimentalist." He explained that it was necessary to have "a

wider distribution of wealth in order to preserve our capital-
istic system." Such nuance was lost on most of the media in
the months before the 1948 election. Two weeks before the
election, the anti-Wallace onslaught had gotten so bad that
his backers bought a full-page advertisement in the *New York
Times*. "WE are for Wallace!" the headline announced, followed
by this declaration:

WE BELIEVE deeply that the words of Henry A. Wallace hold
the promise of peace.

> *"There is no misunderstanding or difficulty between the USA
> and the USSR which can be settled by force or fear and there
> is no difference which cannot be settled by peaceful, hopeful
> negotiations. There is no American principle or public inter-
> est, and there is no Russian principle or public interest which
> would have to be sacrificed to end the cold war and open
> up the Century of Peace which the Century of the Common
> Man demands."*

WE BELIEVE with Henry Wallace that the major parties and
their candidates—Thomas E. Dewey and Harry S. Truman—in
bipartisan alliance have brought us to the brink of war and
fascism; that they represent in their policies the interests of the
few at the expense of the many; that to a Democratic and a
Republican Congress must be attributed inflation (Truman killed
price control and the Republicans buried it); fear and intimidation (Truman's Loyalty Order and the Republicans' Thomas
Committee); repression of labor (Truman charted the course for
the Taft-Hartley law when he broke the railroad strike in 1946).

WE BELIEVE with Henry Wallace that America cannot be free
until all men, regardless of race, color or creed, can live and
work together without fear of discrimination.

WE BELIEVE with Henry Wallace that science, art, literature
and education cannot flourish in an atmosphere of intimidation
and policed opinion.

WE BELIEVE with Henry Wallace that the United Nations must be made effective, not bypassed or used by us or others, as a pawn in the game of power politics.

WE ARE AMERICANS loyal to our nation's heritage. We are deeply convinced that full realization of progress and freedom are possible for the people of this nation. We believe that this is inherent in the program of policy of Henry A. Wallace. As independents, and as artists, scientists and professionals, we are proud to pledge our support to his candidacy.

The signers included Aaron Copland, W.E.B. Du Bois, Dashiell Hammett, Lillian Hellman, Norman Mailer, Thomas Mann, Isamu Noguchi, Clifford Odets, Erwin Panofsky, Linus Pauling, Muriel Rukeyser, Ben Shahn, Artie Shaw, Mary van Kleeck and Frank Lloyd Wright.

On the night before the election, Wallace spoke on the radio. "Tomorrow, when you go to the polls, you will be voting for one world at peace or two worlds in conflict. Without the Progressive Party, there would be no real choice."

"Tomorrow," Wallace said, "the Progressive Party comes of age. Together, we shall march boldly into the future, holding in our hands the promise of a better life."

The Measure of Gideon's Army

But the Progressive Party didn't come of age on November 2, 1948. Gideon's Army numbered 1,157,328, or 2.37 percent of the total vote. Wallace won fewer votes that Strom Thurmond. Unlike Thurmond, who carried Alabama, Louisiana, Mississippi and South Carolina, Wallace won no states and no electoral votes. "In the entire United States, Wallace carried only 30 precincts," Wallace biographers Culver and Hyde note. "With the exception of seven precincts in the Tampa area, where Wallace was popular with the Spanish-speaking cigar crafters, his success was entirely in black and Jewish districts in New York and California."

Wallace and his backers argued that his third-party bid had influenced Truman to campaign as a reasonably progressive populist in the last weeks before the election, and that this helped the president to upset Dewey. "From the time that Mr. Wallace announced he would run for President," the *Wall Street Journal* observed, "Mr. Truman began to suck the wind from Mr. Wallace's sails by coming out for more and more of the Wallace domestic program."

But this was cold comfort for Wallace and his supporters. Truman had borrowed just enough from the left to win a low-turnout election with a minority of the vote. But his biggest message was one of fear. He had waged a campaign that told Americans they should elect him because he was not a Republican. When the election was done, so, too, was the prospect that the Democratic Party might fully renew and extend its commitment to advance the New Deal, the Second Bill of Rights and the Four Freedoms. The Democratic insiders who had seen Franklin Roosevelt's presidency as an interregnum rather than a new era were back in charge—and they would remain a dominant and constraining force in the party for the next seven decades. The *New York Times* got many things wrong in its half decade of editorializing against Henry Wallace. But it spoke a certain truth in an offhand reference within an editorial endorsing Dewey over Truman. "Mr. Wallace," the newspaper of record observed, "has taken the left wing into exile."

7

The Great Unwinding

Hypocrisy and Double Talk on Race, Cold War Compromises and the Degeneration of the Democratic Party

Our greatest weaknesses as a progressive democracy are racial segregation, racial discrimination, racial prejudice and racial fear.
—Henry A. Wallace, 1947

When you feed the head of a dog, you nourish the whole body. Remember, when you vote for a Democratic Senator, Representative or Alderman in New York, Chicago or Detroit— or anywhere—you vote to make EASTLAND and the Southern race-baiters chairmen of the important committees in Congress.
—Eisenhower-Nixon campaign flyer distributed in African-American neighborhoods, 1956

"Unless the bipartisan foreign policy of high prices and war is promptly reversed," Henry Wallace declared on the night of the 1948 election, "I predict that the Progressive Party will rapidly grow into the dominant party as the cup of inequity of the old parties overflows." Defiant in defeat, he proclaimed that "to save the peace of the world the Progressive Party is more needed than ever before." Wallace was disappointed, bitter and mostly wrong. While it was surely true that an alternative was needed to the Red Scare at home and the Cold War abroad, the Progressive Party would not provide it, and neither would the Democratic Party.

Wallace and another top member of the party's leadership, Pennsylvania publisher Josiah Gitt, recognized after the 1948 defeat that the party needed to broaden its base or die. Wallace tried gamely to deliver that message. In February 1950, at the Progressive Party's convention in Chicago, the former vice president used his keynote address to argue that Progressives needed to "stand before the American people as being Americans, first, last and always." To that end, he asserted again that the party needed to reject the Cold War policies of Washington and Moscow. "The United States and Russia stand out today as the two brutes of the world. Each in its own eyes rests on high moral principles, but each in the eyes of other nations is guided by force and force alone." Progressives needed to make it clear that their party's ideals were "vastly different from the Communist Party." Wallace and Gitt both objected to the party's opposition to U.S. intervention on the side of the United Nations in Korea. And by August 1950, each had resigned from the positions of leadership they held and exited the party.

The Cold War against the Left

The Progressives would straggle on for a few more years, running a 1952 ticket led by one of the country's great labor lawyers, Vincent Hallinan, and newspaper editor Charlotta Amanda Spears Bass, the first African-American woman to be nominated for the vice presidency. Hallinan and Bass focused their campaign on many of the same civil rights and civil liberties issues that Wallace and Taylor had raised, but secured only 140,746 votes, barely one-tenth of the support that the Progressives had attained four years earlier—and far less than the Democrat Adlai Stevenson (27,375,090) or the victorious Republican Dwight Eisenhower (34,075,529).

Both the Progressive Party's 1952 nominees had been accused of being communists and persecuted by authorities in the Red

Scare that spread after Truman's re-election in 1948. Hallinan was nominated while serving a six-month prison term on a contempt citation extending from his defense of Harry Bridges, the president of the militant International Longshore and Warehouse Union. A proud Australia-born radical who was one of the most vital figures in the American labor movement from the 1930s to the 1980s, Bridges was charged by federal authorities with lying to immigration authorities when he said he was not a Communist Party member. The labor leader was convicted in 1950 and sentenced to five years in jail; but a year after the 1952 election a 5–3 Supreme Court decision overturned that conviction. Hallinan's ardent representation of Bridges earned him disbarment and decades of federal scrutiny. Bass, like many civil rights campaigners, was monitored for years by the FBI, which still classified her as a potential security threat in the late 1960s, when she was over 90 and living in relative obscurity in a Los Angeles nursing home. Their experiences were not uncommon for backers of the Progressive Party. It didn't matter whether they were active communists or former communists who had participated in a legal political party that had won elections; it didn't matter whether they were socialists who had never joined the CP because of ideological and tactical differences; it didn't matter whether they were self-proclaimed "progressive capitalists" like Henry Wallace.

Progressives were hounded throughout a Cold War era shaped by Wisconsin senator Joe McCarthy's circus-like Senate hearings and by out-of-control House Un-American Activities Committee sessions, by FBI inquiries, trials and the imprisonments of dissenters, by purges of unions and moves to deport immigrants whose utilization of the First Amendment to advance the cause of economic, social and racial justice was deemed too enthusiastic, and by a blacklisting frenzy that left some of the most talented educators, actors and activists in America without work.

Even before World War II was finished, Wallace had predicted that "the greatest threat to the United States will come after the war." Whether or not Americans chose to recognize Joe McCarthy and those who practiced McCarthyism as the American fascists that Wallace warned about in 1944, the climate of intolerance, innuendo, threat and punishment that characterized the "American inquisition" of the 1950s had a profound impact on the nation's politics.

"The political repression of the 1940s and '50s" that historian Ellen Wolf Schrecker describes in *Many Are the Crimes: McCarthyism in America* fostered "a widespread movement that treated dissent as disloyalty, punished thousands of law-abiding Americans and scared millions more into silence, destroying much of the left and seriously narrowing the political spectrum."

So chilling was the moment that, as the 1950 elections approached, a *New York Times* headline announced, "Intellectual Left Is Silent in Campaign." The subhead explained that "Mentors of Roosevelt Social Revolution, Onetime Militant Crusaders, Now Are Cautious." Silence might have been complicity; but the uglier reality was that when liberals spoke out, they often echoed the right's language. "Liberal intellectuals rode the anti-Communist bandwagon," noted historian Howard Zinn. "*Commentary* magazine denounced the Rosenbergs [Ethel and Julius] and their supporters. One of *Commentary*'s writers, Irving Kristol, asked in March 1952: 'Do we defend our rights by protecting Communists?' His answer: 'No.'" Even the American Civil Liberties Union, which traced its roots to resistance to the first Red Scare of the World War I era, hesitated to take the lead in opposing the threat to civil liberties in the second Red Scare of the 1950s.

McCarthy did not just attack those he claimed were Communist Party members. The senator's alcohol-infused crusade against "subversives" extended deep into what had been the political mainstream, as he ridiculed the "pitiful squealing" of "those egg-sucking phony liberals" who "would hold sacrosanct those Communists and queers." After the 1952 election, the Progressives never mounted another presidential campaign and faded from view by the mid-1950s. The party's strongest affiliate, New York's American Labor Party, folded in 1956—six years after Vito Marcantonio, the anti-imperialist and antiracist congressman who had been the ALP's most prominent elected official, was defeated by a challenger who ran with the joint endorsement of New York's Democratic, Republican and Liberal parties.

The Return of the Segregationists

The Progressive Party actually outlasted Strom Thurmond's Dixiecrat party, which dissolved shortly after the 1948 count was completed. But the Dixiecrats had a place to go. Thurmond finished his term as the Democratic governor of South Carolina in 1951 and a few years later would be sitting in the Senate as a member of the Democratic Caucus. Southern Democrats who marched out of the 1948 Democratic National Convention and gave the Dixiecrat party line that year to Thurmond were seated on the floor of the 1952 Democratic National Convention. They successfully nominated one of their own, Alabama senator John Sparkman, for vice president. Sparkman had announced in March 1948 that he could not support Truman. He then joined his fellow Alabama segregationists in securing the Dixiecrat line for Thurmond. Thanks to these machinations, the Dixiecrats won Alabama that fall on a platform that explicitly condemned proposals to ban lynching and the poll tax. Four years later, Sparkman was a star of the Democratic convention, where he crafted what was described as a "compromise" platform plank on civil rights. In fact, it wasn't a compromise; it was a renewal of the awful calculus of a Democratic Party that Wallace had tried to change in 1944 and challenged in 1948.

The Democrats might send some good signals. Their presidents might, under pressure from Randolph and the March on Washington Movement and Eleanor Roosevelt and the liberals, issue executive orders to desegregate war industries and the military. But their leaders were determined to maintain the loyalty of the "solid South" at almost any cost—even the cost of nominating for the vice presidency a man who had refused to support the party's previous nominee because that nominee was insufficiently racist. Remarkably, Sparkman gained that nomination by acclamation ("At no point had there been any serious rival," the *New York Times* reported) and then campaigned as a fervent racist who explained that Truman's attempts to move the party in a modestly more moderate direction had been a "colossal blunder." The 1952 Democratic presidential nominee, Adlai Stevenson, told the delegates that Sparkman "will give me all of the strength that I need." The hapless Stevenson was, as usual, wrong. The party's ticket carried nine Southern and border states but lost the rest of the country—going down to defeat even in Stevenson's home state of Illinois.

According to Curtis MacDougall: "The longer a person stuck to his Progressivism, the more likelihood there was that the price he would ultimately pay would be greater. Whereas the Dixiecrats of 1948 were welcomed back into the Democratic fold with everything forgiven, no such generous attitude prevailed toward the Progressives."

Many Wallace allies were purged in the Democratic primaries of 1950. Senator Glen Taylor, labeled an incorrigible leftist after his 1948 alignment with Wallace, was beaten in Idaho. Senator Claude Pepper was beaten in Florida. California Representative Helen Gahagan Douglas, dubbed the "Pink Lady" for her supposed sympathies with the Soviet Union, tried for the Senate in 1950; she survived a bitter Democratic primary battle only to be beaten in November by Republican red-baiter Richard Nixon.

In Roosevelt's day the Democratic Party had been ideologically adventurous and increasingly, if never quite sufficiently, excited about building coalitions against reaction. Now, however, it turned inward. "As a result of the Cold War, American politicians closed ranks on foreign policy," explained historian Zachary Karabell in assessing the fallout from the 1948 campaign, describing a number of factors that "narrowed the spectrum of choice and debate in national elections." The Democrats became a less distinctive and dynamic party. They no longer drove the debate but instead erred on the side of an increasingly cautious "bipartisan consensus." "Truman's second term began with the upset of the century, but it quickly turned sour," Karabell asserts. "Between Korea, labor unrest and the efflorescence of McCarthyism, Truman spent the remaining years of his term embroiled in constant crisis. The standing of the Democratic Party was so low in 1952 that Eisenhower coasted to an easy victory over Adlai Stevenson, and Republicans retook the House of Representatives."

Race was not the only domestic issue on which the Democrats failed in the 1950s, but it was the critical one. FDR had fallen far short on civil rights, refusing too frequently to hear the pleas of Randolph, Eleanor Roosevelt and Wallace to fully realize the New Deal as a transformational force for economic *and* racial justice. Yet the New Deal years had seen a movement among Northern African-American voters away from the Republican camp with which they had been associated from the end of the Civil War through the early 1930s. As recently as 1920, the Democrats had refused to seat African-American delegates on the floor of their conventions. But FDR's personal popularity, his appointments, his mild embraces of desegregation and his New Deal economic initiatives caused a realignment in many Northern cities. A "combination of civil rights symbolism and economic incentives really compelled black voters to say farewell to the party of Lincoln," explains historian Leah Wright Rigueur. FDR consistently secured roughly two-thirds of the African-American vote for his re-election bids. And yet the Democratic Party continued to be a haven for the most brutal racists in the South, and its surrender on this issue haunted the party morally and politically.

By the late 1940s and early 1950s there were a number of prominent Democrats who were genuinely committed to racial justice, like Minnesota's Hubert Humphrey and Wisconsin's Philleo Nash. But most Democratic leaders accepted the awful arrangement that found a place for segregationists in a supposedly progressive party. Truman and Stevenson were cautious, calculating men who were unprepared to abandon the old order. The party had mounted a liberal campaign in 1948 under pressure from Wallace on the left, but after Thurmond's States' Rights Party backers returned to the party fold, the Democrats returned to their old ways in the 1950s.

Modern Republicanism

At the same time, Eisenhower proposed a "modern Republicanism" that was influenced by New York–based veterans of the Willkie and Dewey campaigns. Eisenhower was not a civil rights champion in the manner of Willkie or Wallace, but he saw the need for change and he accepted it. The new president announced in his first State of the Union address that the go-slow approaches of the Truman administration were done. "I propose to use whatever authority exists in the office of the president to end segregation in the District of Columbia, including the federal government, and any segregation in the armed forces," declared the old five-star general and former Allied supreme commander. Rejecting a request from the secretary of the Navy to delay integration, Ike replied: "We have not taken and we shall not take a single backward step. There must be no second-class citizens in this country."

Eisenhower appointed liberals such as California governor Earl Warren to the federal courts. Barely a year into his presidency the Warren-led Supreme Court handed down the landmark *Brown v. Board of Education* decision that rejected state laws establishing racial segregation in public schools.

A Republican assistant attorney general who had been a key supporter of Eisenhower, J. Lee Rankin, argued on the side of the African-American plaintiffs in the *Brown* case, telling the high court that the doctrine of "separate but equal" facilities for blacks and whites could not be justified. At the same time, one of the leading lawyers defending the segregationist doctrine was John Davis, the Democratic Party's 1924 nominee for president.

Eisenhower was never as outspoken or direct as he should have been on civil rights; after the *Brown* decision, he simply said: "The Supreme Court has spoken, and I am sworn to uphold the constitutional process in the country. And I will obey." What distinguished Eisenhower and his party, for all the president's compromises and personal failures and for all the GOP's political gamesmanship, was a rejection of the position of the powerful Southern Democrats who promised "massive resistance" to integration.

Ninety-nine Democratic members of Congress, including Sparkman, signed the Thurmond-drafted 1956 Southern Manifesto, which denounced the high court's *Brown* decision as "a clear abuse of judicial power." The Southern Democrats, many of them the ranking members of their party on key House and Senate committees, pledged to employ "all lawful means to bring about a reversal of this decision which is contrary to the Constitution and to prevent the use of force in its implementation." The 1956 Democratic platform featured a tortured word salad of language opposing "illegal discriminations" but refusing to get specific about what that meant. With regard to *Brown*, all that could be mustered was: "Recent decisions of the Supreme Court of the United States relating to segregation in publicly supported schools and elsewhere have brought consequences of vast importance to our Nation as a whole and especially to communities directly affected. We reject all proposals for the use of force to interfere with the orderly determination of these matters by the courts."

In contrast, the Republican platform said, "The Republican Party accepts the decision of the U.S. Supreme Court that racial discrimination in publicly supported schools must be progressively eliminated." It also announced: "The Republican Party has unequivocally recognized that the supreme law of the land is embodied in the Constitution, which guarantees to all people the blessings of liberty, due process and equal protection of the laws. It confers upon all native-born and naturalized citizens not only citizenship in the State where the individual resides but citizenship of the United States as well. This is an unqualified right, regardless of race, creed or color."

Eisenhower's "modern Republicans" better recognized the tenor of the times, which were defined not just by court cases and legislation but by growing movements in the South and the North on behalf of civil rights. The August 1955 murder of 14-year-old Chicagoan Emmett Till while he was visiting relatives in Mississippi drew national attention, as the Till family and African-American media forced open a discussion of violent racism in the segregated states of the South. The following December, Rosa Parks was arrested after she refused to move to the "colored section" of a Montgomery, Alabama, bus. The yearlong bus boycott in Montgomery, supported nationally by Randolph and the Brotherhood of Sleeping Car Porters and led on the ground by the new president of the Montgomery Improvement Association, the Rev. Martin Luther King Jr., played out on a schedule that paralleled the 1956 presidential campaign. Change was coming.

Eisenhower's 1956 re-election campaign got it. Republican aides reached out to African-American voters, arguing, in the words of Citizens for Eisenhower strategist Richard Tobin, that during the president's first term "more advances have been made in civil rights for the Negro than during the administration of any president except Abraham Lincoln, and the Negro voter is already beginning to be actively aware of this." Tobin talked up the integration of the District of Columbia and the military but also focused on the number of African Americans who had been appointed to positions in the administration and the Foreign Service. The Republican National Committee published lists of hundreds of appointees—including ambassadors, United Nations delegates, commission chairs and White House aides—as part of an argument in the NAACP's *Crisis* magazine for "Why the Negro Should Vote for the Republican Party." The party claimed it "took the position at the outset that it would do all it could to eliminate second-class citizenship in the United States by executive order, negotiation and education. Whatever could not be achieved by these methods we pledged ourselves to do by legislation. As a result of this pledge a civil rights program was sent to Congress by Attorney General Brownell." The RNC detailed the agenda and concluded by noting, "The Attorney General asked the Congress to pass this legislation, which is not revolutionary, or not considered even controversial, but it did not pass it because of opposition from the Democrats."

That was not a debatable point; Democrats controlled the House and the Senate in the latter stages of Eisenhower's first term. And they included Mississippi senator James Eastland, the ranking Democrat on the Judiciary Committee and a racist who would later try to keep Thurgood Marshall off the Supreme Court. The top Democrat on the powerful Post Office and Civil Service Committee was North Carolina senator Olin Johnston, who as his state's governor in the 1940s had refused to take action to prevent the execution of a 14-year-old African American—the youngest person to be executed by a state government anywhere in the United States during the 20th century. Johnston, who bragged about keeping notes for a 40-hour-long speech in his desk should the need to filibuster civil rights legislation arise, was an especially enthusiastic supporter of Adlai Stevenson.

As the 1956 election approached, and as Stevenson again ran a campaign that sought to align Northern intellectuals with Southern segregationists, a number of African-American leaders signaled that they'd had enough. The most prominent of among them was Representative Adam Clayton Powell, the fiery Harlem preacher who had been elected to Congress in 1944 as a Democrat running with the backing of Vito Marcantonio's American Labor Party. Powell announced that he would organize a "Democrats for Eisenhower" campaign, saying, "Anyone who is endorsed on the one hand by Eleanor Roosevelt and on the other hand by Eastland of Mississippi is either a hypocrite, a liar, a double-talker or a double-dealer." Other prominent African-American Democrats broke with the party in 1956, like Michigan state senator Cora Brown, a pioneering legislator and congressional candidate; she announced that she was backing Eisenhower for re-election because he had displayed "a larger measure of faith" when it came to advancing civil rights.

But it was Powell who carried the campaign to the great African-American voter bases across the country, traveling to Baltimore, Chicago, Cleveland, Detroit, Los Angeles and San Francisco on a crusade that was credited with helping Eisenhower win nearly 40 percent of the African-American vote, a higher percentage than any Republican in a quarter century —and a far greater percentage than any Republican presidential nominee since.

Wallace respected the moves the president had made on civil rights, and he would later tell Richard Nixon that he thought Eisenhower was "in a better position than Stevenson to hold the extreme right in check." Throughout the 1950s, Wallace corresponded with Eisenhower and those around him on a number of international issues, maintaining a particular focus on the need to aid developing nations, work with the United Nations and guard against the burgeoning military-industrial complex. Eisenhower and his brother Milton (who had been spokesman for the Department of Agriculture during the New Deal) displayed considerably more respect for Wallace's insights than did most Democrats. That respect was returned in 1956, when Wallace endorsed the Republican president for re-election.

Wallace expressed his support for Eisenhower because of the president's advocacy for diplomacy and peace—and a proper balancing of global demands and domestic needs. Wallace admitted to being more skeptical about the Soviet Union than he had been in the late 1940s, saying, "I have of course changed my attitude toward Russia several times, as have most Americans over the past twenty-five years." But he also maintained that "I have not changed my basic views, and I have clung resolutely to my ultimate ideal that American security can be preserved by means of an international organization strong enough to enforce peace." In a *Life* magazine article published in the spring of 1956, Wallace explained, "For a good many years now I have cherished a hope and a belief—a hope for world peace and belief that there is a way to achieve it." He wrote of his ongoing faith

in the necessity not only of coexistence but of competitive coexistence between Russia and the Western world. In the final showdown the competition will not be in terms of military might. Even in our economic competition we must remember that the spirit of man is the final arbiter. As the Prophet Zechariah put it, "Not by might, nor by power, but by My Spirit, saith the Lord of hosts." The days of encirclement and threats of the A-bomb and the H-bomb must inevitably give way to a future of imaginative competition for the minds of men, in terms of rapidly changing technology and expanding world trade. In terms of such achievement can we who believe in God and progressive capitalism demonstrate that we can best serve the spiritual and material needs of all men? I say we can, if we think clearly and deeply. That was the only path to peace in 1948. It is the only path today. ...

I am for Eisenhower because I believe that, more than any other person, Republican or Democrat, now evident as a presidential possibility, he is the man most likely to preserve world peace.

Eisenhower was no pacifist. Nor, it needs to be pointed out, was he as pure or good in his approach to international affairs as Wallace's words of encouragement might suggest. The 34th president was a Cold Warrior. Though he maintained reasonably functional relationships with the Soviet leaders of his time, he did so with an ardent "peace through strength" approach that accepted outsized military budgets, nuclear deterrence, spying and CIA meddling in the affairs of other countries that extended to the instigation of a coup d'état against the duly elected government of Iran that was cheered on by British and American oil companies, and the overthrow of the government of Guatemala, where land reformers had dared to challenge the mighty United Fruit Company. Ultimately, Eisenhower pursued rapprochement with the Soviet Union, to such an extent that he was attacked as "a tool of the communists" by leaders of the right-wing John Birch Society as it took shape in the late 1950s. But on Ike's watch, "domino theory" obsessions with the spread of Soviet influence saw the United States acting in ways that undermined the prospect for diplomatic solutions in parts of the world—Vietnam, Cuba, the Middle East—that would eventually become synonymous with flawed and failed foreign policy. "If Eisenhower kept the military on a short leash, he let the feeling-its-oats CIA run amok," noted a generally favorable review of his presidency published in 2012 by the *American Prospect*, which concluded that "our whole sorry Cold War pattern of sub rosa interventions and propped-up dictatorships in the Third World was largely created on Ike's watch. While he's seldom thought of as a villain, Latin Americans—among others—would have every right to call him just that."

It is a measure of how misguided and dysfunctional the leadership of the Democratic Party was during the 1950s that Eisenhower was seen as a better option by Wallace and many others. Author Tom Carson concluded 60 years after Ike's initial election in 1952 that "Eisenhower deserves to be every Democrat's favorite Republican White House occupant this side of Abraham Lincoln." For a great many Americans in the 1950s Eisenhower's vision of a "modern Republicanism" that embraced much of the New Deal at home while recognizing the need to dial down tensions with the Soviet Union made more sense than what the Democrats were offering; indeed, in 1956, while Ike lost most of the South, he carried New York and all of New England. He even carried San Francisco—something no Republican presidential candidate has done since. What the Democrats did not understand was the truth spoken by New York governor W. Averell Harriman, who challenged Stevenson for the party nomination in 1956, when he warned that the party desperately needed "a new vision." "Yesterday's progressivism is today's moderation," Harriman told union leaders in the spring of 1956. "America does not stand still, and the world does not stand still. We need new vision to face the new problems of America, and the new problems of the world—the new capabilities of our country, and the new limitless potentialities of the moral and physical strength of this great nation of ours." Harriman said Democrats needed to become "zealots" on behalf of civil rights and social progress. But the party bosses did not agree; in the same city where they rejected Wallace in 1944, they rejected Harriman's presidential bid in 1956.

Avoiding the "Dread Road"

For Wallace, the necessary vision had to combine a commitment to social progress at home with a commitment to peace. He had argued for two decades that it was impossible to delink the two. Democrats did not get the connection in the 1950s and early 1960s, and only rarely have they done so in the years since then. But, sometimes, it seemed to the former vice president that Eisenhower did.

Sometimes, Ike even sounded like Wallace. Not three months into his presidency, in an April 16, 1953, address, Eisenhower

spoke at length about difficult relations between the United
States and the Soviet Union and addressed the threat of annihi-
lation posed by atomic weaponry. He spoke of the "dread road"
of constant military escalation and warned about "a burden of
arms draining the wealth and the labor of all peoples; a wasting
of strength that defies the American system or the Soviet system
or any system to achieve true abundance and happiness for the
peoples of this earth. ... Every gun that is made, every warship
launched, every rocket fired signifies, in the final sense, a theft
from those who hunger and are not fed, those who are cold
and are not clothed."

Eisenhower continued:

This world in arms is not spending money alone.

It is spending the sweat of its laborers, the genius of its scientists, the hopes of its children.

The cost of one modern heavy bomber is this: a modern brick
school in more than 30 cities.

It is two electric power plants, each serving a town of 60,000
population.

It is two fine, fully equipped hospitals.

It is some 50 miles of concrete highway.

We pay for a single fighter with a half million bushels of wheat.

We pay for a single destroyer with new homes that could
have housed more than 8,000 people.

This, I repeat, is the best way of life to be found on the road
the world has been taking.

This is not a way of life at all, in any true sense. Under the
cloud of threatening war, it is humanity hanging from a cross
of iron.

Eisenhower said that "the greatest task, and the greatest
opportunity, of all," was "the dedication of the energies, the
resources and the imaginations of all peaceful nations to a new
kind of war. This would be a declared total war, not upon any
human enemy but upon the brute forces of poverty and need.

The monuments to this new kind of war would be these: roads and schools, hospitals and homes, food and health. We are ready, in short, to dedicate our strength to serving the needs, rather than the fears, of the world."

Eisenhower's 1953 "Cross of Iron" speech set the tone for an administration that would conclude in 1961 with the famous Farewell Address in which Ike warned: "We must guard against the acquisition of unwarranted influence, whether sought or unsought, by the military-industrial complex. ... We must never let the weight of this combination endanger our liberties or democratic processes. We should take nothing for granted. Only an alert and knowledgeable citizenry can compel the proper meshing of the huge industrial and military machinery of defense with our peaceful methods and goals so that security and liberty may prosper together."

Wallace never returned to the Democratic Party in any formal sense and by 1960 was telling reporters who tracked him down at Farvue, his 115-acre farm north of New York, that he was "permanently out of politics." He maintained friendly relations with President John Kennedy (who, Wallace suggested, might have borrowed one of his signature programs from Wallace's 1934 book *New Frontiers*). But he did not signal actual support for a Democratic nominee until October 1964, when he spoke with some enthusiasm regarding the ticket of Lyndon Johnson and Hubert Humphrey. Humphrey had been a Wallace enthusiast in 1944. Johnson was an old New Dealer who had served in the House during FDR's second term and battled the right-wing "Texas Regulars" on behalf of the party's national candidates in the early 1940s. As a new president after Kennedy's assassination in 1963, LBJ opened a correspondence with Wallace about the ways in which the "War on Poverty" might be used to renew rural America.

However, after Johnson's landslide victory in 1964, which surpassed even that of FDR and Wallace in 1940, the former vice president began to fret about LBJ's increasing commitment of troops and resources to a ground war in Vietnam. It was precisely the sort of pointless Cold War blunder that Wallace had anticipated when he wrangled with Truman and Truman's secretary of state, Jimmy Byrnes, in the period before his break with the Democrats. Suffering from amyotrophic lateral sclerosis (ALS), the degenerative neuromuscular disease that would claim his life on November 18, 1965, Wallace could no longer speak. But he scratched out a message on the tablet he used to communicate.

"The policies of Truman and Byrnes," he wrote, "will yet make this country bleed from every pore."

8

The Party That Lost Its Way

But for the Vietnam War, the Dream of a New New Deal Might Have Been Renewed

War and the tensions leading to war are the great destroyers of the liberal spirit.

—Henry Wallace, Harvard Law
School forum, May 1, 1953

And, all the while, the Democratic Party machinery continued to atrophy.

—Jack Newfield, *Robert Kennedy:*
A Memoir, 1969

This is not a perfect party. We are not a perfect people. Yet, we are called to a perfect mission. Our mission: to feed the hungry; to clothe the naked; to house the homeless; to teach the illiterate; to provide jobs for the jobless; and to choose the human race over the nuclear race.

—Rev. Jesse Jackson, Democratic
National Convention, 1984

In 1965, the Democratic Party finally had a popular president with overwhelming majorities in the House and the Senate. Lyndon B. Johnson had won in 1964 on a promise of diplomacy abroad and social investment at home. He signed landmark civil rights and voting rights bills, beating the segregationists in the party and promising a Great Society that might pick up where the New Deal left off. The promise of an "Economic Bill of Rights" was briefly entertained, when the Johnson administration bowed to pressure from an aging A. Philip Randolph and a young Rev. Martin Luther King Jr. to consider a "Freedom Budget for All Americans." The budget proposed a ten-year program to achieve:

- the abolition of poverty
- guaranteed full employment
- fair prices for farmers
- fair wages for workers
- housing and health care for all
- the establishment of progressive tax and fiscal policies that respected the needs of working families

The Freedom Budget was a visionary document—even now, its language and its ambitions read like excerpts from a campaign speech by Bernie Sanders or Elizabeth Warren, the "Fight for 15" call to establish living-wage protections or even Alexandria Ocasio-Cortez's talk of a Green New Deal.

But it never happened. It proved to be too ambitious. LBJ was willing to meet the organizers of the March on Washington for Jobs and Freedom to discuss the budget. But the Johnson administration was distracted and diverted by the fiscal demands of the rapidly escalating Vietnam war. King recalled the progress of 1963, 1964 and 1965 and the promise of the Freedom Budget in his April 4, 1967, address at Riverside Church in New York.

"A few years ago there was a shining moment in that struggle," he said. "It seemed as if there was a real promise of hope for the poor, both black and white, through the poverty program. There were experiments, hopes, new beginnings. Then came the buildup in Vietnam, and I watched this program broken and eviscerated as if it were some idle political plaything of a society gone mad on war. And I knew that America would never invest the necessary funds or energies in rehabilitation of its poor so long as adventures like Vietnam continued to draw men and skills and money like some demonic, destructive suction tube. So I was increasingly compelled to see the war as an enemy of the poor and to attack it as such."

The pastor was not a partisan. He was, as he announced in 1968, "a drum major for justice ... a drum major for peace ... a drum major for righteousness" who drew inspiration from theologian Walter Rauschenbusch and the Social Gospel tradition, which, in Rauschenbusch's words, identified the sins of "religious bigotry, the combination of graft and political power, the corruption of justice, the mob spirit and mob action, militarism, and class contempt." To the extent that King engaged with politics, it was with an eye toward ushering in the new social order that the Social Gospel movement had identified decades earlier. But King understood the political dynamics of the time in which he lived. He had battled the Tories of both parties, Democratic segregationists and Republicans who were mutating old racist tropes into the crude "law and order" politics that was just then surfacing. He understood the delicate balances of electioneering and governing, and he recognized, as Wallace and others had two decades earlier, that an embrace of militarism and American imperialism would crush hopes for change at home.

King identified "the three evils of society": the "giant triplets of racism, economic exploitation and militarism." In one of his least remembered yet most significant speeches, a Labor Day weekend address in Chicago to the 1967 National Conference on New Politics that was delivered after a long, hot summer of bad news from Vietnam and urban riots at home, he declared:

> We have come because we see this as a dark hour in the affairs of men. For most of us this is a new mood. We are traditionally the idealists. We are the marchers from Mississippi, and Selma and Washington, who staked our lives on the American Dream during the first half of this decade. Many assembled here campaigned assiduously for Lyndon Johnson in 1964 because we

could not stand idly by and watch our nation contaminated by the 18th-century policies of Goldwaterism. We were the hardcore activists who were willing to believe that Southerners could be reconstructed in the constitutional image. We were the dreamers of a dream that dark yesterdays of man's inhumanity to man would soon be transformed into bright tomorrows of justice. Now, it is hard to escape the disillusionment of betrayal. Our hopes have been blasted and our dreams have been shattered. The promise of a Great Society was shipwrecked off the coast of Asia, on the dreadful peninsula of Vietnam. The poor, black and white, are still perishing on a lonely island of poverty in the midst of a vast ocean of material prosperity. What happens to a dream deferred? It leads to bewildering frustration and corroding bitterness.

King was not the first to make these connections. In many senses he was reporting on a reality that had been evolving on the ground for several years. In the summer of 1965, civil rights activists in McComb, Mississippi, reacted to the death in Vietnam of a twenty-three-year-old African-American soldier from the community, John D. Shaw, by issuing a broadside that declared, "No Mississippi Negroes should be fighting in Vietnam for the White Man's freedom, until all the Negro people are free in Mississippi." To those who said the war was a fight for democracy, the young Mississippi Freedom Democratic Party activists declared, "We don't know anything about Communism, Socialism and all that, but we do know that Negroes have caught hell right here under this American Democracy." They added: "No one has a right to ask us to risk our lives and kill other Colored People in Santo Domingo and Vietnam, so that the White American can get richer. We will be looked upon as traitors by all the Colored People of the world if the Negro people continue to fight and die without a cause."

Those statements were denounced not just by the white racist congressman representing McComb but by liberals who imagined the statements to be too extreme, even traitorous.

Yet by the spring of 1967, one of the most prominent African Americans in the United States and, indeed, the world, was refusing to be drafted for reasons that echoed the McComb message. "Man, I ain't got no quarrel with them Viet Cong," announced heavyweight champion Muhammad Ali, who asked, "Why should they ask me to put on a uniform and go 10,000 miles from home and drop bombs and bullets on brown people in Vietnam while so-called Negro people in Louisville are treated like dogs and denied simple human rights?" In short order, John Lee Hooker would be singing, "We got so much trouble at home, we don't need to go to Vietnam."

King saw, better than most of the politicians of his time, that the fabric of the country was being torn apart. Yes, there were antiwar riots on campuses, but the riots that swept through major cities in the summer of 1967 could not be delinked from the broader political context of a time in which the nation's treasure was being dispatched to Southeast Asia rather than the Near East Side of Detroit. As Hooker sang that summer, "Oh, the Motor City's burnin'… my hometown burnin' down to the ground, worser than Viet Nam," King spoke urgently about the need to reconcile politics with economic and social upheavals, and the new movements and ideas that extended from those upheavals. "When scientific power outruns moral power, we end up with guided missiles and misguided men," he said. "When we foolishly maximize the minimum and minimize the maximum we sign the warrant for our own day of doom."

King's words challenged the Democratic Party. He would not live to see the miserable playout of the 1968 election, in which the Democrats failed to embrace that challenge and lost to Richard Nixon. But he saw the future clearly. As a nonpartisan who had the moral courage to call out both major parties, he mapped the battle lines of a fight that would continue through the remainder of the twentieth century and into the twenty-first —a fight over whether the Democratic Party would be as bold and visionary as it had been in the days of the New Deal, and as Wallace had hoped it would be in the post–World War II era. King himself recalled the New Deal favorably, mentioning FDR's Works Progress Administration while calling it "barbarous to condemn people desiring work to soul-sapping inactivity and poverty." The civil rights leader wanted parties and politics to evolve. Unfortunately, as the Democratic Party proved at critical junctures in the 1960s, 1970s and beyond, it was disinclined to evolve too quickly. There would be steps forward, moments of great clarity. But invariably they would be followed by steps backward, and by abandonments of principle that prevented the party from becoming what it needed to be in order to address fundamental changes in society and a rightward drift in the organized politics of the United States.

Imagining the Real Spirit of America

King was prescient about the turbulent moment in which he spoke. More prescient, it turned out, than Johnson. Within months of the pastor's address, LBJ, the master strategist of Democratic politics in the 1950s and 1960s, had been done in by the new politics. On March 31, 1968, Johnson ended his re-election bid after a weak showing in the New Hampshire primary against one dissident Democrat, Minnesota senator Eugene McCarthy, and the entry into the competition of another, New York senator Robert Kennedy.

Of the two challenges, McCarthy's was most clearly identified as an antiwar campaign. Yet from the start, the Minnesotan tried to make the connection between the administration's war agenda and an abandonment of the New Deal vision. He summed up the crisis of LBJ's presidency in a December 1967 address in Chicago to the Conference of Concerned Democrats: "The message of the Administration today is a message of apprehension, a message of fear, yes—even a message of fear of fear. ... This is not the real spirit of America."

McCarthy continued, tapping into a streak of romantic faith that still animated American politics:

This is a time to test the mood and spirit:
 To offer in place of doubt—trust.
 In place of expediency—right judgment.
 In place of ghettos, let us have neighborhoods and communities.
 In place of incredibility—integrity.
 In place of murmuring, let us have clear speech; let us again hear America singing.
 In place of disunity, let us have dedication of purpose.
 In place of near despair let us have hope.

McCarthy, a poet and a philosopher, found plenty of believers in this project of getting America "back on course." His striking success in the first-in-the-nation New Hampshire primary, where he exposed LBJ's vulnerability and suggested the possibility of a new direction for the party and the country, made him a counterculture star. By the time he got to later primary states like Wisconsin and Oregon, he was winning not just the "Clean for Gene" young but suburban voters who embraced an antiwar vision that rejected Cold War fantasies in favor of diplomacy abroad and progress at home. In combination with the support attracted by Kennedy, McCarthy ran up numbers that proved the great mass of Democrats favored a different direction for the party.

When all was said and done, however, McCarthy could not overcome the barriers to change that had been erected within the Democratic Party. Like Henry Wallace in 1944, he won the hearts and minds of grassroots Democrats. But grassroots didn't matter when it came to nominating the Democrat who would bid for the presidency in 1968. Because of those barriers, the party surrendered its future to the Cold War calculus that steered Johnson and his administration into the jungles of Southeast Asia. In truth, however, the surrender had begun much earlier in the decade.

Before Vietnam became a full-blown disaster, retired General Douglas MacArthur had already told the newly elected president, John F. Kennedy, "Anyone wanting to commit ground troops to Asia should have his head examined." And there were prominent Democrats who recognized before the war began that their party needed to move away from Cold War thinking. In 1958, Democrats experienced one of their greatest victories in an off-year congressional election. In a moment of economic downturn that hit farm country especially hard, voters elected 15 new Democrats to the Senate and 49 new Democrats to the House. Among the elected were many young liberals who would pave the way for the Great Society, providing vital support for the Civil Rights Act, the Voting Rights Act and the War on Poverty. But that's not all.

"A new foreign policy was proposed today by a group of House Democrats and nongovernment experts who feel the existing one has failed," announced a May 23, 1960, Associated Press report on what was referred to as the Liberal Project, launched by Representative Robert Kastenmeier of Wisconsin and other members of the Democrats' Class of 1958, along with a handful of more senior members like California Representative James Roosevelt, FDR's oldest son. The AP explained that the group was proposing "a long-range program for universal disarmament and world economic cooperation."

While Henry Wallace now stood outside the Democratic Party that had rejected him, his ideas were being renewed by at least some in the next generation of partisans. "Most of the House members are first-termers, who set out to fashion a liberal program within Congress and enlisted the aid of outside experts," the AP reported. Chief among the experts was economist James P. Warburg, who authored an ambitious report on how the United States should step back from the Cold War brink and begin to apply realism to international relations. Warburg's report called for U.S. support for the reunification of the divided state of Germany, in a move that was to be accompanied by the withdrawal of U.S. and Soviet forces. It proposed recognition of what was then referred to as "Communist China" and its eventual admission as a member of the United Nations.

The Liberal Project went further. In February 1960, 18 House Democrats put forward a resolution calling for the U.S. to renew a moratorium on nuclear weapons testing. And a handful of members even began to crusade against funding the House Un-American Activities Committee. In February 1961, James Roosevelt described HUAC as "a bad institution, which has tended to grow worse in its depredations on our liberties as well as on our democratic reputation in the world today." New York Democrat William Fitts Ryan, who had been elected the previous fall, declared that "many thoughtful, responsible, sincere citizens share my belief that the Committee on Un-American Activities has violated fundamental rights and privileges on which our nation is founded."

Roosevelt and Ryan ended up on the losing end of an overwhelming 412–6 vote. They drew rebukes from fellow Democrats, led by HUAC chair Francis Walter, a Pennsylvanian who charged that Roosevelt was guilty of "faulty reasoning, distortion, falsehood and total failure to comprehend even remotely the nature of communism ... The only way I can interpret his statement is that he objects to the fact that the committee operates on what it believes to be a self-evident principle that communism is evil and un-American. Apparently, he does not share that view." In 1962, when a book of essays edited by Roosevelt, *The Liberal Papers*, was published, Republicans attacked and Democrats scattered. Western New York congressman William E. Miller, chairman of the Republican National Committee and Barry Goldwater's future running mate, charged that Democratic House members had "produced a book containing the most dangerous foreign policy recommendations I have ever seen. ... The proposals not only repeat the Communist line—they go beyond the Communist line."

The dangerous essayists included Warburg, a banker before he became a financial adviser to FDR during the president's first term. Other contributors included Walter Millis, a former editorial writer for the Republican-leaning *New York Herald Tribune*, and Charles E. Osgood, a University of Illinois professor who would in 1964 be chosen to serve on the Social Science Advisory Board of the Arms Control and Disarmament Agency. But Democratic leaders and strategists made no effort to defend the Liberal Project, and most of the House members who had been associated with it abandoned the initiative on the eve of the 1962 election—though Kastenmeier, the initiative's most ardent advocate, and Roosevelt were easily re-elected that fall.

The fate of the Liberal Project offers a reminder of the extent to which the Democratic Party was unwilling to reconsider its approach to foreign policy in the years before the 1964 Gulf of Tonkin Resolution was approved with the support of every House and Senate Democrat, save Alaska senator Ernest Gruening and Oregon senator Wayne Morse, a pair of old-school anti-imperialists. Gruening was in his seventies, Morse in his sixties; both were veterans of the 1924 independent presidential campaign of Robert M. La Follette. Three years later, Morse and Gruening faced well-funded Democratic primary challenges. Gruening lost the nomination in Alaska, while Morse, weakened by the bitter primary in which he was accused of all manner of disloyalty, lost in November 1968.

The New Left and the New Right

It would fall to a new generation, operating outside the Democratic Party, to advance an agenda grounded in the idealism that Wallace had hoped would shape the postwar program of the party. Radicals like a young Tom Hayden saw little room for themselves in the Democratic Party of the early 1960s.

Hayden helped found Students for a Democratic Society, which proposed an "agenda for a generation" in the form of the 1962 Port Huron Statement:

> We are people of this generation, bred in at least modest comfort, housed now in universities, looking uncomfortably to the world we inherit ... As we grew, however, our comfort was penetrated by events too troubling to dismiss. First, the permeating and victimizing fact of human degradation, symbolized by the Southern struggle against racial bigotry, compelled most of us from silence to activism. Second, the enclosing fact of the Cold War, symbolized by the presence of the Bomb, brought awareness that we ourselves, and our friends, and millions of abstract "others" we knew more directly because of our common peril, might die at any time. We might deliberately ignore, or avoid, or fail to feel all other human problems, but not these two, for these were too immediate and crushing in their impact, too challenging in the demand that we as individuals take the responsibility for encounter and resolution ...
>
> We witnessed, and continue to witness, other paradoxes. With nuclear energy whole cities can easily be powered, yet the dominant nation-states seem more likely to unleash destruction greater than that incurred in all wars of human history. Although our own technology is destroying old and creating new forms of social organization, men still tolerate meaningless work and idleness. While two-thirds of mankind suffers undernourishment, our own upper classes revel amidst superfluous abundance. Although world population is expected to double in forty years, the nations still tolerate anarchy as a major principle of international conduct and uncontrolled exploitation governs the sapping of the earth's physical resources. Although mankind desperately needs revolutionary leadership, America rests in national stalemate, its goals ambiguous and tradition-bound instead of informed and clear, its democratic system apathetic and manipulated rather than "of, by, and for the people."

The student activists were sharply critical of the "old parties," noting little distinction between them and arguing for a new politics grounded in an understanding "that the political order should serve to clarify problems in a way instrumental to their solution; it should provide outlets for the expression of personal grievance and aspiration; opposing views should be organized so as to illuminate choices and facilitate the attainment of goals; channels should be commonly available to relate men to knowledge and to power so that private problems—from bad recreation facilities to personal alienation—are formulated as general issues." That sort of thinking gained little traction with Democrats in Washington. But it quickly took hold at the grass-roots in the form of mass protests; it also expressed itself in the form of the fierce opposition of Democrats around the country to the compromises of the Democrat in the White House.

Unless Johnson moved to end the war, Dr. King announced in the summer of 1967, he would "very, very definitely" oppose LBJ's re-election. King, who had eschewed making formal political endorsements, told reporters he would back an antiwar Republican against Johnson. If the GOP nominated a hawk, King said, he would support a third-party "peace" candidate. "We'll go all out to take a stand in voting for someone who's against the war in Vietnam." Around the same time, Americans for Democratic Action, the liberal group that had ardently backed Truman and rejected Wallace in 1948, deplored the Johnson administration's "reckless escalation of the Vietnam War" and announced, "The ADA expresses its intention to support in the 1968 election that candidate, of either party, who offers a genuine hope for restraint in the conduct of the war in Vietnam and for its peaceful resolution on honorable terms, if such a candidate is presented to the American people." With the start of the primary season just months away, the 50,000-member group did not anticipate a meaningful Democratic challenge to LBJ; thus, it argued that it was necessary to "dissolve normal ties of party allegiance." But others had not given up on a making the race for the 1968 Democratic nomination a referendum on the war that might either force Johnson to change course or replace him. Allard Lowenstein was drumming up support for a Dump Johnson movement inside the party, and in August 1967, the politically potent California Democratic Council signaled that it would endorse a peace candidate in the state's 1968 Democratic primary.

As it happened, a peace candidate would win the California primary. But it wasn't McCarthy. Rather, it was Bobby Kennedy.

While many were skeptical of Kennedy as a messenger, his bid actually seemed to be weaving the lost strands of the New Deal coalition together, as he campaigned on campuses and in barrios, on Native American reservations and in the farm country of Nebraska. RFK's message echoed the concern and optimism that Henry Wallace mustered in 1943 and 1944. "It is a revolutionary world we live in. Governments repress their people; and millions are trapped in poverty while the nation grows rich; and wealth is lavished on armaments," Kennedy said. "The future does not belong to those who are content with today, apathetic toward common problems and their fellow man alike. Rather it will belong to those who can blend vision, reason and courage in a personal commitment to the ideals and great enterprises of American society."

But Kennedy would be assassinated on the night of his California primary win, just moments after he promised an "on to Chicago" race to wrest the Democratic nomination from Hubert Humphrey. McCarthy and another antiwar Democrat, South Dakota senator George McGovern, would carry elements of the campaign forward, only to be crushed at that year's violent Democratic National Convention in Chicago. The bosses swept aside the insurgents in that summer of 1968 with the same crude efficiency that they had rejected Wallace in the same city in the summer of 1944. But this time they had no FDR to save them. Humphrey was defeated by Richard Nixon, whose Southern strategy, law-and-order demagoguery and outreach to "Silent Majority" hardhats would further unravel the New Deal coalition.

At a time when the Democratic Party could have seized the moment, it rejected an opportunity to pivot—not just on the issues of the day, but toward the future. Instead of distinguishing itself from the misguided priorities of the Johnson administration, and from a Republican Party that was veering right on so many issues, the party missed the opportunity that King, Kennedy, McCarthy and a rising generation of activists had seen for a new politics. This would become a pattern. At each critical juncture, the party had choices. There would be breakthroughs, brief shining moments. But then the "steady hands" of the party, the Washington insiders and consultants, the fund-raisers and the donors themselves, would guide the party back toward the calm waters of centrist caution and compromise. The struggles between those who wanted politics that erred on the side of boldness and those who favored the managerial path played out in both parties in the aftermath of the 1968 election— the last in the postwar era that saw a substantial portion of electoral votes go to a third party (46 from the Southern states that embraced Alabama governor George Wallace's American Party agenda of warmed-over racism, law-and-order ranting and "bomb them back to the Stone Age" militarism). These were not simplistic fights between good-guy heroes and bad-guy villains, although both major parties had their share of each. These were fights to define politics in a new era of ever more dominant mass media, ever more influential money in politics and an emerging recognition that what was at stake at home and abroad mattered immensely to very rich men and very powerful corporations. The upheavals of the 1960s had not just shaken inner cities and college campuses. They had shaken the corridors of power. Civil rights, women's rights, environmentalism and consumer protection were on the agenda. There were real debates about foreign policy, in which questions were being asked about whether the promise of "making the world safe for democracy" wasn't really code for protecting the profits of multinational corporations.

The rebels of the 1960s, people like consumer advocate Ralph Nader, ranked higher and higher on lists of the most-admired Americans. Social movements were getting better organized and more effective. They might not be capable of stopping wars; they might not succeed in shifting budget priorities as far as the Freedom Budget for All Americans had proposed. But civil rights and voting rights and consumer protection and environmental protection were embraced with growing enthusiasm by leading figures in both parties. Amid all the chaos of the late 1960s, there was a consensus around the idea that government needed to be more activist and stricter when it came to regulating business. That scared the people whom sociologist C. Wright Mills had in the 1950s begun to identify as "the power elite." The most extreme of their number had begun to organize as early as the late 1950s under the umbrella of the John Birch Society, from which many of them had engaged during the 1960s in an effort to shift the Republican Party far to the right. By the early 1970s, however, more mainstream millionaires and corporatists recognized that their power was threatened by a moment in which even Richard Nixon recognized the need for an Environmental Protection Agency. The pushback on the part of the champions of the military-industrial complex, the great polluting industries, the cigarette-peddling tobacco companies and the investors who reaped the benefits of their profiteering took shape in the early 1970s. A Virginia corporate lawyer (with clients such as the Tobacco Institute), whom Nixon would soon make a Supreme Court Justice, circulated a 1971 memorandum that warned of an "Attack on the Free Enterprise System."

"The sources are varied and diffused," Lewis Powell Jr. warned in the memorandum. "They include, not unexpectedly, the Communists, New Leftists and other revolutionaries who would destroy the entire system, both political and economic. These extremists of the left are far more numerous, better financed, and increasingly are more welcomed and encouraged by other elements of society, than ever before in our history. But they remain a small minority, and are not yet the principal cause for concern. The most disquieting voices joining the chorus of criticism come from perfectly respectable elements of society: from the college campus, the pulpit, the media, the intellectual and literary journals, the arts and sciences, and from politicians. In most of these groups the movement against the system is participated in only by minorities. Yet, these often are the most articulate, the most vocal, the most prolific in their writing and speaking."

To counter this threat, Powell urged millionaires, billionaires, CEOs and investors to become dramatically more engaged in shaping the popular debate, with investments in conservative media and pro-business think tanks and policymaking. Above all, he said they had to enter what he referred to as "the neglected political arena." Powell did not tell them that the Republican Party was going to be their vehicle, but this was implicit in the message. And indeed, a Republican president would soon elevate the memo-writing tobacco lawyer from his Richmond office to the bench of the highest court in the land, where Powell would, over the course of a fifteen-year career, go about the work of tearing down barriers to corporate influence on elections and governing.

During those fifteen years, the Grand Old Party was remade into a new formulation that explicitly rejected the notion that government could do good (except, it should be noted, for Wall Street and the industrial side of the military-industrial complex), that reanimated the states' rights politics of the South and that embraced privatization, deregulation and the dismantling of the New Deal. The party became so clearly identified with wealth and privilege that its 2012 presidential nominee was a million-aire investor whose "vulture capitalist" track record would have made the robber barons of old blush, while its 2016 nominee was a real estate mogul who bragged about not paying his taxes. The sensible course for the Democrats was to go the other direction, to make a clear distinction that isolated the party of the billionaire class on the fringe of American politics. There were plenty of Democrats who argued on moral and practical grounds for doing just that. They won some fights. But they lost the war. Instead of seeking "the continuous rebirth of liberalism" that Henry Wallace had proposed, instead of serving as the "vigilant watcher and perpetual guardian of the ramparts of the future," the Democratic Party made itself a managerial movement that softly promised it would never be quite so bad as the Republicans.

Could another history have been written? Yes.

McGovernism and Its Discontents

The reaction of progressives to Chicago and the Humphrey defeat was a demand for the democratization of the Democratic Party, to reform the nominating process so that delegates were selected in primaries and open-and-transparent caucuses rather than the backrooms of closed state conventions. The bosses were disempowered, not just by procedural changes but by affirmative action rules that helped to put the grassroots activists who had been elbowed aside in 1968 at the center of the delegate-selection process for 1972. The change was real and immediate. It allowed McGovern to defeat Humphrey for the 1972 nomination. It was an ironic moment for the party when McGovern, who had joined the Illinois delegation at the 1948 Progressive Party convention that nominated Wallace, defeated Humphrey, who had spoken from the podium at the 1948 convention that nominated Truman. Supported by students, civil rights campaigners and liberal trade unionists, McGovern campaigned on a progressive populist platform that explicitly critiqued militarism and colonialism, called for abolition of the Electoral College, promised full public financing of elections, advocated for abortion rights and gender equity, supported criminal justice reform and embraced economic and racial justice. It was well to the left of any platform the party had written before or has written since.

McGovern, whom I came to know well in his later years, was a savvy politician who won five House and Senate races in the traditionally Republican state of South Dakota. He traveled in the circles of the Kennedys, counseled presidents of both parties and won the nomination of his party for the job. Yet he did not subscribe to the "great man" theory of politics. He was a historian of the labor movement who believed in the power of organized people—and who subscribed to the radical faith that critical junctures created openings for the historically disenfranchised to transform politics and governing. He was more comfortable in a suit and tie than jeans and tie-dyed shirts, yet he relished the societal change that unfolded in the 1960s. If he had an electoral mission, it was to convince the millions of young people who had been enfranchised when the Constitution was amended in 1971 to lower the voting age to 18 that they had something to vote for in 1972. McGovern understood the tenuous nature of a moment when a generation of young Americans felt betrayed by both major parties. He shared their frustrations. "I'm fed up to the ears with old men dreaming up wars for young men to die in," he declared. He joined their demonstrations, speaking at antiwar rallies across the country, including the great October 15, 1969, Moratorium to End the War in Vietnam demonstration on Boston Common.

The senator told that crowd of 100,000: "We must learn that it is madness—not security—to devote 70 per cent of our controllable federal budget to armaments and only 11 per cent to the quality of life. Perhaps out of the blood-soaked jungles of Southeast Asia will come the humility and the national wisdom that will lead us into the light of a new day." Those were powerful words, to be sure. But at the same rally on the same day, many of the speakers challenged the very idea that this mass movement should count on political leaders or parties. Historian

Howard Zinn urged more demonstrations and direct action to "create trouble for the machine," while Peter Camejo of the Student Mobilization Committee warned the crowd to "Watch out for the politicians who turn up now."

McGovern maintained a faith that disenchanted and disenfranchised Americans could be brought back into the system and, moreover, that their engagement could change the system. The key, of course, was to change the Democratic Party. He wanted to open the party up, not just to the young people who were rallying on Boston Common but to the millions, the tens of millions of Americans who had never really had a voice in the party. McGovern pursued this new politics as part of a mass movement to change the party.

"McGovern is often blamed for taking a Democratic Party that represented the working man and refashioning it into a party of blacks, women, gays, environmentalists, college professors, criminals, movie stars, software engineers and personal-injury lawyers," author Timothy Noah wrote thirty-five years after the 1972 campaign. "But to the limited extent that this caricature is true, the change came about through three historic forces over which McGovern had no control. Organized labor was in rapid decline; suburbanization was killing off the urban political machines; and previously marginalized groups of people were no longer willing to suffer in silence. To a small extent, McGovern helped open the Democratic Party to greater influence from minorities and women by leading a party commission formed after the 1968 election that introduced more state primaries and required convention delegations to reflect the racial and sexual composition of their states. But the restlessness of the new constituencies made change inevitable."

What distinguished McGovern was that he welcomed the new constituencies and placed his faith in them, when so many prominent Democrats did not. *Time* magazine, on the eve of the 1972 Democratic National Convention, described McGovern's delegates, so many of them young, so many of them women, so many of them people of color, as "an astonishing new force" in American politics. "The battle lines are drawn," *Time* reported. "The McGovern young can argue with considerable justice that America's alienated youth were invited to work within the system, and (BAM! POW! SPLAT!) they did. Armed with the reform rules that McGovern helped to formulate, the young legions this year shattered political assumptions and shut down political machines that had been grinding on for decades."

McGovern celebrated the change in his acceptance speech. "My nomination is all the more precious in that it is a gift of the most open political process in all of our political history," he said. "It is the sweet harvest of the work of tens of thousands of tireless volunteers, young and old alike, funded by literally hundreds of thousands of small contributors in every part of this nation. Those who lingered on the brink of despair only a short time ago have been brought into this campaign, heart, hand, head and soul, and I have been the beneficiary of the most remarkable political organization in the history of this country." The senator believed that not just the party but the politics of the nation were in the process of being transformed. "In a democratic nation, no one likes to say that his inspiration came from secret arrangements by closed doors, but in the sense that is how my candidacy began.

"I am here as your candidate tonight in large part because during four administrations of both parties, a terrible war has been chartered behind closed doors," said the nominee, who was promising a break with the legacies of two Republican presidents (Eisenhower and Nixon) and two Democrats (Kennedy and Johnson). "I want those doors opened and I want that war closed. And I make these pledges above all others: the doors of government will be opened, and that war will be closed."

McGovern's words had the effect of uniting the establishment wings of both major parties around a shared goal: beating George McGovern. The candidate and his supporters were attacked as radicals throughout the 1972 campaign, first by hawkish Democrats like Senator Henry "Scoop" Jackson and then by Republicans who echoed those attacks. Just as the Federal Bureau of Investigation had spied for years on Henry Wallace, it spied for years on McGovern; especially after he called for the replacement of J. Edgar Hoover, the FBI's famously vindictive director. Hoover had once demanded to know, "What have we got on McGovern?" Vice President Spiro Agnew, Nixon's attack dog, made McGovern's association with the 1948 campaign a regular topic of his 1972 campaign speeches: "Sooner or later, the people of this country are going to find out what George McGovern is really like. They are going to discover his far-out, left-wing voting record. They are going to learn of his former ties with Henry Agard Wallace and his recently affirmed support of the policies of Henry Agard Wallace. And they are going to see how he feels about marijuana and busing, and abortions and amnesty for draft dodgers, and they are going to drop George McGovern like a hot potato."

McGovern's campaign stumbled badly after it was revealed that vice-presidential nominee Thomas Eagleton had undergone electroshock therapy for clinical depression in the 1960s. Eagleton was forced off the ticket and McGovern's clumsy search for a new running mate was long, embarrassing and, it can fairly be said, crippling for a campaign that was challenging an incumbent who had no qualms about employing dirty tricks to prevail.

McGovern might have made up much of the ground he had lost if Democrats had united behind his candidacy. But instead, establishment Democrats organized openly and aggressively to assure the defeat of their party's nominee. Working in close coordination with White House aides such as John Ehrlichman, who would eventually be jailed for his role in the Watergate scandal that ended Nixon's presidency, former Texas governor John Connally organized an exceptionally well-funded national "Democrats for Nixon" campaign. Connally's campaign attracted support from hundreds of current and former

Democratic elected officials. Many were Southern segregationists who were on their way to becoming Republicans, but Connally's project was active across the country, with high-profile supporters in New York, Pennsylvania, Michigan, Ohio, Illinois and elsewhere, and a message that McGovern had "gotten out of touch not only with the mainstream of the Democratic Party but the people of the country." A signal was sent, with generous assistance from the daily and weekly newspapers that overwhelmingly endorsed Nixon, that Democrats could comfortably cast their ballots for the president they had once dismissed as "Tricky Dick."

McGovern, the mild-mannered Midwesterner who had repeatedly been elected in the Republican-friendly state of South Dakota, was turned into a parody of himself. His mistakes were amplified. His record—as a pilot during World War II, as the innovative director of John Kennedy's Food for Peace program, as an able legislator and reformer—was obfuscated, mischaracterized or mocked. The media went along with the charade. Nixon won in 1972 by roughly the same margin as Johnson had defeated Goldwater in 1964.

Like Goldwater, McGovern had taken on a popular president at a time when the economy was strong. Like Goldwater, McGovern had challenged his own party's establishment and brought a new generation of ideologically committed activists into the process. Like Goldwater, McGovern remained politically viable after the defeat, winning re-election to the Senate and continuing to speak out for decades after a rejection that, in McGovern's case alone, polls showed Americans eventually came to regret.

But there was a great difference between the defeat of McGovern in 1972 and the defeat of Goldwater in 1964. While Goldwater was quickly rehabilitated as a Republican elder statesman and heralded as an iconic antecedent of the conservative campaign that would in 1980 secure the presidency for one of his most ardent supporters, Ronald Reagan, McGovern was never forgiven for leading an insurgency. Conservative Republicans saw the 1964 loss as a setback, not a rejection; they leaned into the core values that had been outlined by Goldwater and endorsed by the party convention while at the same time seeking abler candidates, smarter strategies and savvier messaging. They locked in their agendas, adjusted their tactics and started winning in ways that quickly began to realign American politics.

Democrats, for the most part, did the opposite. Party leaders became more cautious, more deferent to economic power and more likely to react than to lead. If anyone suggested that this might not be the right path, they were immediately accused of trying to chart a "McGovernite" course.

In 2016, historian Josh Mound would write in the *New Republic*: "A specter is haunting the Democratic Party— 'McGovernism.' For the past forty years, whenever a Democratic presidential hopeful has given off the slightest whiff of leftish anti-establishmentarianism, party leaders and mainstream pundits have invoked McGovern's name. In 2004, Howard Dean was the new McGovern. In 2008, Barack Obama became the new McGovern. This year, it's Bernie Sanders's turn." But it wasn't just the charge of McGovernism that the establishment long wielded. It also wielded the rules. As in Wallace's day, when party bosses closed down the convention rather than allow Wallace to be renominated, the new bosses of the 1970s and 1980s gamed the process to regain control of "their" party.

After the 1972 election, the party leadership moved swiftly to undo the reforms that had opened up the party and allowed McGovern to prevail that year. McGovern, for his part, would be the last progressive insurgent to win the Democratic nomination. Progressives might still win Democratic nominations in a few congressional districts and even at the state level: a Ron Dellums here, a Bella Abzug there; a Dennis Kucinich and a Paul Wellstone; a Barbara Lee to cast a single vote against George W. Bush's authorization of the use of military force; a Russ Feingold to stand in lonely Senate opposition to the

Patriot Act. But they were the exceptions that proved the rule. Democratic Senate and House leaders retreated from the ideological barricades. They worried more about raising campaign money than stopping wars abroad or launching wars on poverty at home. At the highest levels of the party, the money men and the bosses and the Southern hangers-on tightened their grip in the late 1970s and early 1980s. They retook positions of leadership and moved to ensure that never again would the presidential nomination go to a candidate who would "go down the line unswervingly for the liberal principles of both political democracy and economic democracy," as Henry Wallace said in 1944, or campaign unapologetically on McGovern's "Come Home, America" promise of peace and justice.

The bosses eventually eliminated much of the democratizing infrastructure that had been developed in order to give grassroots activists a greater say in shaping the direction and the agenda of the party. Minnesota congressman Don Fraser, a progressive Democrat, had led a multiyear project to strengthen the party from the grassroots up. Among the proposed innovations, modeled on European parties, were the institution of policy conferences and activist party membership, with dues from people who could afford them. The 1972 party convention had charged the Democratic National Committee with organizing a charter conference in 1974 and midterm "mini-conventions" going forward. By the time the charter conference was to be held, however, DNC chair Robert Strauss and his allies had so successfully gutted the reform initiative that the *New York Times* headlined its report: "Major Changes Have Long Since Been Abandoned."

The Democratic Socialists Step Up

But some Democrats refused to give up on party democracy. One of them was Michael Harrington, the democratic socialist author who had gained national prominence with the publication of *The Other America* in 1962. During the 1960s, Harrington used his prominence to influence Democratic administrations and candidates while at the same time remaining a leading figure in the Socialist Party. In the fall of 1972, just weeks before the presidential election, he abruptly quit as a co-chair of the Socialists—who were deeply divided among old-school radicals, new left activists and more conservative social democrats—charging that "the historic party of Eugene Victor Debs and Norman Thomas is today doing the work of Richard Nixon." While the Socialist Party had endorsed McGovern, Harrington complained that the resolution supporting the Democrat's candidacy was "so reluctant and backhanded—attacking McGovern's foreign policy as 'neo-isolationist and conservative' and his domestic proposals as 'casual, vague and sometimes contradictory' —that it committed the party to the anti-Nixon struggle only in the most formal sense." Declaring that "defeating Nixon is the priority of the democratic left," Harrington argued for the formation of "a genuine coalition that will bring together that majority of Americans" on behalf of what was then referred to as "the New Politics." An instinctual organizer, Harrington saw McGovern's constituency as a base to build from, and he was interested in doing the building within the Democratic Party.

Harrington's decision to enter the Democratic Party, and to encourage others on the left to do the same, was a response to his understanding that America's two-party system left little room for organization to the left of the Democrats. This was a source of frustration for Harrington, who in the early 1960s and 1970s had been intrigued by the prospect of multiparty democracy on a spectrum from the unapologetic right to the center-right Republicans, to the center-left Democrats, to the unapologetic left. His was a hope that many entertained at a time when so much was changing. If society was opening up to new ways of doing things, why not politics? Some "new politics" advocates moved from speculation to action. Unfortunately, their projects were better at generating ideas—often very good ideas—than votes. In 1968 the Peace and Freedom Party drew some 100,000 votes nationwide with a ticket led in some states by Black Panther leader Eldridge Cleaver and in others by comedian Dick Gregory. The People's Party campaign of 1972 drew 79,000 votes with a ticket led by one of the most prominent antiwar activists in the country, Dr. Benjamin Spock. After these very modest results, Harrington proposed an entryist strategy to bring the left into a Democratic Party that the McGovern campaign, for all its fumbles, had at least briefly succeeded in pulling in a leftward direction.

In 1973, Harrington, Deborah Meier and their allies formed the Democratic Socialist Organizing Committee as an explicitly socialist organization in the Democratic Party "to build a new American majority for social change." Harrington argued that a new form of coalition politics was needed to break the losing streak of Democrats. "In 1968, the Center-Right of Nixon and Wallace received almost 58 percent of the votes; in 1972, in a two-way race, Nixon got over 61 percent," he wrote. "In 1968, the American unions were a major, and sometimes sole, force behind Hubert Humphrey, proving that the organized workers are the most cohesive element that can be mobilized for social change. But the '68 election also proved that labor by itself cannot come close to winning. … In 1968 many McCarthyites did not understand that Humphrey was infinitely preferable to Nixon; in 1972, the Meanyites did not understand that McGovern was infinitely preferable to Nixon. If this split continues, the Republicans will hold the presidency for the foreseeable future. Therefore, the only way to build a new majority for social change is for labor and the new politics to come together."

For that to happen, Harrington argued, the Democratic Party had to change. To that end, DSOC activists threw themselves into the work of transforming the party. Their hope was to unite labor and the left and then to use what remained of the reform infrastructure that had been established in the aftermath of the

1968 convention to forge a bolder, more visionary Democratic Party that could run up the sort of majorities that FDR had in the 1930s and 1940s.

Harrington was not a Henry Wallace acolyte. Harrington had moved from youthful conservatism toward an embrace of democratic socialist ideals that extended from Norman Thomas, the 1948 Socialist Party nominee who had been sharply critical of Wallace for accepting the support of the Communists. Yet the vision that Harrington had for a Democratic Party that merged labor and farm organizations with movements supporting racial justice and women's rights, global cooperation and peace, was a reasonable late-century expression of what Wallace and his allies had hoped for in 1944: a Democratic Party that maintained the radical energy of the New Deal, the Four Freedoms and the Economic Bill of Rights, even as goals and priorities were adjusted to address new challenges.

Harrington began to speak of a pragmatic "democratic left politics" that identified "the left wing of the possible." No longer would leftists be satisfied with being "abstractly right" or with gathering "to celebrate ceremonial socialism at occasional banquets." The goal was to develop an American variation on the British Labour Party or the social democratic parties of Scandinavia. Working with brilliant young organizers like Marjorie Phyfe and Jack Clark and allies like Gloria Steinem and actor Ed Asner, Harrington argued that it was possible to move the Democratic Party to the left. "The crying necessity for democratic left programs and ideas is, then, clear enough," he explained. "But what about democratic left politics? We believe that left-wing realism is today found in the Democratic Party. It is there that the mass forces for social change are assembled; it is there that the possibility exists for creating a new first party in America."

The DSOC had some success advancing this argument in the mid-1970s. Harrington and his allies developed working relationships with a number of unions—particularly the United

Auto Workers, the International Association of Machinists and the American Federation of State, County and Municipal Employees—and eventually inspired *Business Week* to observe that "socialism [is] no longer a dirty word to labor." Prominent Democrats like Massachusetts senator Edward Kennedy embraced Harrington, and a new generation of elected officials like California representative Ron Dellums and New York City Council Member and eventual mayoral candidate Ruth Messinger aligned with the DSOC. Members of the DSOC organized a "Democracy '76" project to engage with the upcoming presidential election. But for the most part, the attempt to remake the Democratic Party as a social democratic or perhaps even more radical force was, at best, tolerated.

The governors, mayors and members of Congress who had reasserted themselves as the Democratic Party leadership after 1972 showed little inclination toward visionary politics, let alone radical change, in 1976. They had secured predictable gains in the Watergate election of 1974, and they were looking for an easy win over Nixon's bumbling successor, Gerald Ford. They didn't want to make thing more complicated than they already were. Social movements had transformed and were transforming the nation. An awful war had ended awfully. An oil crisis had shaken the country and the world. The economy was in recession. A president had resigned before he was impeached. His unelected successor now occupied the Oval Office. The rough outlines of a political realignment seemed to be taking shape. Many segregationist Democrats had found a new home in Nixon's "Southern strategy" GOP, and were now enthusiastic about a rising star on the right wing of their re-energized party, former California governor Ronald Reagan, who came close to seizing the nomination from Ford. Big-city bosses were losing their grip in most of the country, even if Richard J. Daley was still clinging to the mayoralty of Chicago.

Amid all the upheaval, however, there remained a Democratic establishment. It warned against "McGovernism," and it counseled that the party could and should make itself the natural party of governance, the manager of the future, by moving back to the center. It did not buy into Harrington's notion that to build a new American majority for social change, there must be a program "bold enough to appeal to millions of men and women," a program "located on the left wing of realism." While many top Democrats were desperate to go back to the old way of doing things, Harrington was pushing to go "beyond the New Deal, the Fair Deal, the New Frontier and the Great Society." We know, he insisted, that "Keynesian policies can pump-prime an underutilized economy. But can we assume that if only Washington will get things moving, then the private market provides the best mechanism for a social allocation of the gross national product. We think not. We think that liberals must discuss going beyond liberalism."

Harrington's project had enough allies, and enough energy, to get a hearing. The unions and the activists he gathered around the Democracy '76 ideal were needed, especially as Eugene McCarthy was busy organizing a quixotic independent campaign that threatened to draw away liberal votes from the party's 1976 nominee, Jimmy Carter. At that year's Democratic National Convention, Carter "instructed his point man on the platform committee, Joe Duffy, to do what he could to satisfy the concerns of the Democratic Agenda caucus," Harrington biographer Maurice Isserman recounts. "As a result, the campaign platform the Democrats adopted in July was full of promises of support for full-employment legislation and national health insurance, as well as pledges to institute limits on defense spending and nuclear arms development."

Carter and his liberal running mate, Minnesota senator Walter Mondale, campaigned and won as reasonably progressive Democrats. Yet a *New York Times* headline from four days before Carter and Mondale were inaugurated in January 1977 declared, "Liberals Rejected." It appeared above a story about the rejection of a plea from Senators Kennedy, Humphrey and Gaylord Nelson of Wisconsin, as well as 47 Democratic House members led by Kastenmeier, for the appointment of Gar Alperovitz to the new president's Council of Economic Advisers. The House members argued that Carter needed a counselor who would be responsible for fostering public engagement and citizen participation on seeking new economic alternatives. Alperovitz, as an advocate for worker participation in economic planning and new models for employee ownership of manufacturing firms, would have been a perfect fit in one of FDR's New Deal administrations. But the *Times* reported that a source in the Carter transition team said "there is no chance that Dr. Alperovitz would be selected to serve."

Nevertheless, Harrington's project, operating as Democratic Agenda, and its labor allies kept up the pressure. In the summer of 1977, they were rallying to urge the administration to approve full-employment legislation proposed by Humphrey and California representative Augustus Hawkins, an old New Dealer who had gotten his start as a backer of author Upton Sinclair's 1934 "End Poverty in California" gubernatorial campaign. The Democratic Agenda also pushed for a host of other progressive initiatives. Their events were large, drawing thousands of activists, and they were historically significant. Writer Harold Meyerson recalls the group's 1977 conference as "a landmark in American liberalism chiefly because of the strategic reconciliations it signified. The conference marked a coming together of leaders of the left movements that had emerged in the 1930s—that is, the progressive unions—with the leaders of the left movements that had emerged in the 1960s—feminist, civil rights, and environmental."

The Democratic Agenda movement sought to turn the December 1978 midterm convention in Memphis into what the *New York Times* referred to as "a virtual vote of confidence" on President Carter. There was much speculation at the time about the prospect that Ted Kennedy would challenge Carter for the party's 1980 nomination, and pundits imagined the Memphis gathering as a showdown between Carter and Kennedy forces. But White House aide Jody Powell told reporters, "The dispute which appears to be on the horizon in Memphis is not between the President and Senator Kennedy but between the administration and Democratic Agenda."

Democratic Agenda proposals for a national health-care program, establishing public-power production to counter the economic and environmental abuses of big oil and big gas corporations and shifting budget priorities in order to steer less money to the Pentagon and more to meet domestic needs won around 40 percent of the midterm convention vote. And the delegates cheered wildly for Kennedy when he called for "health care as a matter of right and not a privilege." The votes and the response to Kennedy shook the Carter forces, including a young floor manager for the president's centrist forces in Memphis, Hillary Rodham. Within weeks, the White House would reverse plans to cut federal health-care spending, and the *Times* reported that "the political pressures generated by Kennedy and others in the liberal wing of the Democratic Party played a role in the restoration of health funds. The impact is likely to be seen in other social programs as well."

Last Gasp of the Liberals

The Memphis conference inspired Harrington and Kennedy to look to 1980 as a moment when the Democratic Party might finally be set on a progressive course. As Meyerson recalled decades later, after Kennedy's death:

> I was fortunate to have been in the room when he was at his greatest, at a succession of speeches beginning at the Democratic Party's Midterm Convention in Memphis in 1978. Kennedy and the United Auto Workers had been pushing the Carter administration to bring an ambitious plan for universal health care to the Hill, but Carter demurred. The administration also began

moving away from classic New Deal economic policies, deregulating industries and cutting back spending as joblessness spiraled. Increasingly, it was Kennedy who spoke out against many of these changes. At Memphis, Carter delivered a lackluster speech that won a tepid response, but Kennedy absolutely electrified the delegates with a passionate address on the need for universal health care. The speech laid out and created the momentum for his coming challenge to Carter. The talk included characteristically elegant affirmations of the causes of women's and civil rights and biting attacks on Republican nominee Ronald Reagan and his crazy notions. It concluded with a moving description of the Americans Kennedy had met while campaigning who were suffering through hard times, and his pledge to continue fighting for them. But read today, what stands out is his opposition to the rightward movement of the economic mainstream and to the Democrats' retreat from their historic commitment to full employment. Even more, what stands out is his apprehension that the unionized, industrial America that anchored the nation's prosperity and the Democrats' popular majorities was giving way to a meaner economic order.

There was a reason for Kennedy to run in 1980, and it was not just that Carter seemed vulnerable. The Democratic Party seemed vulnerable. A Democratic president had been elected in 1976, but Carter had not given the country a new New Deal, not even a new Great Society. He had borrowed as frequently from the right as from the left, embracing deregulation schemes and economic programs that bordered on austerity. It wasn't that he did not try to do good, and even to think big with his talk of energy independence and pursuit of Middle East peace. But it never came together for the Carter administration, as the president struggled to get a grip on skyrocketing gas prices, inflation and a hostage crisis in Iran that transfixed the nation.

"No Democrat would have dared raise a voice against Jimmy Carter had he been clearly successful or more vengeful—or even moderately lucky," Theodore White wrote. "But by 1979 all the sweet memories of the winning Carter of 1976 had faded." Unfortunately for the Democratic Party and for the country, Kennedy's 1980 presidential bid ultimately lacked the ideological coherence and sense of political urgency that might have ended the political malaise. Harrington and others gave Kennedy strong backing, but he ran less as a Democratic Agenda candidate than as, well, a Kennedy.

"Kennedy's exasperation with Carter was so great that, at times, he simply spluttered," White recalled. "I went to visit him in November 1979, shortly after he had announced his candidacy. I wanted to know precisely where it was he differed from Carter so strongly that he must run. He said that a president must direct the government, has to give it vision." But, White asked, where was the specific difference of opinion, where was the argument for taking the party in a different direction. "Then," the author recalled, "details cascading from him more and more rapidly, he concluded in an outburst of frustration: 'We wanted the same things ... [but] this ... this outsider can't solve our problems. ... Even on issues we agree on, he doesn't know how to do it. He was angry, personally, with Jimmy Carter. The job of a leader, insisted Kennedy, was to uplift the people, to sound the call—not to mourn in public, not to find fault with the people. Carter was acting, though Kennedy did not say so, in a way offensive to the entire family tradition, offensive to the heritage of governing skills in which he had been brought up."

When Kennedy finally got around to sounding the call, it was too late. He had already lost the nomination fight, despite a late surge when his campaign gained traction with wins in the New York, Pennsylvania and California primaries. His speech to that summer's Democratic National Convention remains one of the epic statements of liberalism. "I have come here tonight not to argue as a candidate but to affirm a cause," declared Kennedy, whose speech referenced FDR even more than his own brothers as a touchstone. "I am asking you to renew the

commitment of the Democratic Party to economic justice."
The senator understood what many Democrats did not: that
Reagan would devote much of his campaign to dividing the New
Deal coalition against itself by suggesting that the Democratic
Party had somehow grown too liberal. Reagan, a former liberal
Democrat who had once celebrated trade union power and
made radio ads for left-leaning candidates, claimed: "I didn't
leave the Democratic Party. The party left me."

Kennedy recognized the perilous moment in which the party
found itself.

> We heard the orators at [the Republican] convention all trying to
> talk like Democrats. They proved that even Republican nominees
> can quote Franklin Roosevelt to their own purpose. The Grand
> Old Party thinks it has found a great new trick, but 40 years
> ago an earlier generation of Republicans attempted the same
> trick. And Franklin Roosevelt himself replied: "Most Republican
> leaders have bitterly fought and blocked the forward surge of
> average men and women in their pursuit of happiness. Let us not
> be deluded that overnight those leaders have suddenly become
> the friends of average men and women." And four years later
> when the Republicans tried that trick again, Franklin Roosevelt
> asked: "Can the Old Guard pass itself off as the New Deal? I
> think not. We have all seen many marvelous stunts in the circus,
> but no performing elephant could turn a handspring without
> falling flat on its back."

Kennedy's speech earned thunderous applause, but he was
not the party's nominee. Carter lost, horribly. So did McGovern
and many of the Senate's liberals—Frank Church of Idaho,
Birch Bayh of Indiana, Gaylord Nelson of Wisconsin—as the
chamber flipped from Democratic to Republican control for the
first time since the 1950s. (Among the defeated Democrats was
one-term Iowa senator John Culver, who used his subsequent
free time to begin a biography of Wallace.) Democrats held on
to the House, but with 34 fewer seats—and with Southern "Boll

Weevil" Democrats frequently aligning with the Republican House leaders to create a working majority for many of Reagan's domestic and international initiatives. What Kennedy feared had come to pass. The struggle for the soul of the Democratic Party became ever more frustrating for those who sought to move it at the national level. Activists wanted the party to go all in on behalf of labor rights at a time when unions were under attack not just from the new administration but from the recession and deindustrialization. They wanted the party to move to the forefront in addressing a farm crisis that lasted long after the recession of the late 1970s and early 1980s had begun to ease. They developed inside-outside strategies to preserve abortion rights and block Reagan's right-wing judicial nominees. They opposed Oliver North and his dirty warriors in Central America, demanded sanctions against the apartheid regime in South Africa and championed a nuclear freeze. The grassroots campaigners of the 1980s had a far clearer sense than top Democrats of the direction in which the party needed to head if it was going to keep faith with the emerging social and political movements of the era. But the divide between the grassroots and party leadership was growing wider. The consultants and strategists who made their livings placing television ads steered the party away from the precincts of Cleveland and Detroit and Milwaukee and toward the fund-raising circuits of L.A. and New York.

The conflict over the direction of the Democratic Party had its distinct leaders and factions. But this was not just a narrow struggle over who would call the plays for midterm elections or the makeup of the presidential ticket. This was a fight over the right response to a moment of drastic change in global economic arrangements that had a profound impact on the United States, when whole industries were being offshored, and when the industries that remained were fleeing Northern industrial cities and states for rural stretches of the South where unions were weak and wages were low. Wall Street was becoming more dominant than it had ever been, as emerging cable news channels and a rapidly restructuring media system went 24/7 with stock market reports but paid less and less attention to factory closings and began to suggest that a 4, 5 or 6 percent unemployment rate was normal. The balance was shifting away from traditional working-class political strategies that tried to unite hourly-wage workers into a New Deal or Fair Deal coalition.

Michael Harrington and his allies had resisted the shift, as had radicals around the world such as British parliamentarian Tony Benn and his young ally Jeremy Corbyn. Kennedy and Harrington in the United States, Benn in Britain and others like them had a good sense of what was coming. They fought to remake political parties, the Democrats in the U.S., Labour in the United Kingdom, the Social Democrats in Germany. They argued that economic democracy, anti-imperialism and antiracism could form the underpinnings for a new politics, and that this combination would create coalitions capable of curbing Reaganism in the United States, Thatcherism in the U.K. and even crueler manifestations of right-wing politics in countries around the world. They were more right than wrong. But they could not get their own parties on board for the politics that was as bold on the left as the Republicans and Tories of other ilks were becoming on the right.

Going to the Grassroots

Caution, compromise and centrism came to define Democratic Party politics at the national level, while progressives steered their energy into state and local races. Harvey Milk and Harry Britt had shown how to do it in San Francisco, Ruth Messinger in New York City, Maryann Mahaffey in Detroit. In 1983, Representative Harold Washington would go home to Chicago and upend the Democratic machine.

A broad wrestling for the soul of the Democratic Party was taking place at the grassroots. Its roots can be traced to the

1970s, in the places that might be expected: urban centers and college towns. Movement activists who did not mind being referred to as radicals, like California's Ron Dellums and New York's Bella Abzug, entered the House in 1971 after winning primaries where they ran to the left of Democratic incumbents. In 1976, Abzug came within one point of defeating former-Nixon-aide-turned-Democrat Daniel Patrick Moynihan in a New York Senate primary—less than 10,000 votes out of almost a million cast. That same year in California, Tom Hayden disrupted the state's Democratic politics with a primary campaign against liberal Democratic senator John Tunney. The former student radical, who had played a critical role in drafting the Port Huron Statement, campaigned on a promise to remake the Democratic Party he had once battled from the outside. Hayden's campaign was significant because it sought to move beyond the comfort zones of the left and organize a clearly identified "new politics" movement in the nation's largest state, opening dozens of campaign offices and pouring energy into grassroots organizing. As important, Hayden outlined an agenda that went further than Harrington and others had in its efforts to merge economic populism with what would come to be known as "identity politics." Instead of narrowing the party's options by going one way or another, Hayden argued for an all-of-the-above approach that anticipated the Rainbow Coalition politics soon championed by the Rev. Jesse Jackson.

Hayden's bid borrowed several pages from the New Dealers. He outlined his plans in pamphlet form—just as Wallace had with *Sixty Million Jobs* and other publications—with a campaign broadside titled *Make the Future Ours*. It framed out a politics that Hayden would seek to advance from the late 1970s onward with the Campaign for Economic Democracy and other groups, and as a California state legislator. To a greater extent than anyone trying to pull the Democratic Party to the left during the period, Hayden recognized the need to integrate economic, social and racial justice themes into a party message that aimed to attract new supporters. Hayden blended radical economics with a radical embrace of gender equity, LGBTQ rights, criminal justice reform and sustainability. And, like Wallace and those who had battled for the soul of the party in the last days of FDR's presidency, Hayden understood that it was necessary to extend his message beyond domestic issues with a full-throated critique of militarism and a denunciation of permitting multinational corporations to dictate international policymaking. A global view had to frame the party's vision, Hayden argued, and it had to be a new view that broke with the Cold War politics of the past. "Our new foreign policy should revolve around five principles," he wrote:

> First, it must be humanistic, concerned with reducing the suffering of people instead of trying to prop up corrupt governments.
>
> Second, it must respect the right of self-determination, including the right to choose revolution and socialism, instead of focusing on military intervention.
>
> Third, it must seek peace, through reducing armaments and the gap between have and have-not nations, instead of a nuclear arms race and interference in the Koreas, Vietnams, Chiles and Angolas of the world.
>
> Fourth, it must be democratic, carried out with the consent of the American people after full Congressional debate—rather than secret Executive action.
>
> Fifth, it must be of both economic and social benefit for all Americans, not a constant drain of public blood and taxes for the benefit of narrow economic and bureaucratic interests.

Like Wallace's popular writing in the 1930s and 1940s, Hayden's pamphlets blended idealism and practicality, poll numbers and proposals. "The American people are ready for [a new] foreign policy after thirty years of Cold War," Hayden said in 1976, and cited polls showing Americans leaning toward a "New Humanism" in foreign affairs. "Nearly two-thirds of Americans would give up meat one day a week to feed hungry children, or the fertilizer from their lawn to grow crops in other lands. Nearly the same percentage disagrees with (the US) destabilizing of the Allende government in Chile. Public confidence in the CIA is at an all-time low. These public attitudes are the more remarkable since few political leaders have had the courage to defend new directions. It has been the peace movement and the natural awakening of Americans, not public officials, which must be credited for the thaw in Cold War thinking."

Reading now through Hayden's old campaign materials—the platforms, manifestos and leaflets he used to convince voters to push the limits of politics—is at once thrilling and depressing. Thrilling because he articulated the challenges the party would have to address, and he anticipated the progressive politics of Ro Khanna, Alexandria Ocasio-Cortez and the generation of leaders who would come to the fore in the late 2010s. Depressing because reading Hayden reminds us that savvy thinkers, activists and Democratic candidates recognized, even as party leaders were moving to the right, that the party itself needed to move left if it was going to ready itself and the country for the future.

Democrats for the Leisure Class

Why didn't those who wanted the Democratic Party to go big in order to challenge the right-wing drift of American politics that began in the 1978 midterms and took off with Reagan's 1980 victory move left? It had something to do with the undoing of political reforms, which in the early 1970s had held out so much promise. The Watergate-era campaign finance reforms, with their limits on campaign contributions and spending, and their outlines for a system in which public financing might replace special-interest spending, began to be undone with the Supreme Court's 1976 *Buckley v. Valeo* decision. The court struck down restrictions on independent expenditures in campaigns, as well as limitation on expenditures by wealthy candidates on their own behalf. It also rejected limits on total campaign expenditure. Along with decisions that would follow over the ensuing years, the *Buckley v. Valeo* decision created the rough outlines for the big-money politics that make both parties more reliant on organized money. For the Republicans, this was fine. They wanted the special-interest money that was bundled up by political action committees and wealthy donors. They also welcomed the rise of well-financed "new right" groups that developed "independent" campaigns, often focused on issues such as abortion and gay rights, that targeted liberal Democratic senators in states like Iowa.

For the Democrats, however, the money pressure had a redefining effect. The party and its candidates needed campaign cash to compete with the Republicans and their "independent" allies. And there were plenty of donors who were ready to give. But the money often came with strings attached—not in the form of explicit *quid pro quo* demands but in the none-too-subtle pressure to avoid offending the pharmaceutical industry, investment bankers or agribusiness interests that might be "tapped" for checks. Big donors knew the calculus. They started to spread their money around to both parties so that the doors would be open to them no matter who won a particular election. "Unlike the other 99.99 percent of Americans who do not make [very large] contributions, these elite donors have unique access," explained the Sunlight Foundation's Lee Drutman in a 2011 study of the campaign finance system that eventually emerged. "In a world of increasingly expensive campaigns, [major donors] effectively play the role of political gatekeepers. Prospective candidates need to be able to tap into these networks if they want to be taken seriously. And party leaders on both sides are keenly aware that more than 80 percent of party committee money now comes from these elite donors."

The party leaders, strategists and consultants could have developed a different politics that relied on small donors and grassroots politics. But why bother when, as Drutman noted, the clustering of the wealthiest donors in a handful of ZIP codes makes it "easy for candidates to raise substantial sums of money at a single event." Money had always influenced American politics, but by the early 1980s that influence was becoming systematized and increasingly sophisticated. In 1980, the Republican Congressional Campaign Committee raised ten times as much as its Democratic counterpart. A few years later, the *Atlantic* reported that though the Republicans "retain the lead in most forms of money-raising, it is an ever more modest one." But the change came at a cost, as the magazine noted that some Democrats were muttering about how the emphasis on fund-raising was "bartering away the party's populist birthright." Evidence of the sellout was not hard to find. Early in 1981, after Ronald Reagan's election and the Senate's shift to Republican control, the *Atlantic* recalled that "Democrats in the House, the party's sole remaining stronghold, engaged Republicans in a contest to see which side could chop more business loopholes in the 1981 tax-cut legislation. Democrats hoped to win back the hearts—and open the pocketbooks—of businessmen, who in 1980 had overwhelmingly supported Republicans. But the Republicans kept matching and raising the Democrats in the tax-sweeteners game. The final version of the legislation was a bonanza for business that reduced federal revenues even more than the Administration had planned—and, parenthetically, thereby encouraged mega-deficits."

A new generation of Democratic "rising stars," men like Arkansas governor Bill Clinton and Tennessee representative Al Gore, were making their names as "business friendly" politicians who knew how to raise big money and run "modern" campaigns. What might make it hard for Democratic fund-raisers and candidates to run modern campaigns, however, was the prospect that activists might push for a single-payer health-care system in ways that would displease Big Pharma, or that rural progressives might demand a platform commitment to break up Big Ag, or that democratic socialists might propose stricter rules for Wall Street. These threats would come to be generally understood by the 2010s, but the Democrats who managed the party recognized them decades earlier and adjusted not just fund-raising strategies but the small "d" democratic threats to those strategies.

By the early 1980s, the midterm gatherings of the party faithful had been scrapped, out of concern that Democratic Agenda's coalition of industrial unions, civil rights campaigners and democratic socialists had exercised too much influence at the 1978 mini-convention. By the time the 1984 Democratic National Convention rolled around, insiders had so successfully restructured the party that they no longer had to worry about winning delegate spots by backing successful candidates in primaries and caucuses. They could, for the first time, attend as unelected and unaccountable "superdelegates." They named former vice president Mondale as the presidential nominee and picked a woman for vice president—Representative Geraldine Ferraro of Queens, New York, who had been elected as a self-proclaimed "small 'c' conservative" law-and-order Democrat who opposed busing to desegregate schools and supported the death penalty. They enacted a platform that did not merely reject the progressive positions of the 1972 McGovern platform but many of the liberal stances that Carter and Mondale had run on in 1976 and 1980. "The Democratic Party has moved away from some hallmarks of its tradition of liberalism in the eight years since Walter F. Mondale's first national campaign," noted the *New York Times*. "The platform approved this week by the Democratic National Convention as the foundation for the fall campaign favors social policies less generous and less expensive than those espoused in the past."

But even that was not enough. After the 1984 election, the corporate-friendly Democrats augmented their project with the creation of the so-called Democratic Leadership Council, a center-right group that promoted neoliberal economic schemes and neoconservative foreign policy agendas with such ample funding from corporate interests that the Rev. Jesse Jackson referred to the group as "Democrats for the Leisure Class." On the one hand Jackson was frustrated by the fact that the DLC was proudly corporate-tied and corporate funded, collecting checks from Bank One, Citigroup, Dow Chemical, DuPont, General Electric, Health Insurance Corporation, Merrill Lynch, Microsoft, Morgan Stanley, Occidental Petroleum and Raytheon. And on the other he was frustrated by the emphasis the DLC leadership placed on reducing the influence of union and environmental activists, feminists and civil rights and social justice groups. As Dan Balz and Ronald Brownstein explained in their book *Storming the Gates*, within a few weeks of the DLC's formation in 1985, "it counted seventy-five members, primarily governors and members of Congress, most of them from the Sun Belt, and almost all of them white; liberal critics instantly dubbed the group 'the white male caucus.' "

Jackson rejected the premise that advocacy for the rights of women and minority groups needed to be dialed down in order to appeal to the working-class white men who had migrated from the New Deal coalition into what was referred to as the "Reagan coalition." He saw the calculus as absurd and defeatist. Instead of renewing economic populist appeals that might appeal to working-class voters of all races and backgrounds, he noted, the DLC and its allies in the party leadership avoided messaging that might offend corporate donors. Instead, they tried to compete with the Republicans when it came to supporting Wall Street–backed trade deals, increased defense spending and spouting socially conservative rhetoric like that of Virginia governor Chuck Robb, who told a 1986 DLC conference, "While racial discrimination has by no means vanished from our society, it's time to shift the primary focus from racism—the traditional enemy without—to self-defeating patterns of behavior—the enemy within." While Robb and other DLC leaders said they wanted to reform the party, liberals and progressives argued that what was really being proposed was a great leap backward.

The Rainbow Response

Jesse Jackson "changed the Democratic Party, helping it evolve into its modern configuration as a diverse party, not a Dixiecrat party," recalls Steve Cobble, a veteran aide and ally of the civil rights leader. "In the 1980s, the prevailing pundit theory was that the ticket back to relevance for the Democratic Party was to follow the lead of the DLC: to try to win back white Southerners, reach out to 'moderates,' and appeal to the corporate class." But that message held little appeal to working-class voters, who were already experiencing the "creative destruction" that this corporate class demanded to satisfy its multinational investors, in the form of layoffs and plant closings, small business failures and farm bankruptcies. When Jackson bid for the party's presidential nomination in 1984 and again in 1988 as the leader of a Rainbow Coalition of progressives who championed worker rights and civil rights at home and peace and justice abroad, he ran into all the roadblocks that had been created to prevent a modern-day embrace of the New Deal, Four Freedoms and Economic Bill of Rights.

The Jackson candidacies proposed the next New Deal coalition. And Jackson worked hard to achieve the goal, campaigning in the farm country of Iowa and outside the steel mills of western Pennsylvania, arguing that urban and rural voters had far more in common with one another than they did with wealthy suburbanites. Jackson reached out to young people, lesbians and gays, Arab Americans, Native Americans and others who had been neglected by the party. The Jackson campaign won more delegates in 1988 than had any left-wing insurgency since 1972. In 1988, Jackson easily beat Democratic members of Congress who had embraced the DLC line, including then senator Al Gore. Despite limited funds, dismissive media coverage and overwhelming opposition from party insiders, Jackson won 13 primaries and caucuses in key states such as Michigan and Virginia and secured almost 7 million votes—more than any candidate except the nominee, Massachusetts governor Michael Dukakis. Jackson did this with an uncompromising campaign that welcomed endorsements from Democratic Socialists of America, Arab Americans, LGBTQ+ activists and others who were working to make their voices heard within the party. With support from a young professor named Paul Wellstone (who two years later would run a Rainbow Coalition–inspired campaign for a Minnesota U.S. Senate seat, and win) and Burlington, Vermont, mayor Bernie Sanders (who two years later would run a Rainbow Coalition–inspired campaign for Vermont's House seat, and win), he was such a phenomenon that R.W. Apple Jr. of the *New York Times* described 1988 as "the Year of Jackson."

Jackson succeeded in knocking back some of the structural barriers that had been erected by the party bosses, bringing diversity to party committees and rule-making bodies, and he won some recognition of the value of voter-registration drives and investment in grassroots organizing. "I think Jackson has not gotten the credit he deserves," Bernie Sanders told me in 2014, as he prepared to run for president. "His campaigns were revolutionary: we had an African-American minister going to states like Iowa—predominantly white states—and rallying farmers. He came to Vermont; I remember I introduced him, and we had hundreds and hundreds of people out to hear him speak in a state that was then virtually all-white. The idea of bringing together people—the Rainbow Coalition concept of whites, blacks, Hispanics, Asians, gays and lesbians—is absolutely right, and the emphasis, in my view, can be on economic issues. The job right now, the main focus, is to bring people together from an economic perspective, on class lines, and talk about an America that works for the vast majority of our people and not just the top 1 percent."

Jackson was perceived as a threat by the neoliberal donors and Beltway strategists who had little interest in ideological appeals that were designed to expand the electorate. Jackson, a brilliant campaigner, would be invited onto the campaign trail late in the fall of election years, with a charge to rally African-American voters, trade unionists and students. Party leaders knew he could excite the base. Yet he was dismissed as a presidential or vice-presidential prospect.

This refusal to give Jackson his due was painfully evident at the 1988 Democratic National Convention. Jackson was a star of the convention, as Kennedy had been in 1980. And Jackson went where Kennedy had not, into a full-spectrum call for a rethink of American foreign policy. "When Mr. Reagan and Mr. Gorbachev met," he said, "there was a big meeting. They represented together one-eighth of the human race. Seven-eighths of the human race was locked out of that room. Most people in the world tonight—half are Asian, one-half of them are Chinese. There are 22 nations in the Middle East. There's Europe; 40 million Latin Americans next door to us; the Caribbean; Africa—a half-billion people. Most people in the world today are Yellow or Brown or Black, non-Christian, poor, female, young and don't speak English. This generation must offer leadership to the real world. We're losing ground in Latin America, Middle East, South Africa because we're not focusing on the real world. That's the real world."

The crowd at that convention cheered itself hoarse as he continued: "If an issue is morally right, it will eventually be political. Fannie Lou Hamer didn't have the most votes in Atlantic City, but her principles have outlasted every delegate who voted to lock her out. Dr. King didn't have the most votes about the Vietnam War, but he was morally right. If we are principled first, our politics will fall in place."

But when all was said and done, the calls from Jackson backers to nominate him for vice president went nowhere. Those calls to unite the party's top two candidates were not unreasonable. Just eight years earlier, Republican nominee Ronald Reagan had invited his chief rival for the nomination, George H.W. Bush, to join a winning GOP ticket. Carter had invited a former rival, Mondale, to be his running mate in 1976. JFK had done the same with Lyndon Johnson in 1960. In 1988, however, the convention bypassed Jackson and selected Lloyd Bentsen, a Texas senator with close ties to oil and banking interests. In 1970, Bentsen beat liberal Democratic senator Ralph Yarborough with a campaign that exploited anger with the incumbent over his votes for civil rights and against the Vietnam War. Bentsen was so conservative that on the eve of the 1970 senatorial election, liberal economist John Kenneth Galbraith urged Texas liberals to vote for the Republican nominee, Bush, over Bentsen. "As prospective senators they are, so far as one can tell, equally conservative and in the Senate will be equally bad," Galbraith reasoned. "A Bentsen victory will tighten the hold of conservatives on the Texas Democratic Party, force the rest of us to contend with them nationally and leave the state with the worst of all choices—a choice between two conservative parties. The defeat of Bentsen, by contrast, will show Texas conservatives that their only chance of winning and of being with the winner is to become Republican. That is how it should be and what the two-party system is about."

Or not. Bentsen won that 1970 general election, and eighteen years later he was the Democratic nominee for vice president. Southern conservatives were still pulling the Democratic Party to the right. And national strategists were still saying this had to be the case. Why was Bentsen chosen over so dynamic and appealing a candidate as Jackson? The theory was that he could win Texas for the Democrats. That didn't happen. The Dukakis-Bentsen ticket lost Texas by 700,000 votes. In fact, it lost every Southern state.

Would a Dukakis-Jackson ticket have run better than Dukakis-Bentsen? It's worth noting that the 1988 race was much closer than it seemed. Though the Democrats fell down in the South, they surged elsewhere. The Democrats ran 5 percentage points better than they had in 1984, and 2.5 percentage points better than they would in 1992 (when Ross Perot's Reform Party grabbed almost 20 percent of the vote from the major parties). Though Dukakis only carried 10 states and the District of Columbia, he came close in the largest and most diverse states in the country—losing Illinois and Pennsylvania by just 2 percent of the vote, California by only a little over 3 percent and states such as Maryland, Missouri and New Mexico by similarly narrow margins. Adding the 130 electoral votes from these states to the 111 the Democrats already had would not quite have tipped the Electoral College, but it would have marked a big comeback for the party just four years after the Reagan landslide of 1984. Could Jackson really have helped that much in those states? Consider this: the 1988 election drew the lowest turnout in decades, just over 50 percent. Turnout was especially low in Chicago, L.A. and other major cities, while it was notably higher in the Republican-leaning suburbs. Turnout by African-American voters was uninspired, as it was among voters of all races under the age of thirty. So could Jesse Jackson have done a better job of mobilizing African-American and young voters in big cities and diverse Northern and Western states? It is fair to say yes. Just as it is fair to say that the Jesse Jackson v. Dan Quayle debate would have been the highlight of the political year.

But the Democratic Party was not prepared to take a chance on a great big strategy for mobilizing new voters, which could have been built around Jackson. The men who called the shots in the Democratic Party as the 1980s gave way to the 1990s were unwilling to follow the advice Jackson had given the 1988 convention: "If we are principled first, our politics will fall in place." They did not choose to fight the big fights that Jackson or Ted Kennedy or Henry Wallace or FDR had proposed. The Democratic Party was no longer building outward, with the vision of mass mobilization that Jackson and his supporters advanced. It was looking inward, seeking narrow wins on cautious agendas. At the 1992 Democratic National Convention that nominated DLC leader Bill Clinton for the presidency, author Joan Didion observed that "no hint of what had once been that party's nominal constituency was allowed to penetrate prime time, nor was any suggestion of what had once been that party's tacit role, that of assimilating immigration and franchising the economically disenfranchised." After winning just 43 percent of the vote in a three-way contest with Republican George H.W. Bush and billionaire gadfly Ross Perot, Clinton promptly appointed the man John Kenneth Galbraith had tried to read out of the party, Lloyd Bentsen, as secretary of the treasury. The die was cast. Democrats would be, at best, a managerial party; at worst, a neoliberal party that did the work assigned by Wall Street more efficiently than had the Republicans. Voters noticed. Party loyalties frayed, coalitions pulled apart, turnout declined.

Bill Clintonism

From 1980 until 2008, no Democratic presidential nominee won 50 percent of the vote. The party might still prevail with a plurality of the vote, as Bill Clinton did with 43 percent in 1992 and 49 percent in 1996, but it became a party of "triangulation" that collected campaign money from many of the same plutocrats who funded the GOP. On issues such as trade policy and deregulation, the Clinton administration implemented the programs that Republicans had long proposed. And when Clinton got in trouble politically after Democrats lost control of the House and Senate in 1994, he shifted even further to the right, advocating for and eventually signing laws that blocked same-sex marriage; implementing draconian criminal justice policies that would contribute to a 60 percent increase in the number of people incarcerated during his eight years in office; and upending welfare protections for women and children, in what Peter Edelman, a Clinton administration aide who resigned over the issue, referred to as "an unspeakable blow to millions of utterly powerless people." Clinton built up the military, supported weapons systems that even Republicans like Arizona senator John McCain identified as boondoggles and worked with the Republicans in Congress to balance budgets in the Pentagon's favor.

Eventually, Clinton went after the New Deal legacy, supporting deregulation schemes that undid Glass-Steagall protections against the speculative abuses of investment firms. "The tragedy of the Clinton administration is that none of this was inevitable," observed historian Nelson Lichtenstein in 2018. "Bill Clinton and most 'Friends of Bill' were not neoliberals, yet they ended up presiding over a political economy that advanced that ideological and financial project. Their first instincts called for a novel form of managed capitalism, not markets, to revitalize the domestic economy, reform health care and labor relations, and ameliorate the social disruptions engendered by globalized commerce. But they caved before those, within the administration and without, who had a firmer set of ideological prescriptions. This was most notable in the emphasis on deficit reduction, in the seemingly gratuitous decision to drive NAFTA down the throat of a resistant Democratic majority in Congress, and the radical deregulation of financial markets. The Clintons presided over a generational changing of the governmental guard, but not the emergence of a new social movement or the revitalization of an old one."

What Lichtenstein referred to as "the tragedy of the Clinton administration" became the tragedy of the Democratic Party. When Clinton took office, in 1993, Democrats had overwhelming majorities in the Senate (57–43) and the House (258–176). They held 30 governorships, versus just 18 for the Republicans. By 2000, as Clinton was finishing his second term, Republicans controlled the Senate (55–45), the House (223–211) and the governorships (30–18). The party was collapsing at the state legislative level and decaying in the county courthouses that had once been the backbone of its national strength. "Clinton's time in office had its successes and its failures," Ezra Klein wrote.

"But politically speaking, Clinton enjoyed the successes and the party often endured the failures. Large Democratic majorities had given way to total Republican dominance."

Clinton deserved blame. But trying to blame the decline of the Democratic Party on one man misses the point of the party's ongoing crisis. The crisis was that the party that once nominated FDR and Henry Wallace was now perfectly satisfied to nominate Bill Clintons and Joe Liebermans, Hillary Clintons and Tim Kaines. Its default position had become the centrist dialectic that says, "Well, we may not be perfect, but we are maybe a little better than the Republicans." Every compromise, every sellout, every surrender was explained away as a necessary "triangulation" that would avert Republican hegemony. The quest for big, bold solutions, for a New Deal or a Four Freedoms or an Economic Bill of Rights, was replaced with the quest for the campaign dollars of the bankers and CEOs whose hatred FDR had once welcomed.

If anyone dared to suggest that the Democratic Party ought to stand for something real, they were attacked by the likes of Obama White House chief of staff Rahm Emanuel as "fucking retarded," as the offensive operative called those who advocated for more ambitious health-care reforms than the administration was prepared to initiate. Emanuel, a Clinton and Obama White House fixture who made himself one of the most definitional figures in the party from the 1990s through the 2010s, responded to pleas for help from embattled unionists by declaring "Fuck the UAW." At its highest levels, the leadership of the Democratic Party had become openly disdainful of liberal idealism.

When Emanuel ran the Democratic Congressional Campaign Committee in 2006, it was his job to recruit House candidates in an election year when polls and pundits predicted the party would retake the chamber. After the Democrats did just that, Emanuel worked the "refs," claiming credit for the wins and suggesting that they wouldn't have occurred without him. But as a savvy 2015 assessment by Rick Perlstein of Emanuel's long career noted, "that achievement disintegrates the more closely it's examined. At the D-Trip, as the DCCC is known, Emanuel aggressively recruited right-leaning candidates, frequently military veterans, including former Republicans. But many of his hand-picked choices fared poorly, losing in general elections. Some even lost in their primaries, to candidates backed by liberals —many of whom won congressional seats resoundingly, even after the DCCC abandoned them. Victory, like defeat, can have a hundred fathers, and we can't know what was ultimately responsible for the Democrats' success that November. Anger at Republicans for the Iraq War (which Emanuel supported) certainly drove many voters' decisions. What is indisputable is that the 2006 majority proved to be a rickety one."

That eventually became a problem for the president Emanuel would serve as White House chief of staff, Barack Obama. "Critics argue that, even where Emanuel's strategy succeeded in the short term, it undermined the party over time," noted the *New Yorker*. "One of his winners, the football star Heath Shuler, of North Carolina, would not even commit to vote for Nancy Pelosi for Speaker of the House, and was one of many Rahm recruits to vote against important Obama Administration priorities, like economic stimulus, banking reform and health care. Many are no longer congressmen. Some Democrats now argue that, in the long run, 2006 might have weakened the Party more than it strengthened it." Retired record executive Howie Klein, who had worked to elect progressive Democrats in 2006, dubbed Emanuel's strategy "catastrophic." Rick Perlstein's 2015 article on Emanuel, highlighted Klein's conclusion that Emanuel's biasing of the process toward the centrists had actually "contributed to the massive GOP majorities we have now, the biggest since the 1920s."

Klein was onto something with his observation that even when it won, a visionless and compromise-prone Democratic Party planted the seeds of defeat—and it is notable that he made it toward the end of Barack Obama's second term. The 2008 election campaign, which Obama waged as a notably more pro-gressive Democrat than Bill Clinton, suggested the possibility of the party. The young senator from Illinois was not campaigning as a classic outsider; he enjoyed the support of Ted Kennedy, many other party elders and key unions. Nevertheless, he pulled off an upset by thwarting what pundits had imagined would be a triumphal run for the nomination by Hillary Clinton. The problem was, while he beat the Clinton machine and may have initially rattled some of the party leadership, Obama proved to be every bit as adept at scrambling to the empty center as previous Democratic presidents.

The first time I interviewed Obama, when he was an Illinois state senator bidding for a seat in the U.S. Senate, he told me that if he got to Washington his role model would be Wisconsin senator Russ Feingold, the maverick Democrat who cast the sole Senate vote against George W. Bush's USA Patriot Act, vehemently opposed the Iraq War and broke with the Clinton administration not only on war and peace issues but also on Wall Street regulation and trade policy. Once a senator, however, Obama did not take Feingold as a role model. In fact, they differed on essential constitutional, trade and presidential accountability issues, with Obama consistently taking more cautiously centrist positions. One of Obama's first votes in the Senate was to confirm Bush's nominee for secretary of state, Condoleezza Rice. The new senator's personal physician, friend and mentor, Dr. Quentin Young, wrote to express his concern. "I told him I was disappointed in him," the veteran campaigner for peace and social and economic justice recalled. "Rice was the embodiment of everything that was wrong with this adminis-tration. So, he called me back and he said, 'Why didn't you pick up the phone and call me?'" Young was appalled. He had not imagined that he would have to explain to Obama that voting to confirm a neoconservative champion of the Iraq War was a bad idea. When Obama started opining on the importance of letting presidents name their Cabinet members, Young recalled,

"I said: 'You are a constitutional lawyer. It's about advice and consent, right? You should have denied him your consent.'" Young was right to be concerned. But most Democratic primary voters paid little attention to Obama's actual record. They embraced his promise of "hope and change," imagining it as a commitment to break not just with eight years of Republican folly but with the compromised politics of Bill Clinton and the Democratic leadership in the 1990s.

Obama was nominated and elected in 2008 by progressives, both younger tech-savvy activists who made his candidacy an early favorite of the blogosphere and old-school liberal precinct walkers who saw in his candidacy an extension of the frustrating work of opposing all that was Bush and Cheney. Obama got a leg up in the race for the Democratic nomination because he was the one top-tier contender who could say that he had opposed authorizing Bush to take the country to war with Iraq. In the Iowa caucuses that would define the 2008 race, those antiwar credentials, above all other factors, made the young senator a contender. Similarly, as he campaigned in key states such as Wisconsin, Obama's call for a new approach to free trade agreements and for massive infrastructure investments allowed him to secure backing from labor and liberal farm activists at critical stages in the process. The progressives who committed to Obama early on were the essential foot soldiers of his long march through the caucuses, the primaries, and the fall campaign.

For all the progressive support he assembled, however, Obama was not going to be "the most liberal ... nominee to ever run for president," as Tennessee Senator Fred Thompson would claim at that 2008 Republican National Convention that nominated Arizona Senator John McCain for the presidency. Obama was not "more liberal than a senator who calls himself a socialist [Bernie Sanders]." McCain could rant and rave about how his rival "began his campaign in the liberal left lane of politics and has never left it." But the truth was that Obama exited the left lane long before the roll call of Democratic National Convention delegates at their midsummer gathering in Denver.

Making Nice with Wall Street

As soon as Obama had secured the delegates he needed to claim the nomination, the candidate who had positioned himself in primary states like Wisconsin, Michigan and Ohio as something of an economic populist immediately made nice with Wall Street. In a June 2008 *Fortune* magazine interview, the senator explicitly rejected what he had said during the primary campaign about challenging corporate-friendly trade deals. "Sometimes during campaigns the rhetoric gets overheated and amplified," he told *Fortune*'s Nina Easton, after she reminded him of the heated language he had deployed against Clinton and others who were linked to the unpopular North American Free Trade Agreement. By the time he claimed the nomination that summer, Obama was starting to sound a lot like the man who would nominate Hillary Clinton to serve as his secretary of state, hire on key members of the Clinton administration's economic policy team and eventually propose a Trans-Pacific Partnership trade deal that was opposed by the same labor, environmental and human rights groups that had opposed NAFTA. Still, grassroots Democrats stuck with Obama, and new voters, many of them young progressives, flocked to the polls to support him in the fall. They wanted a Democratic victory, and they got it.

It wasn't just that Obama was an agile campaigner whose vague rhetoric made it possible for liberals, moderates and even some conservatives to get excited about his candidacy. It wasn't just that the prospect of electing an African-American intellectual who wrote best-selling books and who had opposed the Iraq War to replace George W. Bush seemed to represent a great leap forward for the nation—one that at least some Obama backers imagined held out the promise of an enlightened era of "post-partisan" progress. The Republicans helped the Democrats by getting everything wrong, starting with the nomination of Alaska governor Sarah Palin as their vice-presidential nominee, then standing by idly as the nation's economy blew apart following the Wall Street meltdown of September 2008. Obama was elected president with the highest percentage of the vote secured by any Democratic nominee since Johnson in 1964. And his coattails were long. Democratics secured robust majorities in the House and Senate. The election results seemed to suggest that everything was possible, just as it had been 1932 or to an only somewhat lesser extent in 1964.

Obama did not choose to be so bold as FDR, or even LBJ. Elected at a point when the country was hemorrhaging jobs, he had two choices: a new New Deal or a continuation of the managerial approach that had defined Clinton's presidency. Within hours of election, he signaled that he would not be welcoming the hatred of Wall Street: he announced that Rahm Emanuel would be his White House chief of staff. Obama, the "agent of change," had selected a militant advocate for free-trade policies favored by the Clinton and Bush administrations, Clinton's point man in the fight for NAFTA and an alphabet soup of similar deals that were passionately opposed by the very labor, environmental and farm groups that had just finished working to elect Obama. Picking Emanuel reassured Wall Street and its amen corner in the DLC, but it gave no comfort to Main Street. The selection of Emanuel also sent a subtler signal that would soon by amplified as the president-elect named his cabinet. When Obama was establishing his credentials with progressive Democrats by opposing the 2002 congressional resolution that authorized President Bush to go to war with Iraq, then representative Emanuel supported the resolution and remained one of the steadiest Democratic apologists for the Bush administration's failed foreign policies. And who would serve as Obama's secretary of defense? The man who had held the position for the last two years of Bush's presidency: Robert Gates.

Obama was not going to govern as any kind of democratic socialist or even as the great reformer that his most ardent supporters imagined him to be. His would be a cautious, calculating presidency that did many good things but that was never as bold or adventurous as was needed in a moment of deep recession, mounting inequality and forever wars.

In Illinois, when I had first covered him, Obama stood to the left. This is a man who moved to Chicago to be part of the political moment that began with the 1983 election of Harold Washington, a progressive Democratic congressman who as a Roosevelt College (now Roosevelt University) undergraduate had in 1948 been active with the campus "Students for Wallace" club, as the city's first African-American mayor. In Chicago, Obama studied the organizing techniques of *Rules for Radicals* author Saul Alinsky; who worked with proudly radical labor leaders to defend basic industries and avert layoffs. The future president used his Harvard-minted legal skills to fight for expanded voting rights; he was mentored by civil libertarian legislator and federal judge Abner Mikva; he discussed the intricacies of Middle East policy with Edward Said and Rashid Khalidi; he learned about single-payer health care from Quentin Young, the longtime coordinator of Physicians for a National Health Program. And famously, Obama did not just make antiwar sounds before Iraq was invaded, he appeared at an antiwar rally in downtown Chicago beside a "War Is Not an Option" sign. Obama knew not just the rough outlines of the left-labor-liberal-progressive agenda, but the specifics. He did not need to be presented with progressive ideas for responding appropriately to an economic downturn, to environmental and energy challenges, to global crises and democratic dysfunction. He had spoken of, written about and campaigned for them over the better part of a quarter century. In his first bid for the Illinois State Senate in 1996, he had run with the endorsement of the New Party, the labor-left movement of the mid-1990s that sought to move the Democrats toward an understanding that "the social, economic and political progress of the United States requires a democratic revolution in America—the return of power to the people." He knew that the Democratic Party needed to move away from the cautious center where Bill Clinton had wedged it. Yet, as president, he often retreated to that very center.

Why? Because parties matter as much as individuals when it comes to defining presidencies. Even in a moment of seeming strength, with control of the White House and both chambers of Congress, the Democratic Party remained divided. It did not know what it was fighting for. It was ready to manage the affairs of state, and to do so more ably than the wrecking crew that had been assembled by Dick Cheney and George Bush. It was prepared to push for some agenda items, including meaningful reforms to a creaking health-care system. Yet it was not prepared to overturn the politics that had empowered Cheney and Bush. It was not ready to take on Wall Street and the military-industrial complex and to end the corruption of campaigning and governance by special interests. It was not ready to be radical at a time when radicalism was required. The pressure on Obama, not just from Republicans but from many in the leadership of his own party, was to conform to the systems and structures he had inherited, rather than to change them. Even in the fight for the Affordable Care Act, the great struggle of the period when he had the congressional majorities he needed to act boldly, Obama erred constantly toward the center, and even to the right. The man who had told a 2003 AFL-CIO gathering in Illinois, "I happen to be a proponent of a single-payer, universal health-care program," was, in 2010, rejecting that option as unrealistic.

"On one end of the spectrum, there are some who have suggested scrapping our system of private insurance and replacing it with government-run health care," the president announced. "Though many other countries have such a system, in America it would be neither practical nor realistic." And most Democrats, some grudgingly, some enthusiastically, were getting on board with a president who seemed to suggest that there was a flaw in the DNA of the public employees who would run a single-payer program. "I don't believe we should give government bureaucrats or insurance company bureaucrats more control over health care in America," he declared. It is easy to get mad at Obama when we read lines like that. It is harder to recognize that if the Democratic Party had maintained a clear commitment not just to a single-payer health-care reform but to the sort of social welfare state that FDR and Wallace had envisioned when they looked to the postwar era, Obama would very probably have been a bolder and better president. Doubt that? Consider the success of the conservatives in the Republican Party who adopted a virulent antitax, austerity-focused "government is the problem" stance in the late 1970s and, though it was cynical and unworkable, stuck with it so consistently and so resolutely that they ultimately reframed debates, drew many Democrats into their rhetorical trap and won elections. The Republicans were radical in the wrong direction, but Democrats were not sufficiently radical in the right direction.

There were times when Obama seemed to recognize this reality, as when he prepared to seek re-election in 2012. In his first term he had narrowly won approval of his chief legislative priority, the Affordable Care Act, and then led the country on a slow path toward recovery from the 2008 meltdown. At this point Obama clearly understood that frustration with conservative economic policies, whether gleefully advanced by Republicans like Paul Ryan or accepted with apologies by Democrats who chose not to fight, was turning Americans against both parties. More attuned than his rivals to the tensions of the moment, the president saw the political import of the Occupy Wall Street movement and state-based protests against austerity. He may have been a centrist, especially on economic issues, but Obama was a savvy centrist. He saw which way the wind was blowing and he went with it, delivering the essential address of his presidency on December 6, 2011. Speaking in Osawatomie, Kansas, where a century earlier Theodore Roosevelt had delivered one of the most radical speeches of the Progressive era, Obama echoed concerns expressed by the occupiers of New York City's Zuccotti Park who had inspired a national outcry. "Inequality," the president declared, "distorts our democracy. It gives an outsized voice to the few who can afford high-priced lobbyists and unlimited campaign contributions, and runs the risk of selling out our democracy to the highest bidder. And it leaves everyone else rightly suspicious that the system in Washington is rigged against them—that our elected representatives aren't looking out for the interests of most Americans." It was the right message, as was the Obama campaign's targeting of Republican Mitt Romney's record as a "vulture capitalist." Obama was re-elected with ease, making him the first Democrat since FDR to win his initial election and his re-election with more than 50 percent of the vote.

But Obama did not maintain the message. By the summer of 2013, he was proposing to make Larry Summers, the secretary of the treasury under Clinton whom Obama had brought in as the director of his National Economic Council, the next chairman of the Federal Reserve. Key Democratic senators warned that they could not confirm a man who so frequently opposed needed regulation of the financial sector of the U.S. economy. "The truth is that it was unlikely he would have been confirmed by the Senate," said Senator Bernie Sanders, the Vermont independent who caucused with the Democrats but had emerged as an outspoken critic of the party's willingness to empower Summers and others like him. "What the American people want now is a Fed chairman prepared to stand up to the greed, recklessness and illegal behavior on Wall Street, not a Wall Street insider whose deregulation efforts helped pave the way for a horrendous financial crisis and the worst economic downturn in the country since the Great Depression." Summers withdrew his name from consideration. But the fact that he was even proposed revealed the incoherence of the Democratic approach not just to economics but to so many fundamental issues. To the extent that the party had definition, it came not from its platform or its values but from charismatic individuals who sought, and sometimes won, the presidency.

Obama won twice, but his wins did not translate into long-term success for the party. After the great victories of 2008, in fact, it all started to come apart. The 2010 elections were devastating for Democrats at the national and state levels. The party lost sixty-three House seats and seven Senate seats, as well as six governorships and twenty state legislative chambers. Because 2010 was a census year, Republicans were able to gerrymander congressional districts in a way that secured their House majority. Four years later, in the next round of midterm elections, the Republicans picked up nine Senate seats and full control of the Congress. And it just kept getting worse. "In his eight years in office, Obama oversaw the rapid erosion of the Democratic Party's political power in state legislatures, congressional districts and governor's mansions," wrote election analyst Clare Malone early in 2017. "At the beginning of Obama's term, Democrats controlled 59 percent of state legislatures, while now they control only 31 percent, the lowest percentage for the party since the turn of the twentieth century. They held twenty-nine governor's offices and now have only sixteen, the party's lowest number since 1920."

A Weak and Inoffensive Democratic Party

There are those, even now, who want to blame Obama for this decline. But that's a misread. Surely Obama made his share of political and policy missteps, a good many of which he acknowledges. But the party was desperate and weak, ill-defined and inept. It worried more about raising money than expanding its membership. Its leaders got excited when they recruited former

Republicans as candidates, or millionaires, or drab centrists who were willing to repeat the talking points that pollsters promised would offend no one. Democrats stood for so little that even the party faithful lost interest in platform fights. If Obama was at the top of the ticket, the party could excite enough voters to build a winning presidential coalition. If not, the machine sputtered and ground to a halt. And a space opened for Donald Trump.

Henry Wallace had warned the delegates to the party's 1944 convention that "Democrats who try to play the Republican game inside the Democratic Party always find that it just can't work on a national scale." By the 2010s, too many Democrats were playing the Republican game. The Democrats promised to be better managers than the Republicans. They pulled their punches, proposing minuscule minimum-wage hikes when the earning power of working Americans was in decline, supporting free trade deals that served Wall Street rather than Main Street, recognizing the reality of climate change but never developing the sense of urgency that was required, and accepting budget priorities that invariably prioritized the Pentagon over the social safety net.

The thing was, at a point when tremendous numbers of Americans from across the political spectrum said that the country was headed in the wrong direction, voters weren't looking for managers. They were looking for champions who proposed a more visionary and radical politics that might actually address the anxieties generated by globalization and automation, by mounting inequality and the scorching evidence of environmental catastrophe. This did not incline them to vote for Republicans—at least in most instances—but it did create an "enthusiasm gap" and lead strikingly high numbers of potential Democratic voters to stay home or back third-party contenders in the 2016 election that made Trump president. The vast majority of Americans did not back Trump; 54 percent of them rejected his candidacy. But as roughly seven million voters rejected both major party nominees and supported third-party contenders, as turnout slipped in Milwaukee, Detroit and other key cities, and as just enough voters gave in to the Republican nominee's appeals to their worst instincts, Trump was able to lose the popular vote yet win the Electoral College. The 2016 election was not a Trump victory. It was a Democratic Party failure that would produce enormous consequences for the politics and the governance of the nation.

What Henry Wallace proposed in 1944 was a Democratic Party sufficient to beat fascism abroad and at home, that recognized the systemic flaws which gave rise to injustice and addressed them, that did not merely respond to issues as they arose but, rather, was sufficiently dynamic to shape the debate. Like FDR at his best, Wallace had no taste for a Democratic Party that ran up the center in hopes of being all things to all people. He imagined a Democratic Party that pointed to a North Star and marched in its direction. He wanted a Democratic Party that had a soul. Unfortunately, the Democratic Party of 2016 had traded its soul for campaign contributions from investment bankers and the caution of a centrist politics that did not speak to the moment, or to the future.

9

"I Want Us to Be that Party Again!"

How the Democratic Party Might Recover Its Soul in the Twenty-First Century

*Our choice is between democracy for everybody or for the few—
between the spreading of social safeguards and economic opportunity to all the people—or the concentration of our abundant
resources in the hands of selfishness and greed.*
> —Henry Wallace, speaking on a hot summer
> afternoon to autoworkers in Detroit, 1944

*I think we need to be a party that is first and foremost account-
able to working-class people again, and to marginalized people.
I don't want that to be something that we just talk about, but
something that we are about.*
> —Alexandria Ocasio-Cortez, speaking on a hot summer
> night after a day of campaigning in Detroit, 2019

The simple farmhouse where Henry Wallace was born and
came of age can be found in Orient Township, on the southern
side of Iowa's Adair County, just off what is referred to as a
"Minimum Maintenance Road." Drivers are advised to travel it
"at your own risk." That pretty well sums up the approach that
has been taken to Wallace over the seventy-five years since he
battled for the soul of the Democratic Party at its 1944 convention, struggled to keep alive the promise of the New Deal and
eventually retired to the political wilderness. On the December

morning when I visited the Wallace farm, no one was there. I brushed the snow off a stone with a plaque that read: "Henry A. Wallace. Birthplace 1888."

Wallace had hoped to live to the age of 100. If he had, I like to think he might have attended an Iowa caucus meeting on behalf of Jesse Jackson. In an effort to draw rural voters for their 1988 campaign, Jackson and his supporters set up their Rainbow Coalition headquarters in Adair County, just up the street from the county courthouse in Greenfield (population 1,982). But Wallace passed at age sevety-seven, barely twenty years after he finished his vice presidency. The death of a former vice president who would almost certainly have succeeded to the presidency had he beaten the corporatists and the segregationists in 1944 was briefly noted. Wallace's old ideological nemesis, the *New York Times*, headlined its November 19, 1965, obituary: "Ex-Vice President, Plant Expert." Wallace's end was not the big story that morning. Rather, it was a report on the burgeoning U.S. military presence in Southeast Asia, under another headline: "Casualties High." Wallace's funeral took place at an Episcopal chapel near his farm north of New York City. It featured no eulogy, no sermon and no hymns. A reading from Psalm 46 was chosen ("He maketh wars to cease unto the end of the Earth; he breaketh the bow, and cutteth the spear in sunder, he burneth the chariot of fire ..."), as was a reading from Psalm 121 ("He will not suffer thy foot to be moved ...")

The most prominent of the 300 attendees, John Gardner, who was then Lyndon Johnson's secretary of health, education and welfare, had like Wallace started as a liberal Republican and become the conscience of a Democratic administration. He brought a wreath of red and white carnations from the White House and said he was honored to pay tribute to "an extraordinary American." As Wallace had been in the mid-1930s, Gardner in the mid-1960s was a true believer in a presidency that sought to balance the scales a little more on the side of the common man and woman. ("To his admirers," the *Times* said in Gardner's own obituary in 2002, "Mr. Gardner was a modern-day Plato, needed by Americans looking for optimism and idealism.") Unlike Wallace, however, Gardner would not finish his tenure with the administration in which he oversaw the launch of Medicare and championed its War on Poverty. A month before Johnson announced his own decision to forego a bid for re-election, Gardner quietly left the White House at a point when, the *Times* noted, "the war in Vietnam was increasingly occupying the president, and the nation's domestic problems were relegated to a lower priority, as reflected in budget cuts."

This was the long, sad story of the Democratic Party in the postwar years. It might see a New Frontier on the horizon, or imagine a Great Society, but it never really got around the generals and the profiteers of the military-industrial complex. It might grasp at the promise of hope and change, but it was invariably derailed by the campaign donors and consultants who counseled that it would not do to invoke the hatred of Wall Street, as FDR once had, or to propose, as Henry Wallace did, that instead of an "American Century" what was really needed was "the century of the common man." And, yet, on that morning in 2018, as I wandered across the barnyard where a young Henry Wallace came to recognize the great possibility of the American experiment, I felt as if the Democratic Party that Wallace championed, the morally driven and future-oriented party he imagined in 1945, might yet emerge.

"Change is on the way"

The midterm elections of the previous month had produced a striking rebuke to Donald Trump and Trumpism. Wisconsin, Michigan and Pennsylvania, the three states where Trump had built his Electoral College win while losing the popular vote in 2016, had all elected Democratic governors. Democrats now controlled the House of Representatives. And the Democrats who were coming to Washington promised more than just a shift from "R" to "D." Before the 2018 elections, one of the most dynamic of the new members, Massachusetts's Ayanna Pressley, had promised that "change is on the way," a show of respect for the #ChangeCantWait calculus of the millions of young voters, people of color and women who organized for the Democrats in 2018. Their sense of urgency helped Pressley displace an older Democratic incumbent in a primary that drew national attention, as part of a transformational moment that ushered into Congress a new generation of intersectional activists—among them Alexandria Ocasio-Cortez from New York, Rashida Tlaib from Michigan and Ilhan Omar from Minnesota. They had been given a charge not merely to dissent against Trump but to present a governing alternative, and they outlined this alternative along with progressives who had taken leadership positions in the Congressional Progressive Caucus: Ro Khanna from California, Pramila Jayapal from Washington and Mark Pocan from Wisconsin. They said they had been elected to enact a $15-an-hour minimum wage, expand health-care guarantees, end price-gouging by pharmaceutical corporations, avert austerity, protect immigrants and revoke blank checks for military interventions. Trump still had the White House. Mitch McConnell still ran the Senate. The Democratic mandate was not overwhelming. But it was real. And it was more than sufficient to frame the debate going forward.

That debate would, necessarily, involve the future of the Democratic Party. Bernie Sanders had assured this would be the case in 2016, with a presidential bid that unsettled not just Hillary Clinton's campaign strategists but the entire Beltway establishment.

Sanders amused the crowds that showed up to launch his second bid by recalling: "During our 2016 campaign, when we brought forth our progressive agenda we were told that our ideas were 'radical,' and 'extreme.' We were told that Medicare for All, a $15-an-hour minimum wage, free tuition at public colleges and universities, aggressively combating climate change, demanding that the wealthy start paying their fair share of taxes, were all concepts that the American people would never accept. Well, three years have come and gone. And, as a result of millions of Americans standing up and fighting back, all of these policies and more are now supported by a majority of Americans."

Campaigning as a democratic socialist, Sanders had in 2015 and 2016 jump-started the ideological discourse in a party and nation where the "s" word for decades was relegated to the fringe. Sanders's identification as a socialist was not a liability in 2016. It was a strength. It made him an intellectually exciting contender who addressed America's anxieties—not merely with the solutions he proposed but in the way he talked about battling "oligarchy" and "plutocracy" and "the billionaire class." At a time when Americans were sick and tired of the political "competition" between right-wing dogma and centrist double talk, Sanders focused on existential questions and provided essential answers.

In 2016, the candidate who was borrowing from the playbooks of the Scandinavian social democrats, as well as from Eugene Victor Debs and the Socialist Party mayors who once ran cities like Milwaukee, won twenty-three Democratic primary and caucus contests. Sanders's incipient revolution extended beyond the nomination fight. Twenty-eight-year-old Alexandria Ocasio-Cortez's victory over Joe Crowley, a ten-term incumbent who was the fourth-ranking Democrat in the House, was arguably New York's most remarkable congressional election result since thirty-one-year-old Elizabeth Holtzman narrowly beat House Judiciary Committee chairman Emanuel Celler in a 1972 Democratic primary that was all about war and peace, reform and rebellion. It wasn't even close in 2018. Ocasio-Cortez won 57.5 to 42.5, despite the fact that Crowley overwhelmingly outspent her and enjoyed support from almost every top-ranking Democrat in New York as well as the Working Families Party and leading progressives in Washington.

The success of a young working-class woman who had worked for the Sanders campaign illustrated the volatility within a Democratic Party, where too many leaders failed to recognize the intense yearning for economic and social change among its own base and among the millions of young voters who could be rallied to the party. "We were so clear about our values," Ocasio-Cortez said. "We were always naming what we wanted to accomplish." She told voters: "In the wealthiest nation in the world, working families shouldn't have to struggle. It's time for a New York that's good for the many. I am an educator, organizer, Democratic Socialist and born-and-raised New Yorker running to champion working families in Congress. This movement for Congress is about education and health care; it's about housing, jobs, justice and civil rights. It's about preparing for the future of our environment, energy and infrastructure. It's about championing the dignity of our neighbors. And it's about getting money out of politics."

That upfront referencing of her democratic socialism signaled that Ocasio-Cortez was a different kind of candidate. Asked by *Vogue* about what drew her to DSA, she said that what she found was that "every time I saw myself showing up for something that was important to my community, when I was one of the many people who showed up in Union Square for the 100-day vigil after Hurricane Maria, DSA was there. Every time I was joining my brothers and sisters in the Movement for Black Lives, DSA was there. When I saw these actions, it was like, OK, this is clearly an extension of our own community." She added:

> When we talk about the word socialism, I think what it really means is just democratic participation in our economic dignity, and our economic, social and racial dignity. It is about direct representation and people actually having power and stake over their economic and social wellness, at the end of the day. To me, what socialism means is to guarantee a basic level of dignity. It's asserting the value of saying that the America we want and the

America that we are proud of is one in which all children can access a dignified education. It's one in which no person is too poor to have the medicines they need to live. It's to say that no individual's civil rights are to be violated. And it's also to say that we need to really examine the historical inequities that have created much of the inequalities—both in terms of economics and social and racial justice—because they are intertwined. This idea of, like, race or class is a false choice. Even if you wanted to separate those two things, you can't separate the two, they are intrinsically and inextricably tied. There is no other force, there is no other party, there is no other real ideology out there right now that is asserting the minimum elements necessary to lead a dignified American life.

In another time, Ocasio-Cortez might have opted for a third-party candidacy. The hope of breaking the grip of the Democratic-Republican duopoly and opening up American politics to multiparty democracy has often attracted able and idealistic young candidates. These candidacies have raised issues and influenced the major parties. But they have only rarely prevailed on Election Day—and usually only in the handful of states where ballot laws and election procedures have been liberal enough to create an opening for a broader politics. But in 2018, AOC saw her opening inside the Democratic Party. And she was not alone. Across the country, hundreds of first-time candidates won 2018 Democratic primaries as members and allies of DSA, or as Justice Democrats, as bold progressives, muscular liberals, unapologetic leftists and proud radicals. Some pushed beyond the boundaries of the two-party system, as Greens and Socialist Party stalwarts. Others won as "fusion" candidates associated with the Working Families Party in states such as New York, where the WFP frequently fused with the Democrats. Up in Vermont, Lieutenant Governor David Zuckerman, a veteran activist in that state's Progressive Party, won the Democratic primary and secured election as a

Progressive/Democrat. This was not quite the Popular Front, but something seemed to be changing.

After 30 years of globalization, 20 years of digital revolution and decades of automation, with climate change posing an existential threat and inequality surging, the United States was at a critical juncture. The Trump administration had crystallized long-simmering concerns about the rightward drift of the Republican Party, and of an American Fascism of the sort Henry Wallace had warned about. Democrats' nostalgia for the party's managerial days seemed absurd to a rising generation of activists who sought a bolder politics. They were no longer prepared to defer to the party establishment. The old tears, the old cautions, the old words and labels, were being rejected.

Josh Mound argued early in 2016 in the *New Republic* that "the Democrats' belief that they needed to steer clear of McGovernism, assuming it was ever correct, now looks increasingly misguided. With each passing decade, the types of voters drawn to McGovern's 1972 campaign have become a larger and larger share of the American electorate, while the issues championed by McGovern have become more and more salient." To Mound, it was "hard to view the demographic trends of both the Democratic Party's electoral coalition and the country as a whole as anything other than 'George McGovern's Revenge.' The U.S. is well on its way to becoming majority nonwhite, while the support of people of color, women, and gays and lesbians —the political alliance mocked by conservative Democrats at the '72 convention—have become crucial to the victory of any Democratic candidate. Likewise, it's clear in retrospect that the seemingly quixotic appeal of McGovernism to white-collar workers was part of a longer trend in both the composition of the American workforce and the Democratic coalition. Whereas many at the time assumed that social liberalism was the only factor attracting white-collar workers to McGovern, the continued 'proletarianization' of many service-sector workers makes clear in retrospect that McGovern's economic populism was key, too. From the vantage point of 2016, McGovern's message on economic inequality and the political power of the rich seems prophetic."

But that is just part of the radical prophecy Democrats need to borrow from the past. When McGovern spoke at the dedication of the Henry A. Wallace Room in the U.S. Department of Agriculture's headquarters in Washington in 1999, he recalled that he had won the 1972 Democratic nomination with a "similar platform" to that of Wallace. He was right about that. Just as Wallace had said in 1944 that "the future belongs to those who go down the line unswervingly for the liberal principles of both political democracy and economic democracy regardless of race, color or religion," so McGovern spoke to the Democratic convention of 1972 in a similar language:

> Together we will call America home to the ideals that nourished us from the beginning.
>
> From secrecy and deception in high places: come home, America.
>
> From military spending so wasteful that it weakens our nation: come home, America.
>
> From the entrenchment of special privileges in tax favoritism; from the waste of idle lands to the joy of useful labor; from the prejudice based on race and sex; from the loneliness of the aging poor and the despair of the neglected sick: come home, America.
>
> Come home to the affirmation that we have a dream. Come home to the conviction that we can move our country forward.

McGovernism does not seem so radical today. Nor do the preachments of Henry Wallace about racial and gender equity, about political and economic democracy and about a proper balancing of budget priorities so that the cross of iron might not hang too heavily around the neck of humanity. This, of course, is the point at which we find ourselves, asking the question that FDR and his 1940 Republican challenger, Wendell Willkie, asked, that Henry Wallace kept asking after both of his political compatriots had died too young: can we win the peace as surely as we won the war against Adolf Hitler's Nazism and Benito Mussolini's fascism? Can we see off the threat of American fascism? Can we, as Wallace proposed in the language of the prophets, do all to wrestle against the rulers of the darkness in the world, against spiritual wickedness in high places?

The Folly of Surrender

The cautioners and the compromisers will always be present, reminding us that Wallace was rejected and McGovern was defeated, and they will extend the list to include all the others who have failed to usher in the next politics of a nation where polling tells us that ever-increasing numbers of Americans believe that the United States has veered disastrously off course. The surrender caucus is right about the past, but not about the future. Necessary change always begins in failure. The abolitionist Liberty Party of the 1840s never won more than 2.3 percent of the vote for its presidential nominee, yet it gave way to the Free Soil Party and then to the Republicans who would win the presidency in the 1860s. Would we tell Abraham Lincoln not to try because James Birney was rejected? The Progressive Party of 1924 won just 16 percent of the national vote and carried only Robert M. La Follette's home state of Wisconsin. Would we tell Franklin Roosevelt not to bid on a platform that drew liberally from that of the Progressives, because La Follette was defeated? The conservative cause crashed and burned in 1964. Would we tell Ronald Reagan not to try in 1976 or again in 1980 because Barry Goldwater never got near the presidency?

The notion is absurd. And it is equally absurd to write off the visionary figures of the postwar left because they were prematurely antiracist or too certain that détente would come, because they believed that budgets were moral documents and dared to argue for a "policy of placing human rights above property rights," because they declared, as Henry Wallace did, that "I am committed to using the power and prestige of the United States to help the peoples of the world, not their exploiters." At some point, the Democratic Party must recognize that while the arc of the moral universe is long, it does bend toward justice. And that the passage of time evolves our politics toward a point where it is entirely plausible—and even more entirely necessary—to get on the right side of the future.

This is about more than a single issue or a platform. It is about vision. The New Deal was not one initiative, it was thousands of attempts to overcome the disaster created by economic royalists and their Tory allies in Congress. It was about a willingness to try and fail, and to try again and succeed. It was a different discipline from the politics it replaced. New Dealers said it was possible to master Wall Street and the markets, and then they said it was possible to defeat Hitler and fascism. And when the greatest war was done, they proposed a future of Four Freedoms and an Economic Bill of Rights. Their vision was true in their time, but their party yielded to caution and compromised its vision. Yet the vision survives and is, in many senses, more popular now than it has ever been. What is unknown is whether the party that abandoned the New Deal vision in the postwar era will continue the politics of caution and compromise.

That is *the* issue, not a single issue but every issue wrapped up in one. Henry Wallace knew it. It is why he spoke in sweeping terms, of creating tens of millions of jobs, of ending poverty, of breaking the grip of fascism abroad and of seeing off the threat of a homegrown variation, of building a future where peace and prosperity were not political promises but the foundation on which a better world might be built.

The New New Deals

On the day before I visited Wallace's farm in Adair County, I had traveled to a town an hour up the road, Jefferson, with

Ro Khanna. One of the newest members of Congress, Khanna worked in the Obama White House and then ran against a Democratic incumbent in 2016. His win, in a Silicon Valley district, anticipated the victories of Ocasio-Cortez and Pressley, and, like them, he arrived with a determination to push the limits. Khanna was in Jefferson to announce a plan to bring tech investment, training and high-paying jobs to the community of 4,150 in rural Greene County. "The digital revolution is one that every community should and can participate in," Khanna told local leaders who had gathered with tech industry executives the congressman had convinced to support an investment initiative that the *Guardian* imagined "could be a blueprint for revitalizing other rural communities."

Wallace would have loved what Khanna was doing—not merely because of the commitment to Wallace's beloved Iowa but because of the ambition of a project that said no corner of the United States should be left behind. This was New Deal thinking, and Khanna and I talked a lot about FDR and his second vice president during our drive across Iowa. But we also talked about whether the Democratic Party could again be so ambitious and visionary. "The question is: What is the Democratic Party? When we go to Youngstown, Ohio, when we go to Beckley, West Virginia, when we go to Paintsville, Kentucky, what are we saying the vision is for those kids to participate in the economic future? I believe that the answer has to be: partly with a role for government with the private sector to invest in new-energy industries, to make massive investments in fiber and broadband, massive investments in new vocational schools and expanding universities and making universities debt-free. People say it can't be done. South Korea's got 70 percent graduation! College graduates! And their broadband is huge! So the government, in cooperation with the economy and in cooperation with cities, can create that kind of investment."

Khanna was talking about a new New Deal. Instead of a $1.5 trillion tax cut for billionaires and corporations, he was arguing for the twenty-first-century equivalent of the Works Progress Administration, the Public Works Administration and the National Youth Administration.

"If you care about the forgotten Americans," Khanna said, "you would use the funding to build those cities, to invest, to make college debt-free, to expand universities across this country, to put tons of money into vocational and educational apprenticeships, to have fiber and broadband all across America. We could transform America's heartland for $1.5 trillion. ... We're going to go forward. The question is whether the future is going to include the communities that have been forgotten, that have been left behind by both parties. Democrats should be talking about what we're going to do to create economic opportunity in all these communities. We should be saying, 'We want to bring the future to you.'"

This notion of bringing the future to you was not new. This was the Rural Electrification Act of 1936, here updated for the twenty-first century. This was the sweeping "no one left behind" program that inspired Woody Guthrie to sing of how "your power is turning our darkness to dawn." The idea of big, bold government plans to wire up America so that everyone could share in progress was once embraced by democratic socialists and self-identified "progressive capitalists" alike. They recognized, as Wallace did, that "no private industry should have the right to bid unfairly for private profit against government and public necessity." The recognition faded over time, as Democrats got scared of the word "socialism," and then by the word "liberal." In the aftermath of the 2016 election, when Bernie Sanders and his supporters put democratic socialism back on the agenda in the United States, the discourse about how to address the failures of monopoly capitalism opened up. Conservative commentators noted the similarities between reforms proposed by democratic socialists like Sanders and progressives like Massachusetts senator Elizabeth Warren, who spoke of breaking up monopolies, encouraging public options and establishing "Accountable

Capitalism." Neither Warren nor Sanders objected. Rather, they stood together on debate stages and defended many of the same premises—just as socialists and New Dealers did in Wallace's day. The idea of great public works projects undertaken not to enrich investors but to empower citizens returned to the public debate as the 2010s gave way to the 2020s—not in the vapid discussions of infrastructure pitched by political charlatans as a meeting ground where Republicans and Democrats could agree to bid out contracts to road builders, but in the serious talk of Sanders, Warren and other 2020 Democratic presidential candidates about using the power of the federal government to achieve a measure of equity. Warren's "I have a plan for that" politics echoed the blend of technocratic idealism and practical economics that Wallace sought to advance in his stack of New Deal–era books and pamphlets: *New Frontiers* (1934), *America Must Choose* (1934), *Technology, Corporations, and the General Welfare* (1937) and, ultimately, *Sixty Million Jobs* (1945). Nowhere was that more true than when she began to speak of realizing the full promise of the digital age.

Warren asserted that "both corporate America and leaders in Washington have turned their backs on the people living in our rural communities and prioritized the interests of giant companies and Wall Street instead." As a 2020 presidential contender she barnstormed across Iowa with a promise of an $85 billion federal grant program for nonprofits and local governments that seek to build independent fiber networks and provide low-cost broadband Internet services. "I will make sure every home in America has a fiber broadband connection at a price families can afford," she declared. "That means publicly owned and operated networks—and no giant ISPs running away with taxpayer dollars."

Rooting out the corruption that guides public dollars to the profiteers was a prime theme of Warren's candidacy as she rose in the Democratic polls of 2019, and she even had a plan to take on the blank-checkbook militarism that Wallace had warned about. "The coziness between defense lobbyists, Congress and the Pentagon—what former President Dwight D. Eisenhower called the military-industrial complex—tilts countless decisions, big and small, away from legitimate national security interests, and toward the desires of giant corporations that thrive off taxpayer dollars," Warren said. "It's past time to cut our bloated defense budget. Defense contractor influence is a big part of how we ended up with a Pentagon budget that will cost more this year than Ronald Reagan spent at the height of the Cold War. That's more than the federal government spends on education, medical research, border security, housing, the FBI, disaster relief, the State Department, foreign aid—everything else in the discretionary budget put together. What's worse, it's how we end up spending money on the wrong things—too much investment in the technologies of the past, and not enough focus on the needs of the future."

Ro Khanna, in collaboration with Sanders, took the argument further. "We need Democrats clearly speaking out against the last 15 years of foreign policy and saying, 'This is not in our national interest,'" he said. "If we're mealy-mouthed about it, if we don't have a clear distinction, then people will default to what they perceive as strength. Gandhi was strong, King was strong, Mandela was strong, because they had the strength of conviction to overcome the strength of force. But if you don't have that all-consuming, authentic strength of conviction, people will default to the easier, 'Well, let's just go with the strong man.' And I don't think the Democratic Party has really had that—in the Congress, at least—that passion and conviction to say, 'We've got an alternative vision for foreign policy, which is actually more consistent with our ideals and far more consistent with the world that the millennials want for the twenty-first century.'"

This, he explained, was one of the reasons he would back Sanders for president. The senator was not just arguing, as a number of Democratic contenders were, for cracking down on the corruption of empire in general, and the military-industrial complex in particular. He was talking about a whole new framework.

"Terrorism is a very real threat, which requires robust diplomatic efforts, intelligence cooperation with allies and partners, and yes, sometimes military action," Sanders acknowledged in a spring 2019 article he wrote for *Foreign Affairs* headlined "Ending America's Endless War." "But as an organizing framework, the global war on terror has been a disaster for our country. Orienting U.S. national-security strategy around terrorism essentially allowed a few thousand violent extremists to dictate the foreign policy of the most powerful nation on earth. We responded to terrorists by giving them exactly what they wanted."

Sanders wrote in concluding the article:

The American people don't want endless war. Neither do we want a foreign policy that is based on the logic that led to those wars and corroded our democracy: a logic that privileges military tools over diplomatic ones, aggressive unilateralism over multilateral engagement, and acquiescence to our undemocratic partners over the pursuit of core interests alongside democratic allies who truly share our values. We have to view the terrorism threat through the proper scope, rather than allowing it to dominate our view of the world. The time has come to envision a new form of American engagement: one in which the United States leads not in warmaking but in bringing people together to find shared solutions to our shared concerns. American power should be measured not by our ability to blow things up, but by our ability to build on our common humanity, harnessing our technology and enormous wealth to create a better life for all people.

"We have to rethink politics in America"

I went with Sanders to Wallace's birthplace on a rainy afternoon in the summer of 2019.

The two of us were in a room where the windows looked out upon cornfields and wind turbines—an image, I suspect, Wallace would have adored. We paused to consider a photo of FDR and his vice president, beaming in delight with each other during a 1940 campaign appearance; the man Wallace described as "the greatest liberal in the history of the United States" and the vice president who sacrificed his power, career and proper place in American history for the liberal vision that the Democratic Party had abandoned.

"You seem to have made it a mission of this campaign to renew the Economic Bill of Rights, to take this seventy-five-year-old idea and bring it to the present," I said. "Why?"

Sanders started answering with specifics, references to proposals for a Medicare for All single-payer health-care plan and tuition-free college. Then he stopped himself. "I want to start again," he said. "The answer is that we have to rethink politics in America. We have to ask questions that the establishment does not want us to ask. What Roosevelt said back in 1944 is we have a Bill of Rights, which protects our political freedoms, and that's very important. But we have nothing to guarantee economic freedoms. So the question in essence that Roosevelt was asking is: if today you're making $9 an hour, if today you have no health care, if today you can't afford a higher education, how free are you really? And that's the kind of discussion that we need. What does freedom mean?"

I asked Sanders how he answered that question. "Freedom does not mean that you're sleeping out on the streets," he replied. "Freedom does not mean that you're $100,000 in debt because you went to college. Freedom does not mean that you can't go to the doctor when you're sick. So we have to redefine what freedom means, and that's what fighting for an Economic Bill of Rights is about. All that we are saying—and this is not radical, some of it already exists in other countries around the world—is this: Health care is a human right. OK? Then the United States has got to join every other major country in guaranteeing that.

If you work 40 hours a week, and you can't make it on $10 an hour, then we have to raise that minimum wage to at least $15 an hour and make sure that workers can join a union. All over this country now, we have a massive housing crisis. It's not just half a million people sleeping out on the streets. It's people paying 50 to 55 percent of their limited incomes on housing. Freedom means that you have decent housing at a cost that you can afford. Freedom means that, when you turn on your water faucet, the water that comes out is not toxic but drinkable."

I looked up at a *Time* magazine cover from September 1940, a little less than a year before Sanders was born, with an iconic portrait, *Wallace of Iowa* by Grant Wood—the *American Gothic* painter who was born a few hundred miles away in Anamosa, Iowa. It was from a time when the media portrayed Wallace as a heroic figure. But the dynamic contender of one election year could be portrayed as the threat of the next, and the also-ran of the one after that. I reminded the senator that Wallace's advocacy for an Economic Bill of Rights had run afoul of the segregationists in the Democratic Party. "They had segregationists leading the party!" Sanders interrupted.

"What Roosevelt understood, is that you have entrenched economic interests—he called them economic royalists; we call them the billionaire class—who will do anything that they can to protect their incredible wealth and their incredible power," Sanders said. "So one of the points of this campaign is to ask the questions the corporate media will not ask, of course, and Congress does not discuss. Where is the power in America? Why aren't things changing? How do you end up with three people owning more wealth than the bottom half of America? Those issues we don't discuss. And I want to force discussions on those issues because I've said it a million times and I'll say it again: No president, not Bernie Sanders or anybody else, can do it alone. We can't transform this economy, this government, unless millions of people are involved in an unprecedented grassroots political movement to challenge the power structure of this country."

It was not necessary to approve or disapprove of Sanders's candidacy to recognize that to be a proper prescription. This is what Democrats must do if they hope to be more than just an electoral machine, if they hope to transform our politics in ways that might finally address militarism and inequality, racism and xenophobia, the automation of the economy and the climate crisis. Democrats have to think as Roosevelt and Wallace thought, when they spoke of a New Deal and Four Freedoms and an Economic Bill of Rights and "winning the peace" with a global vision. And they have to do so with an understanding that addressing existential issues with bold responses is the best way to avert the threat of the American authoritarianism that the 33rd vice president began warning about three years before the 45th president was born.

"It's not over"

So why be optimistic? Why not give in to the pessimism that has shaped so much of the postwar era? I found some of the answer in Orient, but not all of it. This is because, while the story of Henry Wallace is much associated with those Iowa cornfields, it also passes through Detroit, where, in the summer of 1943, he made the connection between the struggle against European fascism and "an Americanized fascism." When I visited Detroit 75 years after Wallace raised the issue of American fascism, in the summer of 2018, I found no memorials recalling the former vice president. But I heard an echo of the New Deal language he spoke, of the overarching faith in the prospect of making real the promise of these United States. I was traveling with Alexandria Ocasio-Cortez, as she campaigned for progressives in the state's Democratic primaries. The days were hectic. We did not get enough time to discuss things in much depth. So we agreed to meet at a café in a predominantly Arab-American neighborhood of Dearborn. It was a little bit before midnight.

AOC had been going all day. She was tired, yet she still wanted to talk. When I asked her how she hoped to see the Democratic Party change, she blended the language of the past and the future, speaking of "a twenty-first-century New Deal" and a new New Deal Coalition.

"There is a hunger for an assertive, strong, ambitious, defined effort to establish and advance economic and social and racial justice for working-class Americans," she told me. "That requires a plan. It requires ambitious ideas. People I think are searching for those champions, searching for that movement. I think [the way we do that is by] linking all of the individual movements that we see happening across the country and taking up those causes as our own. Taking up Ferguson as our own. Taking up Flint as our own. The Bronx as our own. Rikers as our own. Rural America as our own. I think that's what it's about, and that's why it needs to be a movement."

Could it be done again? Could it be done better? Could this talk of a twenty-first-century New Deal move from the pages of a platform to the program of a government and then to the reality of a nation? Could the movement become the Democratic Party, and could that party transform America? Ocasio-Cortez recognized that the New Deal had fallen short in too many ways. But she refused to believe that the spirit of the thing, the striving energy that FDR embraced at his best and that Henry Wallace never surrendered, had died. If rural electrification was possible, then why not a Green New Deal? "I want us to be the party that wired, and electrified, literally, the nation," she said, as the weariness of the late hour dissipated. "Because it's not over. We did that. And now we have a lot more to do."

Democrats once dreamed the biggest dreams, of thwarting the politics of hatred and seeing off the threat of American fascism, of achieving economic and social and racial justice and peace and prosperity. This is history. But it need not be history alone. Just blocks from where a Democratic vice president of the United States threw down the gauntlet and proposed a fight against racism and inequality that would finally extend the American dream to all Americans, here was a young Democratic leader who spoke of the New Deal as it should be spoken of. Not as some majestic memory, but as a touchstone. Beaming now, filled with energy and excitement, Alexandria Ocasio-Cortez spoke of forging a party that would again extend from the bottom up, that would be "first and foremost accountable to working-class people again, and to marginalized people." She looked up toward the North Star above the great American city of Detroit. "I don't want that to be something that we just talk about, but something that we are about," she said. "I want us to be *that* party again!"

Acknowledgements

I tweet a lot about history, especially history as it relates to the present. Over the past few years, I've frequently tweeted quotes from Henry Wallace's 1944 essay on the dangers of American fascism. People often reacted with surprise that a vice president of the United States would say such things. I mentioned this to my longtime editor at Verso, Andrew Hsiao. That's how this book got started. Andy was the perfect editor: encouraging, cajoling, demanding and enthusiastic. The same goes for the Verso crew and associated comrades, especially patient Mark Martin and copy-editor extraordinaire Jeffrey Klein.

I also got the best encouragement from my longtime cowriter Bob McChesney, my *Nation* editor and friend Katrina vanden Heuvel, historian Paul Buhle, bookseller Russell Freedman, Willard Olesen of Greenfield, Iowa, and innumerable grassroots Democrats and independent progressives who got excited when I said I was writing a book on where the party went off the rails. My wife, Mary Bottari, put up with incessant chattering about rallies in Detroit and the 1944 convention and why George McGovern and Jesse Jackson were right. Mareme asked generous questions. Whitman was a great traveling partner on the way to the Wallace farm in Orient, Iowa; and she kept Bernie Sanders entertained when we got there.

A Note on Sources

Henry Wallace died before my time, but I have been lucky enough over the years to meet a number of people who campaigned for him, and even a few who knew him. When I was a young labor writer, Wallace's name came up frequently, especially when I was interviewing activists with historic left-wing unions such as the United Electrical, Radio and Machine Workers of America and the International Longshore and Warehouse Union. Many years ago, when I did a series of oral histories with veterans of the Abraham Lincoln Brigade that fought in the Spanish Civil War, Wallace's name was invariably a part of conversations about the postwar activism of Steve Nelson, Clarence Kailin and others. These conversations inform this book, as do discussions about Wallace's 1948 campaign with Jack O'Dell, a brilliant civil rights activist and progressive campaigner across many generations (who died at 96, when I was finishing this book), and with Annette Rubinstein, the great chronicler of the New York City left, again across many generations. These conversations and interviews helped me to understand what Wallace meant to his supporters. I had many illuminating conversations over the years with George McGovern, who, especially in his later years, shared his insights as a young Wallace supporter and, just as importantly, as an able historian of the Democratic Party in which he made a bit of history of his own. I've enjoyed extended conversations with Noam Chomsky and others who recalled their youthful support of the 1948 Wallace campaign; as well as folks like former Milwaukee mayor Frank Zeidler,

Wisconsin state representative Mary Lou Munts and others, who recalled why they most definitely were not Wallace backers that year. In researching and writing a history of Madison, Wisconsin's *Capital Times* newspaper (with my colleague Dave Zweifel), I came to understand the journey of those who championed Wallace in 1944 and opposed him in 1948—a group that included the paper's founder and editor, William T. Evjue.

I never thought of writing a book about Wallace until several years ago, however, and it was then that I began a more thorough exploration of the remarkable speeches, books, articles, pamphlets, letters and assorted papers that form the underpinnings of this narrow examination of his story. The most important of the books are those written by Wallace. Most of them are short and to the point. Wallace is best understood as a pamphleteer, in the tradition of Tom Paine and the other founders he revered. The best of his writing and thinking, and that which is most relevant to this book, can be found in *The Century of the Common Man* (1943), *Democracy Reborn* (1944) and *Sixty Million Jobs* (1945). His 1948 campaign book, *Toward World Peace*, is valuable as an expression of the idealism that he brought to that campaign, and "Where I Was Wrong," the sober 1952 essay in which he described his growing disillusionment with the Soviet Union, is an instructive read. So, too, is Wallace's May 14, 1956, *Life* magazine essay, "Henry Wallace Tells of His Political Odyssey." Three Wallace books from his tenure in FDR's cabinet, *New Frontiers* (1934), *America Must Choose* (1934) and *Statesmanship and Religion* (1934), are worth a look. My favorite Wallace book is his 1936 "inquiry into the general welfare" titled *Whose Constitution?* It brings the reader deep into New Deal–era debates about where political and economic democracy might intersect. (Wallace books were generally published by Reynal and Hitchcock, the New York publishing firm founded in 1933 by Eugene Reynal and Curtice Hitchcock, and that in 1948 became associated with Harcourt, Brace.)

I was able to review different editions of Wallace's books, and many of Wallace's shorter pamphlets from the 1940s (some of which are now hard to come by), thanks to Russell Freedman, the co-owner of Second Life Books in Lanesborough, Massachusetts. After I ran into Russell in the fall of 2018 and told him about this project, a large package arrived at my home, with a simple note from Russell that read, "These belong with you." In it were the books and pamphlets of the Wallace canon, as well as notes from the former vice president and assorted ephemera. I am eternally thankful to Russell.

In addition to the books and pamphlets, Wallace kept an extraordinary diary, which was edited by the great historian John Morton Blum and published, in part, as *The Price of Vision: The Diary of Henry A. Wallace, 1942–1946* (Houghton Mifflin, 1973). Blum's commentaries on the man and his era were invaluable to me. So, too, was an extended essay on the diaries, "A Loner Who Believed in the Common Man," by Cabell Phillips, which was published as a *New York Times Book Review* section on October 14, 1973.

In preparing this book, I reviewed materials from a number of collections of Wallace's papers. The best of these is maintained by the University of Iowa Libraries as the Henry A. Wallace Collection. (The digital collection, at http://wallace.lib.uiowa .edu, is a superb resource.) The Library of Congress collection in Washington is valuable and so, too, is the New Deal collection at the Franklin D. Roosevelt Library and Museum in Hyde Park, New York. The FDR Library is home to the Henry A. Wallace Visitor and Educational Center. Finally, I made several trips to the Wallace farm near Orient, Iowa, which maintains a small collection and is a delight to visit.

Of the many books on Henry Wallace, three are, to my mind, essential. The first is *American Dreamer: A Life of Henry A. Wallace* (W.W. Norton & Co., 2000) by John C. Culver and John Hyde. This book introduced a new generation of Americans to Wallace. I share the view of John Kenneth Galbraith, who called it "an indispensable document on both the man and the time." For my purposes, it was invaluable for its detail and for its analysis—especially of the power struggles within the Roosevelt administration during Wallace's vice presidency. Also of immeasurable value is Russell Lord's *The Wallaces of Iowa* (Houghton Mifflin, 1947), a meticulously researched book that is rich in insight and perspective. Finally, I relied a great deal on Curtis D. MacDougall's *Gideon's Army* (Marzani & Munsell, 1965) for details of the struggles Wallace engaged in and for a sense of the times. MacDougall's personal reflections as well as his conversations and correspondence with Wallace and other key figures provide a touchstone for anyone who wants to understand the latter stages of Wallace's vice presidency, his wrangling with Truman and his presidential run.

In many senses, the same can be said for Norman D. Markowitz's thoroughly researched and thoughtful book *The Rise and Fall of the People's Century* (Free Press, 1973). Markowitz's insights into Wallace and the left are especially valuable. Thomas W. Devine's *Henry Wallace's 1948 Presidential Campaign and the Future of Postwar Liberalism* (University of North Carolina Press, 2013) covers the same period from a very different perspective, yet offers a valuable set of insights—as does "Uncommon Man: The Strange Life of Henry Wallace, the New Deal Visionary," a fine essay by Alex Ross, which was inspired by the book and appeared October 7, 2013, in the *New Yorker*. The other books that provided both details and insight are *Prophet in Politics: Henry A. Wallace and the War Years, 1940–1965* (Iowa University Press, 1970), by Edward and Frederick Schapsmeier, and *Henry A. Wallace: Quixotic Crusade 1948* (Syracuse University Press, 1960), by Karl M. Schmidt.

Wallace's radical politics continue to inspire analysis and interpretation, and controversy. A few years back, the former vice president was the subject of considerable interest and speculation based on the arguments made by Oliver Stone and Peter Kuznick in the book *The Untold History of the United*

States (Gallery Books, 2012) and the accompanying much-watched and much-discussed Showtime series. I use the reaction to the project in Chapter 1 of this book to illustrate the way in which Wallace continues to inspire ideological passion and intellectual fascination.

This has always been the case, as I discovered when reviewing the *New York Times* and *Time* magazine archives from the 1930s to the 1960s, with regard to Wallace. Both publications tangled with him. But they covered him thoroughly and the reporting they did informed my research and this book. I also reviewed and valued coverage of Wallace by the *Nation*, the *New Republic* and a number of other publications that are referenced in the book and in this essay.

Finally, in preparing the later chapters of this book, and in my regular reporting, I have interviewed Bernie Sanders, Elizabeth Warren, Mark Pocan, Pramila Jayapal, Ro Khanna, Alexandria Ocasio-Cortez and other figures mentioned in this book. Many of those interviews have appeared in the *Nation*, the *Capital Times* and the *Progressive*. I have also drawn on published interviews and tapes from interviews done over the years with George McGovern, Jesse Jackson, Tom Hayden, Robert Kastenmeier and a number of the other figures mentioned in these chapters.

Preface

The Howard Zinn quote comes from the essay, "If History Is to Be Creative," which can be found in the book *A Power Governments Cannot Suppress* (City Lights, 2006). The Wallace Global Fund's very thoughtful and thorough website can be found at http://wgf.org/henry-wallace. Eisenhower's quote on the perils of a right-wing Republican Party was included in a November 8, 1954, letter to his brother, Edgar Newton Eisenhower, which can be found in *The Papers of Dwight David*

Eisenhower, ed. L. Galambos and D. van Ee. Wallace's speech to the 1944 Democratic National Convention, which is examined in greater detail in Chapter 5, can be found in the collection managed by the Library of Congress Manuscript Division in Washington, D.C. The Claude Lévi-Strauss book *Tristes Tropiques* (Librairie Plon, 1955) was published in English by Hutchinson & Co. in 1961. It was a favorite of Alexander Cockburn's.

1. The Prophetic Politics of Henry Wallace

A number of fine books reflect on the role Pete Seeger played in the Wallace campaign, including David K. Dunaway's *How Can I Keep from Singing: The Ballad of Pete Seeger* (McGraw Hill, 1981) and Alec Wilkinson's *The Protest Singer: An Intimate Portrait of Pete Seeger* (Knopf, 2009). Susanna Reich's *Stand Up and Sing! Pete Seeger, Folk Music and the Path to Justice* (Bloomsbury, 2017) is also instructive. In the notes for the CD set *Songs for Political Action*, Ronald Cohen and Dave Samuelson discuss Seeger's adoption of the song "Passing Through" and how he sang it on the campaign trail in 1948. (I also had an opportunity to interview Pete Seeger several times on his music and his politics.) *Pitchfork* magazine writer Marc Hogan discusses Leonard Cohen's engagement with the song in a November 11, 2016, essay, "7 Covers Leonard Cohen Made His Own." Cohen's best version of the song is heard on the album "Live Songs" (Columbia, 1973). Leonard Cohen attended a number of Jewish summer camps in Quebec, an experience described in Ira B. Nadel's *Various Positions: A Life of Leonard Cohen* (University of Texas Press, 2007) and Sylvie Simmons's *I'm Your Man: The Life of Leonard Cohen* (Ecco, 2013). The FDR quote is from his State of the Union address on January 11, 1944. A fine reflection on the Progressive Party's campaigning in the South and its outreach to African-American voters and supporters of civil rights, "A Rock in a Weary Lan': Paul Robeson's Leadership in 'The Movement' in the Decade before Montgomery" was written by Jack O'Dell for the Freedomways collection *Paul Robeson: The Great Forerunner* (Dodd, Mead, 1965). Martin Duberman's classic biography is *Paul Robeson* (The New Press, 1995). I also appreciate *No Way but This: In Search of Paul Robeson* (Scribe, 2018) by Jeff Sparrow. Wallace's statement on liberalism is found in a speech, "What I Mean by a Liberal Person," which he delivered to an Independent Voters Committee of the Arts and Sciences rally at Madison Square Garden, New York City, September 21, 1944. The Detroit Historical Society tells the story of the "Race Riot of 1943" at https://detroithistorical.org/learn/encyclopedia-of-detroit /race-riot-1943. Wallace delivered his speech "Common Man Economics" to a mass meeting of Detroit labor and civic organizations on July 25, 1943. The Associated Press reported on Wallace's Detroit speech in the July 25, 1943, article "Wallace Assails American Fascists as 'Big Business' Roosevelt Haters." United Press reported July 26, 1943, "Peace Initiative Urged by Wallace On America Now; For 'Common Man' He Asks Full Production, Employment and Security With Democracy for All; Vice President, at Detroit, Accuses 'Fascists' of Trying to Undermine Roosevelt." CBC first broadcast "Flirting with Fascism: America's New Path?" on November 29, 2018. Dwight Macdonald's extended essay "Henry Wallace," which is sharply critical of the former vice president's failure to adopt a sharper anti-Soviet line in the period, appeared in the March–April 1947 edition of the journal *Politics*. Jim Farley's assessments of Wallace (and the vice presidency) are contained in *Jim Farley's Story: The Roosevelt Years* (Pickle Partners, 2017). Lillian Hellman wrote extensively about her association with Wallace and the 1948 campaign in her book *Scoundrel Time* (Little Brown, 1976) and an April 11, 1976, *New York Times* essay, "On Henry Wallace." The great historian of American political campaigns David Pietrusza recounts the Hellman-Hammett story in his superb book *1948: Harry Truman's Improbable Victory and the Year That Transformed America* (Union Square Press, 2011). In that book, he also recounts many sharp assessments of Roosevelt's decision to select Wallace, including that by historian Doris Kearns Goodwin. I have written extensively about third-party politics over the years, on my own and in conjunction with Robert W. McChesney. We reflect on the barriers to third-party campaigns in a number of our books, including *Dollarocracy: How the Money and Media Election Complex Is Destroying America* (Nation Books, 2013). D.D. Guttenplan recounts I.F. Stone's assessment of the Wallace campaign in his excellent book *American Radical: The Life and Times of I.F. Stone* (Farrar, Straus and Giroux, 2009), which features a thoughtful consideration of how the left struggled with that campaign. The Congressional Progressive Caucus's bold infrastructure proposal, entitled a "21st Century New Deal for Jobs" was issued May 25, 2017. I interviewed Ro Khanna on some of these issues as part of an extended conversation on December 8, 2018.

2. Hope in a Time of War

I have written a great deal about Paine over the years, and read even more. My touchstone for considering his legacy is Harvey Kaye's majestic book, *Thomas Paine and the Promise of America* (Hill & Wang, 2006). Kaye is also the author of a brilliant book on FDR, *The Fight for the Four Freedoms: What Made FDR and the Greatest Generation Truly Great* (Simon & Schuster, 2015). Throughout this book, I rely on reports from the *New York Times* and *Time* magazine for background on the events that are referenced in speeches by FDR and others. Roosevelt's February 23, 1942, Fireside Chat was titled, "On the Progress of the War." The University of Virginia's Miller Center has archived it, along with other chats, at millercenter.org.

Freda Kirchwey's columns, which are quoted in a number of chapters, are archived by the *Nation* at thenation.com. Sara Alpern's *Freda Kirchwey: A Woman of the Nation* (Harvard University Press, 1987) reflects at length on the editor's writing on FDR and Wallace, and it informed my understanding of the era. I interviewed H.L. Mitchell many years ago about this period, but my understanding has been informed particularly by Jervis Anderson's essential biography of Randolph, *A. Philip Randolph: A Biographical Portrait* (Harcourt, Brace, Jovanovich, 1973), by the writings of Manning Marable and, more recently, by books such as *Reframing Randolph: Labor, Black Freedom, and the Legacies of A. Philip Randolph* (New York University Press, 2015), which was edited by Andrew E. Kersten and Clarence Lang. For more on Woody Guthrie and World War II, check out *That's Why We're Marching: World War II and the American Folksong Movement* (Smithsonian Folkways Recording, 1996). Norman Markowitz's *The Rise and Fall of the People's Century* is especially useful for insights on the debates among social liberals regarding the harnessing of energy for the postwar era. You can find the FDR Library's resources on the Four Freedoms speech at fdrlibrary.marist.edu. Wallace's remarks on "a lesser or part-time democracy" are found in his "America Tomorrow" speech of July 25, 1943. For a great reflection on La Guardia, check out Michael Winship's "La Guardia's the Name and Boy, Could We Use Him Now: Like Donald Trump, Fiorello La Guardia Was Supremely Self-Confident and Brash, and Loved Publicity. But unlike Trump, This Republican Backed Up His Big Talk with Action and Genuine Concern for His Constituents," which was published October 3, 2016, and can be found at billmoyers.com. There are many fine biographies of Wendell Willkie, including *The Improbable Wendell Willkie: The Businessman Who Saved the Republican Party and His Country, and Conceived a New World Order* (Liveright, 2018) by David Levering Lewis, and Steve Neal's *Dark Horse: A Biography of Wendell Willkie* (University

Press of Kansas, 1989). For this book, I relied heavily on coverage of Willkie by the *New York Times* and *Time* and, most of all, on Willkie's book, *One World* (Simon & Schuster, 1943). Wallace's February 12, 1939, speech was titled "On the Genetic Basis of Democracy." A reflection on its influence can be found in Lord's *The Wallaces of Iowa*. Krock's column on Wallace was published in the *New York Times* of July 23, 1940. The *Times* reported on Wallace and Willkie in a December 18, 1943, article, "Willkie, Wallace See New Freedoms; Better World after the War Is Visualized by Speakers on 'Beyond Victory' Program." *Prefaces to Peace* was published by Simon & Schuster in 1943. Willkie's speech "America Cannot Remove Itself from the World" was delivered January 8, 1941, to the Women's National Republican Club meeting at the Hotel Astor in New York. Howard Jones's assessment of Willkie is found in *Wendell Willkie: Hoosier Internationalist* (Indiana University Press, 1992), which was edited by James H. Madison. For a detailed reflection on the Republican Party's rejection of Willkie, see Roland Snyder's "Wisconsin Ends the Political Career of Wendell Willkie" (*Wisconsin Magazine of History*, Autumn 2004).

3. "You Drew Blood from the Cave Dwellers"

Robert E. Herzstein's *Henry R. Luce, Time, and the American Crusade in Asia* was published by Cambridge University Press in 2005. James Baughman, a friend and mentor, wrote *Henry R. Luce and the Rise of the American News Media* (Twayne Publishers, 1987). Luce's article "The American Century" was published by *Life* on February 17, 1941. Freda Kirchwey and the *Nation* worked closely with the Free World Association, as Sara Alpern recounts in *Freda Kirchwey: A Woman of the Nation*. Wallace's "The Price of Free World Victory" speech was delivered May 8, 1942, at the Commodore Hotel in New York. It was published in many forms, including the short book by the same title (L.B. Fischer, 1942). The writer Dorothy Thompson said it contained "a hard clear streak of Biblical righteousness in Henry Wallace. With it goes humaneness and mercy." Donald Wallace White reflects on reactions to the speech in *The American Century: The Rise and Decline of the United States as a World Power* (Yale University Press, 1999). Blanche Wiesen Cook's extraordinary three-volume biography concludes with *Eleanor Roosevelt, Volume 3: The War Years and After, 1939–1962* (Viking, 2016). Mandalit del Barco produced an excellent reflection on Copland's thinking, "On 'Fanfare for the Common Man,' an Anthem for the American Century," which aired July 19, 2018, on NPR. Russell Lord and Culver and Hyde recount reactions to Wallace's speech, including the pushback within the White House and the debates it inspired. The same authors ably outline the ensuing struggles between Jesse Jones and Wallace, as does Norman Markowitz. FDR's reflection on Allied unity came in his March 1, 1945, "Address to Congress on Yalta." For insight on FDR's approach, I turned to a number of books, including *My Own Story: From Private and Public Papers*, a collection of Roosevelt documents selected by Donald Day, which was published by Routledge in 2017. Roosevelt's 1943 State of the Union address was delivered on January 7. Two useful books on Jones and his wrangling with Wallace are Steven Fenberg's *Unprecedented Power: Jesse Jones, Capitalism, and the Common Good* (Texas A&M University Press, 2011) and Paul Koistinen's *Arsenal of World War II: The Political Economy of American Warfare, 1940–1945* (University Press of Kansas, 2004). I found coverage of these struggles in the *New York Times* useful, as well. Wallace's December 1941 *Atlantic Monthly* article, "Foundations of the Peace," remains one of the outstanding statements of the war's goals. There are many fine collections of Eleanor Roosevelt's wartime essays and speeches; I made use of *What Are We For? The Words and Ideals of Eleanor Roosevelt* (Harper Perennial, 2019). The very good *St. Louis Post-Dispatch* report on the Jones-Wallace conflict appeared

April 14, 1942. *Time* magazine profiled Leo Crowley as "Leo the Lion" on March 23, 1942, and I relied on clippings from the *Capital Times* files to get a fuller picture of this Wisconsinite. Wallace's March 8, 1943, speech to the Conference on Christian Bases of World Order, in Delaware, Ohio, was titled, "Avoid a Third World War." Culver and Hyde recount the reference to "bipartisan American fascism." The Detroit speech, referenced earlier, was titled, "America Tomorrow." The *New York Times* editorial, "Mr. Wallace on 'Fascists,'" appeared July 27, 1943. A fine description of FDR's reaction to the speech, including the reference to "cave dwellers," can be found in the notes for Blum's edited edition of Wallace's diary, *The Price of Vision.*

4. The Fight against American Fascism

The original version of Henry Wallace's article "The Danger of American Fascism" can be found in the University of Iowa Libraries collection of his papers, and in its digital archive at http:// digital.lib.uiowa.edu/cdm/ref/collection/wallace/id/65433. It was published by the *New York Times* on April 9, 1944, with the headline "Wallace Defines 'American Fascism'; the Vice President Says It Pollutes Public Opinion, Encourages Intolerance and Presents a Challenge to Our Democratic Way of Life." An editorial response from the *Times*, "Mr. Wallace on 'Fascism,' " was published the same day. Letters responding to the article were published on April 13, 1944, by the *Times* under the headline "Mr. Wallace on Fascism; Readers Discuss Vice President's Article and Editorial Analyzing It." The *Snopes* piece on the article, "Did FDR's Vice-President Write an Op-Ed About 'American Fascism'? Henry A. Wallace's 1944 Piece Included a Warning Regarding the Alliance of Racists and 'Deliberate Poisoners of Public Information,' " was written by Arturo Garcia and published November 28, 2018. Wallace's grandson, Henry Scott Wallace, wrote a reflection on the article

"American Fascism, in 1944 and Today," which appeared in the *Times* on May 12, 2017. A valuable essay on the American fascists of the 1930s and early 1940s, "Revisiting the American Nazi Supporters of 'A Night at the Garden,'" was written by Margaret Talbot and appeared in the *New Yorker* on February 22, 2019. Dorothy Gallagher's *All the Right Enemies: The Life and Murder of Carlo Tresca*, published by Rutgers University Press in 1988, provides a good look at these issues, as well. Joe William Trotter Jr., the Giant Eagle Professor of History and Social Justice and past History Department Chair at Carnegie Mellon University, has written brilliantly on issues of prewar and wartime employment of African-American workers, in books such as *From a Raw Deal to a New Deal: African Americans 1929–1945* (Oxford University Press, 1996). His writing has informed my understanding of the struggles around FDR's executive order, as has Jervis Anderson's writing on Randolph. Historian Jon Wiener wrote about Sinatra's film and his lefty activism in "Frank Sinatra: His Way: The Bell Ring-a-Ding-Dings for Ol' Blue Eyes," for the *Nation* on June 15, 2009. The video of *The House I Live In* can be found on YouTube. Elizabeth Blair provided great insight into Abel Meeropol with her September 5, 2012, NPR report, "The Strange Story of the Man behind 'Strange Fruit.'" Philip Roth's *The Plot against America* was published by Houghton Mifflin in 2004. The *New Yorker* wrote about his reaction to Trump in "Philip Roth E-Mails on Trump," a January 22, 2017, article by Judith Thurman. Wallace's *Our Job in the Pacific* (American Council of the Institute of Pacific Relations, 1944) ticked off Churchill and brought Roald Dahl into Wallace's orbit—as Jennet Conant recounts in *The Irregulars: Roald Dahl and the British Spy Ring in Wartime Washington* (Simon & Schuster, 2008). Max Lerner wrote for the liberal New York paper *PM* in the 1940s and many of his best columns are compiled in *The Unfinished Country* (Simon and Schuster, 1959); his papers are archived at Yale University. Wallace's Chicago speech, titled, "Each Age Demands a New

Freedom," was delivered September 11, 1943. Blum recounts the exchange of letters with William Allen White as "a more unexpected compliment" in notes on the vice president's diary, while Lord publishes the exchange in full in *The Wallaces of Iowa*. Wallace's "Jackson Day" speech was delivered January 22, 1944, in Washington. The next day, the *Washington Post* reacted with its announcement that "the New Deal today is Henry Wallace." Peter Dreier wrote about Wallace as "America's Forgotten Visionary Politician" in a *Huffington Post* column published November 16, 2015. Hubert Humphrey's correspondence with Wallace can be found in the Wallace archives at the University of Iowa libraries. For details on Humphrey's enthusiasm for Wallace in 1944 and political activism during this period, see Arnold A. Offner's *Hubert Humphrey: The Conscience of the Country* (Yale University Press, 2018) and Carl Solberg's *Hubert Humphrey: A Biography* (Minnesota Historical Society Press, 2003). The *New York Times* provided steady coverage of Wallace's "America Tomorrow" tour and reprinted several of the speeches. The 1943 War Department film *Don't Be a Sucker* (and a 1947 version) can be viewed on YouTube. Details on African-American employment in defense industries are drawn from the Urban League reports in the National Urban League Collection at the Library of Congress and Charles D. Chamberlain's *Victory at Home: Manpower and Race in the American South during World War II* (University of Georgia Press, 2010). Janice D. Tanaka's 2016 documentary *Act of Faith* tells the story of the Rev. Emery Andrews and the Japanese Baptist Church in Seattle. Details of the Fair Play Committee's work can be found in a *Los Angeles Times* obituary, "Frank S. Emi Dies at 94; Japanese American Fought Effort to Draft WWII Internees," which was written by Elaine Woo and published December 9, 2010. Among the many important books on the internment of Japanese Americans during World War II is Michi Weglyn's *Years of Infamy: The Untold Story of America's Concentration Camps* (Morrow, 1976). Annette T.

Rubenstein compiled *I Vote My Conscience: Speeches, Writings Debates of Vito Marcantonio* (Vito Marcantonio Memorial, 1956). It was reprinted in a new edition in 2002 by the John D. Calandra Italian American Institute at Queens College, City University of New York. Gerald Meyer's *Vito Marcantonio: Radical Politician 1902–1954* was published in 1989 by the SUNY Series in *American Labor History*. I also relied on the extensive *New York Times* coverage of Marcantonio. *New Yorker* writer Adam Gopnik's article "Being Honest about Trump" appeared July 14, 2016. Henry Giroux commented as part of the *Flirting with Fascism: America's New Path?* program broadcast November 29, 2018, by CBC Radio.

5. July 20, 1944, 10:55 P.M.

The night of July 20, 1944, was one of high drama for those who attended that summer's Democratic National Convention. There are literally dozens of accounts of the events surrounding Wallace's speech, the demonstration that followed Roosevelt's speech and the closing down of the convention. As part of this project, I tried to read them all, watched the old footage and endeavored to create a narrative that captures events accurately. My touchstone was the account provided in MacDougall's *Gideon's Army*. A journalism professor and activist, MacDougall was in the hall. He also spoke and corresponded with a number of the participants. To supplement his account, I relied also news accounts from the time, including those of the *New York Times*, *Time*, *Life*, *PM*, the Madison *Capital Times* and the *Chicago Tribune*. I also reviewed Wallace's notes and his correspondence and oral histories from key participants, especially that of Claude Pepper. The best Pepper interview, conducted by journalist Jack Bass in 1974, can be accessed in the Southern Oral History Program Collection, Southern Historical Collection, Wilson Library, University of North Carolina at Chapel Hill. Pepper's memoirs (written with Hays Gorey), *Pepper: Eyewitness to a Century* (Harcourt Brace Jovanovich, 1987), are quite useful for insights regarding the man and his times, as is James C. Clark, *Red Pepper and Gorgeous George: Claude Pepper's Epic Defeat in the 1950 Democratic Primary* (University Press of Florida, 2011). William Greider has written extensively about the rise of a managerial sensibility in the Democratic Party; two of the best of these articles are "Rolling Back the Twentieth Century," which was published May 12, 2003, by the *Nation*, and "How the Democratic Party Lost Its Soul: The Trouble Started When the Party Abandoned Its Working-Class Base," published November 11, 2014, by the *Nation*. Jack Bell's AP piece appeared in papers across the country on Sunday, November 21, 1943. Wallace writes about it extensively in his diary, as do Culver and Hyde. There's an oral history of Bell at the Harry S. Truman Library in Independence, Missouri. Harry Woodring's machinations were reported extensively by the Associated Press, and the *New York Times* published detailed articles on March 5, 1944 ("Woodring Discusses 3d Party Candidate; Move Likely if President Is Renominated, He Says") and April 4, 1944 ("Anti-4th Term Group Busy 'up to Election'; Archer, Successor to Woodring, Tells Committee's Plans"). Charles Hurd's article was published March 5, 1944, in the *Times*, under the headline, "Wallace Keeps New Deal Alive as Politic Issue; the Vice President, It Is Now Believed, Has a Good Chance to Be Renominated." For a good take on the labor movement, especially the CIO, and the 1944 election, see Steven Fraser's *Labor Will Rule: Sidney Hillman and the Rise of American Labor* (Cornell University Press, 1993). The Tamiment Library and Robert F. Wagner Labor Archive at NYU maintains a good collection of NMU papers. George Gallup's thoughts on the vice presidential race appeared in the *Times*, March 5, 1944, under the headline, "Wallace Top Choice for Vice President of Party's Voters, Gallup Poll Finds." Stanley Weintraub's *Final Victory: FDR's Extraordinary World War II Presidential Campaign* (Da Capo Press, 2012) has a good chapter on FDR's consideration of the vice presidential pick, titled "Missouri Compromise," while Markowitz titled his chapter "The Missouri Compromise of 1944," and Culver and Hyde go with "The Same Old Team." All provide useful details and insights. David McCullough's reflection on the fight, "I Hardly Know Truman," appeared in the July/August 1992 volume of *American Heritage*. Norman Littell recounted the July 19, 1944, conversation with Wallace in *My Roosevelt Years* (University of Washington Press, 1987). Wilfred Binkley's assessment of the convention was published in the September 14, 1944, issue of *Social Action*. *Time* magazine, which saw in the convention the "defeat for the C.I.O. and the Native Radical wing of the Democratic Party," published its report on Wallace as "the best loved and most hated man" on July 31, 1944. See also "Truman Nominated for Vice Presidency: Real Fight Ends with Big Shift by Illinois—Ready, Says Senator," by Turner Catledge, *New York Times*, July 21, 1944. Culver and Hyde recount the Pepper and Arnall addresses. Lord recounts much of the media reaction, as does MacDougall. Mark Etheridge's papers are archived at the Wilson Library at the University of North Carolina at Chapel Hill; Culver and Hyde unearthed Etheridge's stinging letter to FDR, as they did the remarkable "lancing the boil" comment from Wallace's Columbia University Oral History project, a transcript of which can be found in the University of Iowa's Henry Wallace collection. The *New York Times* coverage of every nuance of Wallace's support for Truman was intense throughout the rest of the campaign; a key article (detailing the Madison Square Garden rally and its aftermath) appeared September 23, 1944, as "Wallace Backing Truman Candidacy."

6. Into the Wilderness

Max Lerner's article appeared August 1, 1944, in *PM*. A fine account of FDR's fall 1944 campaigning can be found in *FDR,*

Dewey, and the Election of 1944 (Indiana University Press, 2011) by David M. Jordan. FDR's "We Are Not Going to Turn the Clock Back" speech in Chicago was delivered October 28, 1944. On September 11, 1945, Claude Pepper entered a detailed reflection of communications between FDR and Wallace after the Chicago speech and the development of the 60 million jobs commitment in the Congressional Record. Wallace's book *Sixty Million Jobs* (Simon & Schuster, 1945) reflects on the same, as does Wallace's diary, which contains excellent detail on the campaign. Russell Lord provides a detailed picture of the fight over Wallace's nomination for secretary of commerce, and media coverage of the struggle. Freda Kirchwey's article "The End of an Era" appeared April 21, 1945, in the *Nation*. FDR delivered his "The President Reports on the Yalta Conference" address to the Congress on March 1, 1945. Susan Butler's *FDR and Stalin* (Alfred A. Knopf, 2015) provides a detailed examination of the complex relations between the leaders of the United States and the USSR. Thomas Fleming's book *The New Dealers' War: FDR and the War within World War II* (Basic Books, 2008) also deals with the relationship, and it reflects a good deal on Wallace's role. Wallace's "Way to Peace" speech was delivered September 12, 1946. There are many accounts of the reaction to the speech in the Truman White House by David McCullough, Markowitz and Culver and Hyde. Lawrence Lader's detailed examination of the struggle appeared in the December, 1976, edition of *American Heritage* as "… To Serve the World—not to Dominate It: United States Policy, Henry Wallace Said in His Spirited Challenge to Truman and Dewey in 1948." In *Gideon's Army*, MacDougall recounts Wallace's fall 1946 campaigning. For a taste of segregationist John Rankin's rhetoric, see the Congressional Record of May 1, 1947. In *Thirty Days a Black Man: The Forgotten Story That Exposed the Jim Crow South* (Rowman & Littlefield, 2017), Bill Steigerwald offers a sampling of the racist and anti-Communist ranting of Theodore Bilbo and his segregationist allies. A jarring portrait of Bilbo was published December 16, 1946, in *Life* magazine as "Bilbo Hearing: Senate Group Meets in His State to See If He Should Be Unseated." The *New York Times* wrote about reactions from labor to the 1946 election in a December 15, 1946, article, "Reuther Appeals for Labor Peace; Sees Danger of a Depression because Workers Can't Buy Enough Goods They Make." MacDougall writes at length about this. Walter Reuther's comments appeared in the November 1946 edition of the *United Auto Worker* magazine. Carl Bernstein's *Loyalties: A Son's Memoir* was published by Simon & Schuster in 1989; Eric Foner's review, "Bernstein's Complaint," was published April 9, 1989, by the *Los Angeles Times*. MacDougall reprints the text of Wallace's PCA speech from December, 1946. David Plotke writes about Robert Kenny and others who sought to work within the Democratic Party in *Building a Democratic Political Order: Reshaping American Liberalism in the 1930s and 1940s* (Cambridge University Press, 2006), and MacDougall writes about Kenny's Democrats for Wallace effort. Kenny's major address on the issue was delivered July 19, 1947, at a Democrats for Wallace event in Fresno, California. The *New York Times* reported on July 21, 1947, "Wallace Democrats to Fight Any Pledge to Truman in California Committee Session." Mary A. Hamilton's January 1994 article on J.W. Gitt for *Pennsylvania History: A Journal of Mid-Atlantic Studies*, "A Pennsylvania Newspaper Publisher in 'Gideon's Army'": J.W. Gitt, Henry Wallace and the Progressive Party of 1948, explores some of the concerns of Wallace allies about a third-party run. Culver and Hyde examine Michael Straight's doubts. The *New York Times* reported on Wallace's May 19, 1947, speech in a lengthy article May, 20, 1947, "Warns Big Powers Lean to New War; Wallace, in Los Angeles, Says Russia Is One of Them—20,000 Hear Him." MacDougall's coverage of this period is detailed and illuminating, as is that provided by Culver and Hyde. Wallace delivered his speech on the Red Scare on March 31, 1947, in New York; Idaho senator Glen Taylor inserted the full speech in the Congressional Record on April 9, 1947. Wallace's March 27, 1947, radio address on the Truman Doctrine can be found in *We Who Dared to Say No to War: American Antiwar Writing from 1812 to Now* (Basic Books, 2008), by Murray Polner and Thomas E. Woods Jr. The records of the Progressive Party can be found in the University of Iowa Collections. You can read the 1948 Progressive Party platform online at davidpietrusza. com, and author David Pietrusza does an able job of recounting the platform debates in his book *1948: Harry Truman's Improbable Victory and the Year That Transformed America* (Union Square Press, 2011). So, too, does Zachary Karabell in *The Last Campaign: How Harry Truman Won the 1948 Election* (Knopf Doubleday Publishing Group, 2007). F. Ross Peterson writes about the frustrations of Rexford Tugwell and others in *Prophet without Honor: Glen H. Taylor and the Fight for American Liberalism* (University Press of Kentucky, 2015). George McGovern expressed his thoughts on the 1948 race in an interview with Jonathan Ellis, which was published December 4, 2011, in the *St. Augustine Record* under the headline "At 89, St. Augustine Snowbird George McGovern Is Revered as 'National Treasure' in His Home State." Henry Wallace's NBC radio address on campaigning in the South was broadcast September 13, 1948. James Clark of the *Orlando Sentinel* wrote on "Claude Pepper's Brief Presidential Campaign" for the *Orlando Sentinel* on November 29, 1992. The *New York Times* reported on October 12, 1948, "Brooklyn Hears Pepper; Florida Senator Urges Liberals to Vote for Truman." Truman delivered his "I detest communism" speech October 27, 1948, at Mechanics Hall in Boston. Culver and Hyde recount Wallace's 1948 comments on the Progressive Party's Communist ties costing him support. Mary A. Hamilton's book, *Rising from the Wilderness: J. W. Gitt and His Legendary Newspaper: The Gazette and Daily of York, Pa.* (York County Heritage Trust, 2007) reprises Gitt's columns and does a terrific job of telling his story. The "We Are for Wallace" ad appeared in the *New York Times* on

October 20, 1948. Zachary Karabell recounts Wallace's final radio address in *The Last Campaign: How Harry Truman Won the 1948 Election*. For a link to the *New York Times* endorsement of Dewey, see "New York Times Endorsements Through the Ages," published on September 23, 2016.

7. The Great Unwinding

The *New York Times* reported on its August 9, 1950, front page, "Wallace Deserts Progressive Party in Split on Korea; Curtly Resigns from Group He Founded, the Better to Serve 'Cause of Peace' Lamont Backs His Action." A biography of Hallinan, *San Francisco's Hallinan: Toughest Lawyer* (Presidio, 1982) was written by James P. Walsh. The *New York Times* published a lengthy obituary, "Vincent Hallinan Is Dead at 95; an Innovative Lawyer with Flair," on October 4, 1992. Charlotta A. Bass published a memoir, *Forty Years: Memoirs from the Pages of a Newspaper*, in 1960. The *Los Angeles Sentinel* obituary appeared on April 17, 1969. *Raising Her Voice: African-American Women Journalists Who Changed History* (University Press of Kentucky, 1994), by Rodger Streitmatter, is a valuable source of information on her. The *New York Times* article "Intellectual Left Silent in Campaign" appeared November 2, 1950. Howard Zinn's *A People's History of the United States* was published by Harper & Row in 1980. The *New York Times* reported "A.L.P. Is Dissolved after Twenty Years; A.L.P. Dissolves; Inactive Since '54" on October 8, 1956. Allan Wolfe wrote about "The Withering Away of the American Labor Party" for the *Rutgers University Library Journal*, 31 (1968). Kari Frederickson wrote about the States' Rights Democratic Party in *The Dixiecrat Revolt and the End of the Solid South, 1932–1968* (University of North Carolina Press, 2001). "Sparkman Chosen by Democrats as Running Mate for Stevenson; Senator Hails Party Solidarity: Nominees Pledge

Strong Campaign: No Ballot Taken on 2d Place," reported the *New York Times* on July 27, 1952. Leah Wright Rigueur discussed her book *The Loneliness of the Black Republican: Pragmatic Politics and the Pursuit of Power* (Princeton University Press, 2016) on an August 25, 2016, NPR report on "When African-American Voters Shifted away from the GOP." Jean Edward Smith discusses Eisenhower's approach to desegregation in *Eisenhower: In War and Peace* (Random House, 2012). The Southern Manifesto and a list of its signers can be found in the Congressional Record of March 12, 1956. The Democratic and Republican platforms of 1956 can be reviewed online at UC Santa Barbara's American Presidency Project website: presidency.ucsb.edu. The *Crisis*, the NAACP's national magazine, devoted its October 1956, issue to a pair of detailed articles making the case for the Democratic and Republican tickets; they provide a wealth of information that informed this chapter. Wil Haygood's masterful biography of Powell, *King of the Cats: The Life and Times of Adam Clayton Powell, Jr.* (Houghton Mifflin Harcourt, 1993) includes a terrific examination of Powell's activism before and during the 1956 campaign. The *New York Times* coverage of Powell's decision to back Eisenhower was excellent; key articles included "Powell's Support Keyed to Rights; Will Demand Ban on Federal Help to States Defying Law as Condition of Backing Seeking Seventh Term Uses Riders Effectively" (October 3, 1956), "Powell, Switching, Backs Eisenhower" (October 12, 1956), "Harlem Perplexed by Powell's Defection to Eisenhower" (November 1, 1956), "Democrats Face Negro Vote Loss; A Sizable Switch to GOP Could Hurt Stevenson in the Close States" (November 2, 1956) and "Powell Sees Shift of Negroes to GOP" (November 7, 1956). A brilliant examination of the fight for the African-American vote in 1956 was written by Lincoln Fitch; it is titled "Throwing the Switch: Eisenhower, Stevenson and the African-American Vote in the 1956 Election" and can be found online at cupola.gettysburg.edu. I also gained information and insight from Theodore H. White's long August 17, 1956, essay for *Collier's*, "The Negro Voter: Can He Elect a President?" The Dwight D. Eisenhower Presidential Library and Museum has frequently noted and highlighted the Eisenhower-Wallace correspondence; the Eisenhower Library even tweeted about it: twitter.com/IkeLibrary/status/965677833510096896. Wallace wrote about his thinking on Eisenhower and peace for *Life* magazine, in a lengthy May 14, 1956, article titled "Henry Wallace Tells of His Political Odyssey." The *New York Times* reported, on December 2, 1955, that "Wallace Favors Eisenhower." Tom Carson's *American Prospect* article, "The Republican Socialist: A New Biography Shows That Dwight Eisenhower Was a More Cunning and Active President Than He Gets Credit For," appeared on March 9, 2012. The *New York Times* reported on May 13, 1956, that "Harriman Urges Democrats Adopt 'New Vision' in '56; Tells Garment Union Broad Social Action Is Needed—Criticizes Eisenhower. Harriman Urges Dems Identify Selves as 'Zealots' on Rights Issue." Eisenhower delivered his "Cross of Iron" speech to the American Society of Newspaper Editors, in Washington D.C., on April 16, 1953. He delivered his "Farewell Address" on the military-industrial complex in a national television broadcast on January 17, 1961. As the 1960 election approached, the *New York Times* reported on November 4, 1959, that "Wallace Remains Aloof; Ex-Vice President Denies He Will Rejoin Democrats." The *Times* reported on October 30, 1964, that, "Henry A. Wallace, on Farm, Hails Johnson and Humphrey." Culver and Hyde wrote about Wallace's note on Vietnam in the "Coda" section of their biography. The *New York Times* reported on Wallace's method of communication in his last days in a November 20, 1965, article, "Wallace Wrote Notes to Doctors; Fatal Illness Prevented Oral Communication Near End."

8. The Party That Lost Its Way

Civil rights leaders A. Philip Randolph and Bayard Rustin presented the "Freedom Budget for All Americans" after meeting with Lyndon Johnson and his aides in 1966. It was published in summary form by the A. Philip Randolph Institute in January 1967. The project is examined in "For Jobs and Freedom: An Introduction to the Unfinished March," by Thomas J. Sugrue, which was published August 5, 2013, as an Economic Policy Institute report. I wrote a piece, "A. Philip Randolph Was Right: 'We Will Need to Continue Demonstrations,'" for the *Nation* on April 15, 2014. King's "Beyond Vietnam" speech was delivered April 4, 1967, at Riverside Church in New York. King's "The Drum Major Instinct" sermon was delivered at Ebenezer Baptist Church in Atlanta on February 4, 1968. King's "The Three Evils of Society" speech was delivered at the National Conference for New Politics on August 31, 1967. Howard Zinn wrote about the McComb, Mississippi, protest in *A People's History of the United States*. Documents from the protest can be viewed on the SNCC Digital site at: snccdigital.org. David Remnick wrote a fine reminiscence on Ali's opposition to the war, "Recalling Muhammad Ali's Vietnam War Resistance in the Age of Trump," on September 24, 2017. Dave Zirin's *Muhammad Ali Handbook* (M Q Publications, 2007) is brilliant. John Lee Hooker's "The Motor City Is Burning" came out in 1967. Eugene McCarthy's speech denouncing the Vietnam War was delivered December 2, 1967, in Chicago. The Associated Press report "Changes in U.S. Foreign Policy Proposed by New Liberal Group" was published in papers across the country on May 23, 1960. The *New York Times* reported on the House debate over the Committee on Un-American Activities in the article "House Committee Upheld; Un-American Activities Group Is Backed in Fight on Communism," published on March 11, 1961; see also "James Roosevelt Scores House Unit," published on February 23, 1961. *The Liberal Papers* (Doubleday

& Company, 1962) was edited by James Roosevelt, who wrote an extended introduction. The *New York Times* reviewed it April 8, 1962, in "Out of a Search for Ideas, an Anthology of Dissent." See also in the *Times*, "A.D.A. Is Target of Republicans; Humphrey Linked to Group Described as Subversive," October 11, 1964. Tom Hayden's book *The Port Huron Statement: The Vision Call of the 1960s Revolution* was published in 2005 by Public Affairs. I interviewed Tom Hayden at length about the Port Huron Statement at public events marking its 50th anniversary. For the *Nation*, on October 24, 2016, I wrote "Tom Hayden Taught Us How to Get Beyond Trump and Trumpism." The *New York Times* article "Dr. King to Back Peace Candidate; Will Oppose Johnson Unless He Changes War Stand," appeared August 18, 1967. John Kenneth Galbraith, a leading figure in the ADA, was particularly outspoken with regard to LBJ and the war; see "Galbraith Scores President on War; Says a Long Conflict Could Bury Democratic Party," the *New York Times*, April 3, 1967. The ADA ultimately backed Eugene McCarthy's candidacy; see, "National Board of ADA Endorses McCarthy Candidacy in 65–47 Vote," *Harvard Crimson*, February 12, 1968. Massachusetts senator Edward Kennedy recalled his brother Robert's words in his tribute address at St. Patrick's Cathedral in New York City on June 8, 1968. *The Power Elite* by C. Wright Mills was published by Oxford University Press in 1956. Robert W. McChesney and I wrote at length about the Powell memo and about the role it has played in transforming the Republican Party and our politics in *Dollarocracy: How the Money and Media Election Complex Is Destroying America* (Nation Books/Public Affairs, 2013). See also, "The Lewis Powell Memo: A Corporate Blueprint to Dominate Democracy" at greenpeace.org. George McGovern wrote eloquently and frankly about his 1972 campaign in *Grassroots: The Autobiography of George McGovern* (Random House, 1977). McGovern's 1969 Moratorium speeches were well covered by local media; a good report can be found in the *Heights*, October 21, 1969,

"M Day: People and Peace ..." Timothy Noah wrote "The Liberals' Moment" for the *New York Times*, November 11, 2007. The *Times* article "The Battle for the Democratic Party" appeared July 17, 1972. McGovern delivered his "Come Home America" acceptance speech at the Democratic National Convention on July 14, 1972. The *Sioux Falls Argus Leader* reported July 25, 2015, on J. Edgar Hoover's machinations in "The FBI Mined Secrets from George McGovern's Past." The *New York Times* reported June 27, 1972, that "Agnew Links McGovern to Henry Wallace Views." See also "M'govern's Record Criticized by Agnew," the *New York Times*, June 11, 1972. The *Times* reported "Connally Sees More Democrats Supporting Nixon" on September 21, 1972. I wrote a lengthy essay, "The Genius of McGovern's 'Come Home, America' Vision: The Great Liberal Scoped Out a Vision for Less Military Spending and More Investment in Domestic Renewal. Now, Even (Some) Conservatives Get the Point," for the *Nation* on October 18, 2012. Joshua Mound's article, "What Democrats Still Don't Get about George McGovern," appeared in the *New Republic*, February 29, 2016. The *New York Times* piece, "Major Changes Have Long Since Been Abandoned," appeared December 1, 1974. The article "Harrington Quits as Socialist Head" appeared in the *New York Times*, October 23, 1972. I interviewed Harrington several times in the early 1980s regarding DSOC and working within the Democratic Party, and I wrote a great deal about the founding of DSA, Democracy '76 and Democratic Agenda in my book *The "S" Word: A Short History of an American Tradition ... Socialism* (Verso, 2011). Harrington wrote "The Left Wing of Realism" for *Democratic Left*, March, 1973. Harrington's essay "Out Beyond Liberalism" appeared March 3, 1973, in the *New York Times*. Maurice Isserman's brilliant biography *The Other American: The Life of Michael Harrington* was published by Public Affairs in 2000. The article "Liberals Rejected" appeared in the *New York Times*, January 16, 1977. Harold Meyerson wrote "The Ghost of

Democratic Agenda" for the *American Prospect*, February 13, 2009. Hedrick Smith wrote on the Democratic midterm conference in "The Message of Memphis" in the *New York Times*, December 11, 1978. See also "Democrats Girding for Midterm Parley," the *New York Times*, December 7, 1978. The *Times* reported January 4, 1979, that "White House Cancels Some Cuts in Health Funds in 1980 Budget." Meyerson's article "Keeper of the Liberal Flame: Kennedy Was the Champion of the Uninsured, the Undocumented, and the Forgotten" appeared August 26, 2009, in the *American Prospect*. Theodore White wrote about the Democratic Party losing its way in *America in Search of Itself: The Making of the President, 1956–1980* (Harper & Row, 1982). Ted Kennedy delivered his "The Dream Shall Never Die" speech August 12, 1980, at the Democratic National Convention in New York. To get a sense of Tony Benn in these times, see *The End of an Era: Diaries, 1980–1990* (Hutchinson, 1992). Benn and I spoke frequently about these issues during the last two decades of his life. The Tom Hayden campaign published and distributed "Make the Future Ours" in 1976. Hayden shared copies of the pamphlet and we discussed the 1976 campaign several times over the years. Lee Drutman's "The Political One Percent of the One Percent" was published December 13, 2011, at sunlightfoundation.com. Gregg Easterbrook's "The Business of Politics" appeared in the October 1986 issue of the *Atlantic*. The *Washington Post* explored Ferraro's politics in "Ferraro: Liberal to a Point," July 21, 1984. The *New York Times* reported "Democrats' Platform Shows a Shift from Liberal Positions of 1976 and 1980," on July 22, 1984. I covered early gatherings of the Democratic Leadership Council as a young reporter for the *Toledo Blade* and the *Pittsburgh Post-Gazette*, and I wrote about the DLC for the *Progressive* in an October 2000 article headlined "Behind the DLC Takeover." *Storming the Gates*, by Dan Balz and Ronald Brownstein, was published by Little, Brown in 1996. Steve Cobble wrote "Jesse Jackson's Rainbow Coalition Created

Today's Democratic Politics" for the *Nation*, October 2, 2018. I wrote about Bernie Sanders and Jesse Jackson in "Recalling the Rainbow Roots of the Bernie Sanders Presidential Run," the *Nation*, March 11, 2016. Jesse Jackson delivered his Democratic National Convention address on July 19, 1988, in Atlanta. John Kenneth Galbraith's letter on the Yarborough-Bentsen race appears in *The Selected Letters of John Kenneth Galbraith* (Cambridge University Press, 2017). Joan Didion wrote about the Democrats in "Eye on the Prize," the *New York Review of Books*, September 24, 1992. I covered the 1992 Democratic convention, as I have every Democratic convention since. The *Washington Post* covered Edelman's resignation in "2 HHS Officials Quit over Welfare Changes," September 12, 1996. Edelman wrote about the welfare bill in *Searching for America's Heart: RFK and the Renewal of Hope* (Houghton Mifflin Harcourt, 2001). Nelson Lichtenstein wrote about Clinton in "A Fabulous Failure: Clinton's 1990s and the Origins of Our Times" for the *American Prospect*, January 29, 2018. Ezra Klein's article "Bill Clinton's Party of One" appeared June 5, 2008, in the *American Prospect*. Steven Rattner wrote about Emanuel's UAW slur in *Overhaul: An Insider's Account of the Obama Administration's Emergency Rescue of the Auto Industry* (Houghton Mifflin Harcourt, 2010). Rick Perlstein wrote about "The Sudden but Well-Deserved Fall of Rahm Emanuel" for the *New Yorker*, December 31, 2015. I wrote about Dr. Quentin Young and Obama in "How to Push Obama," the *Progressive*, January 5, 2009. I wrote on Obama's *Fortune* magazine interview in "Obama Goes Soft on Free Trade," the *Nation*, June 25, 2008. I wrote about Emanuel and Obama in "Rahm Emanuel: Face of Change?" in the *Nation*, November 5, 2008. Obama's comments on government bureaucrats can be found in "Excerpts from the President's Remarks on Health Insurance Reform Today," White House release, March 3, 2010. Obama gave his populist economic speech December 6, 2011, in Osawatomie, Kansas. The Bernie Sanders statement on Lawrence

Summers was issued September 15, 2013. Clare Malone's "Barack Obama Won the White House, but Democrats Lost the Country. What Happened?" was published January 19, 2017.

9. "I Want Us to Be that Party Again!"

The *New York Times* on November 19, 1965, reported, "Henry A. Wallace Is Dead at 77; Ex-Vice President, Plant Expert; Henry A. Wallace, Vice President in New Deal and Plant Geneticist, Is Dead at 77; Led Progressives in 1948 Election; Ex-Secretary of Agriculture and Commerce Retired to Westchester Farm," and on November 21, 1965, reported, "New Dealers among the 300 at Simple Service for Wallace." The *Times* obituary for Gardner appeared February 18, 2002, as "John W. Gardner, 89, Founder of Common Cause and Adviser to Presidents, Dies." I wrote about Ayanna Pressley for the *Nation*, September 4, 2018, in "Ayanna Pressley Wins a Fight for the Soul of the Democratic Party." I interviewed Alexandria Ocasio-Cortez, Ilhan Omar, Rashida Tlaib, Ro Khanna, Mark Pocan, Pramila Jayapal and Bernie Sanders while writing this book. Sanders delivered his 2020 announcement speech at a March 2, 2019, rally in Brooklyn. I profiled AOC in "The Alexandria Ocasio-Cortez Effect: The Democratic Party's New Rock Star Is Storming the Country on Behalf of Insurgent Populists," the *Nation*, August 15, 2018. Bridget Read wrote about AOC for *Vogue* in "28-Year-Old Alexandria Ocasio-Cortez Might Just Be the Future of the Democratic Party." George McGovern delivered the keynote address at the September 29, 1999, dedication of the Henry A. Wallace Room in the USDA's headquarters in Washington, D.C. Wallace spoke about serving people, not exploiters, in accepting the Progressive Party nomination in Philadelphia, July, 24, 1948. Lauren Gambino wrote on Ro Khanna for the *Guardian*, "Silicon Valley in Iowa: Congressman's Fight for Tech Jobs in

Rural America," December 16, 2018. I traveled with Khanna on his trip to Iowa, and interviewed him on December 8, 2018. I was in Iowa again in August 2019 to cover Elizabeth Warren and wrote, "Elizabeth Warren Has a Plan to Finish What FDR Started: And It Could Give Democrats a Fighting Chance in Farm Country and Small-Town America," the *Nation*, August 20, 2019. Elizabeth Warren unveiled her plan to reduce corporate influence at the Pentagon on May 16, 2019, with a column for *Medium*. Bernie Sanders wrote "Ending America's Endless War" for *Foreign Affairs*, June 24, 2019. I visited Wallace's birthplace with Sanders on August 11, 2019. I interviewed Alexandria Ocasio-Cortez on July 29, 2018.

Index

Devine, Thomas, 11–2, 127
Dewey, Thomas, 13, 85, 105, 136
Didion, Joan, 203
Dies, Martin, 79
Dies Committee, the, 79
digital revolution, 229
Dixiecrats, 13, 88, 141, 142
domino theory, 150
Don't Be a Sucker (film), 76–7
Double V campaign, 20
Douglas, Helen Gahagan, 92,
120, 142
Douglas, William O., 92, 93
Dreier, Peter, 74
Drutman, Lee, 194–5
Du Bois, W.E.B., 3, 129
Duffy, Joe, 183
Dukakis, Michael, 85, 199, 201–2

Eagleton, Thomas, 175
Eastland, James, 147
Easton, Nina, 209
Economic Bill of Rights, xii, 12,
24, 104, 109, 156, 181, 228,
234–5, 236
economic constitutional order, 3
Economic Defense Board, 49
economic democracy, 90, 190
economic interests, 235
economic power, consolidations
of, 79
economic royalists, xii–xiii, 235
Economist Intelligence Unit, the,
7
Edelman, Peter, 203–4
Ehrlichman, John, 175
Einstein, Albert, 3
Eisenhower, Dwight, ix–x, xv, 9,
138, 143, 231–2
Cross of Iron speech, 152–3
Farewell Address, 153
HW and, 148–9
modern Republicanism,
144–51
Soviet policy, 150, 151–3

emancipation, 33
Emanuel, Rahm, 205–6, 210
Environmental Protection
Agency, 169
equal protection, failure of,
77–8
Equal Rights Amendment, 73
equality, 4
Erlander, Tage Fritjof, 4
Ethridge, Mark, 101
Executive Order 8802, 63
Executive Order 8839, 49
Executive Order 9346, 63
Executive Order 9361, 52
Executive Order 9835, 119

Fanfare for the Common Man
(Copland), 42
Farley, James, 8
fascism
definition, 76, 80–1
HW's definition, 6
rise of, 6
soft, 7
Fascist League of North America,
60
fear, freedom from, 23
Federal Bureau of Investigation,
175
Federal Reserve, 214–5
Feingold, Russ, 207
Fenberg, Steven, 52
Ferraro, Geraldine, 196
Fight for 15, 156
Fleming, Thomas, 111
Flynn, Edward, 93
Foner, Eric, 119
Foot, Michael, 4
Ford, Gerald, 182
Foreign Affairs, 233
foreign policy, 192–3, 196–7,
232
Forrestal, James V., 114
Fortress America, 65
Fortune (magazine), 209–10

DISCARD